THE

GYMNASIUM

OF

CHRIST

STEPHEN KAUNG

Christian Fellowship Publishers

ISBN 13: 978-0-935008-99-9

Available from the Publishers at:
11515 Allecingie Parkway
Richmond, Virginia 23235
www.c-f-p.com

Printed in the United States of America

PREFACE

"Exercise thyself unto piety [or, godliness]; for bodily exercise is profitable for a little, but piety [godliness] is profitable for everything, having promise of life of the present one and of that to come" (1 Timothy 4:7b-8). People nowadays are most conscious of the need to engage in physical exercise, but unfortunately God's people are considerably negligent regarding the need for spiritual exercise. They may have had some experience of being in the *school* of Christ where they learn something of God's truth mentally, yet they are quite ignorant when it comes to the *gymnasium* of Christ where through spiritual exercise they may learn of Christ himself and grow up in Him daily. This causes them to be large in head but small in feet. They know a lot but advance very little along the pathway towards spiritual maturity.

In view of this disappointing situation, brother Stephen Kaung gave a series of twenty messages on the necessity for Christians to be attendees and participants daily in the gymnasium of Christ. He delivered this series of messages before a gathering of Christians in Richmond, Virginia from September 2009 to April 2011. They are now being published for the benefit of other Christians elsewhere. May the Lord Jesus be magnified in our lives.

Contents

PREFACE 3

PART ONE: SPIRITUAL EXERCISE OF THE SPIRIT

1. INTRODUCTION: THE GYMNASIUM OF CHRIST 9
2. CONSCIENCE 27
3. INTUITION 47
4. COMMUNION 71

PART TWO: SPIRITUAL EXERCISE OF THE SOUL AND THE BODY

5. EMOTION 95
6. MIND 115
7. WILL 139
8. BODY 159

PART THREE: HOW SPIRITUAL EXERCISE AFFECTS PRESENT LIFE

9. PERSONAL LIFE 179
10. FAMILY LIFE 201
11. CHURCH LIFE 221
12. SOCIAL LIFE 245

PART FOUR: HOW SPIRITUAL EXERCISE AFFECTS OUR FUTURE LIFE

13. THE SECOND COMING OF THE LORD 267
14. THE KINGDOM OF THE HEAVENS 289
15. THE OVERCOMERS 315
16. THE NEW JERUSALEM 337

PART FIVE: FOUR LIFE-CHANGING LESSONS OF SPIRITUAL EXERCISE

17. CONSECRATION 361
18. DIVIDING OF SOUL AND SPIRIT 381
19. THE BREAKING OF THE OUTWARD MAN AND THE RELEASE OF THE SPIRIT. 401
20. LIFE WITHIN THE VEIL 421

PART ONE:
SPIRITUAL EXERCISE OF
THE SPIRIT

Chapter 1

INTRODUCTION
THE GYMNASIUM OF CHRIST

I Timothy 4:7b-10—Exercise thyself unto piety [i.e., unto godliness]; for bodily exercise is profitable for a little, but piety [godliness] is profitable for everything, having promise of life [life here in Greek is *zoe*, eternal life], of the present one, and of that to come. The word is faithful [or, is true] and worthy of all acceptation [i.e., we should accept it]; for, for this we labour and suffer reproach, because we hope in a living God, who is preserver of all men, specially of those that believe.

I would like to share with you that which is very basic but quite important, and it is this matter of spiritual exercise. The apostle Paul, writing in I Timothy, tells us that bodily exercise is profitable for a little; and, interestingly, in recent days we have heard and been bombarded with reports concerning the need for physical fitness. This country has begun to realize that our young people are not physically fit because they spend so much time before the computer and do not exercise. It has been observed that eating well, drinking well and sleeping well do not necessarily give us a healthy body. Hence, we are told again and again we need to exercise; therefore, physical fitness is one of the popular cultural themes in much of the world today.

Indeed, bodily exercise is profitable; but by comparison with something else which we would like to address during these coming weeks together, physical exercise profits only a little and is limited primarily to our body. Although such exercise may help our soul a little, in that if we have a healthy body we may think better, it does not benefit our spirit. Physical exercise is important, but its benefit is only for this present physical life we are living. It does not sanctify us nor prepare us for life eternal. Having said this, however, it does not mean that, because physical exercise only profits a little, we can ignore it. On the contrary, if we do that, we will suffer for it.

GOD'S PURPOSE FOR HIS PEOPLE

Nevertheless, for us who are Christians there is something far more important and essential than physical exercise; and that is, exercise unto godliness. In other words, the reason God has saved us is because He has a godly purpose to fulfill in each of our lives. It is not His purpose simply to deliver us out of hell and put us into heaven, as though there is so much vacancy in heaven that He needs us to be there to help fill it up. His purpose consists of far more than that. God's will for each and every one whom He has brought into this world is that He wants those of us whom He has redeemed to be conformed to the image of His beloved Son—that is to say, to be like God, which is what godliness actually means. He desires His character to be formed in our lives in order that we may truly manifest His glory. That is the glorious purpose of God for each of us (Romans 8:28b-29a). And in order to arrive at this goal He has made every provision for us to arrive there; but there is one condition which He requires of us—that we must learn to exercise ourselves unto godliness by exercising our spirit. And by exercising our spirit—not our body or our soul—we will come to realize that His grace can and will bring us there.

GOD BREATHED INTO THE HUMAN BODY

Unfortunately, many believers do not have any idea that they have a spirit nor, if they do, they do not know how to exercise it. Now with respect to those who do not know the Lord this is not surprising because they are not aware that God created man with three constituent elements or parts. We are tripartite beings—God having created us with a spirit, a soul, and a body. He used red earth with which to form our body (Genesis 2:7a); therefore, our body has the same composition of materials as is found in the soil of the earth. Accordingly, that gives us world-consciousness and enables us to contact the world because we are of the same nature. Then the Bible in its book of Genesis explains further what next occurred: "God breathed His breath into the nostrils of man" (see 2:7b). Here we learn that something came directly from God himself. After He formed the body with the earth of the ground God breathed into it. Now that is truly a great marvel! This breath is what comes directly from God into man. To put it simply: when He breathed into man, that breath became the human spirit.

Now because God is spirit, we cannot contact Him unless we ourselves have a spirit. So this is the beauty and the wonder of man. What makes man different from all the other beings and from all the things in this world—the animals, the mountains, the trees, and all the other created things on this earth—is this, that man has a spirit. There is that which is of God within us, which is our spirit; and because we have this spirit we are able to communicate with God. It requires us to have the same nature if we are going to be able to communicate with Him.

I recall that many years ago Russia sent into outer space an astronaut or cosmonaut (as "space men" were then being called). This atheistic Communist cosmonaut, upon returning to earth, declared to the world: "There is no God. I have been to outer space and have looked all around, but I did not see God." What utter foolishness! How can the physical body with only its physical senses, contact God who is spirit? The dignity and nobility of man comes not from his having a body. When compared with a mountain one's body is almost nothing. The nobility of man does not even lie with his soul, though his soul does indeed possess huge capacities. Nevertheless, the dignity and nobility of man derives from the fact of his having a spirit that can receive God's life and commune with Him, that he can be transformed and be like God, taking upon himself or herself the character of His holy Son Jesus. How truly wonderful!

MAN SINNED AND DIED

We will recall that in the Garden of Eden God had said to the first man, Adam: "There is a particular tree here, the tree of the knowledge of good and evil, whose fruit you must not eat, because if you do, you will die immediately" (see Genesis 2:17). Now we know that Adam and Eve, our ancestors, ate of that forbidden tree, but back then they and their offspring lived much longer than we do today. If today a person lives to be a hundred years old, people will say, "Wow! You are a rarity!" But our forefathers lived for hundreds of years, so far

Introduction

as their bodies were concerned, and they begot children by means of their physical relationships. Yet the word of God to that first man was true; for on the day that Adam and Eve ate of the forbidden tree, something in them did in fact die; and that was the spirit part in them. The human spirit, which constitutes the dignity and nobility of man, was forfeited. Man could not contact God, and so he henceforth had to live exclusively by his own wisdom and ingenuity. As a result of this, what a tragedy we find in the world! Hence, it is no wonder that unbelievers do not know they have a spirit because their spirit is dead towards God.

When I was a young boy, we had an American grandmother from the state of Virginia who lived with us. She was a missionary to China. She loved China so much that after she retired she did not return to America but stayed with us, and we called her Grandma. Oftentimes, when she was exasperated, she would cry out: "Oh, my soul and body!" In this rather common exclamation, the spirit is never mentioned! With us believers, however, we know that when we believed in the Lord Jesus for salvation, something extraordinary happened in us—that is, in what we call the human spirit. And this is, in part, what I would like for us to consider together today.

THE MEANING OF SALVATION

I am not going to approach this subject of salvation from the theological or doctrinal standpoint. Instead, I want to discuss it with the experiential and practical aspect in view with regard to what it means when we say we are saved. Nevertheless, such an approach will be Biblically based. If we believe that Jesus is the Christ and that He is the Son of God, then we are begotten of God (I John 5:1). He that believes in the Son of God has life and he who does not so believe does not have life (I John 5:12).

So what does being saved or being "born again" mean? It is to be born a second time but born from above (John 3:3-8). When we believe in Jesus, we are saved; and that means that, speaking of the negative aspect, all our sins have been forgiven through the blood of the Lord Jesus. And on the positive side, we receive eternal life: the life of Christ comes into us, and we are born into the family of God (Ephesians 2:19b).

We read in John 3:6 that the Lord Jesus said: "He that is born of the Spirit is spirit." Now that is what is meant by being born again. He who is born of the Holy Spirit has a renewed human spirit that formerly was dead. Therefore, when we are saved, we receive eternal life and the life of Christ comes into us. But where does that life reside in us? Does that life dwell in our body? Does that life dwell in our soul? No, it is too divine to dwell in either of those parts in man; it must therefore dwell in that which answers to God's nature, which is spirit. Consequently, if we do not have a new spirit, the life of Christ we receive has nowhere to dwell in us.

Let us be reminded again that whoever is born of the Spirit is spirit. Our dead spirit is quickened by the Holy Spirit, renewed by the Holy Spirit, and has thus become a new spirit. God is spirit, and now that our spirit is renewed, His life can dwell in our spirit. When we are saved, we receive Someone who is so precious—even the Spirit of God—who comes and dwells in our spirit.

A NEW LIFE

Do you know what happens and what you receive when you are born again? Not only are your sins forgiven, you also have a new life. Christ the Son of God has become your life, and that life dwells in your new spirit. The Holy Spirit has also come to dwell in your spirit, and He bears witness with your spirit that you are a child of God and consequently you can cry, "Abba, Father" (Romans 8:15). In other words, your relationship with God is recovered and renewed. And that is your first experience of what you receive when you are born again.

THE NEW LIFE—BOTH FOR TODAY AND ETERNITY

Why does Christ come into our life? What is this gift of life for? People think that eternal life is for the future—not for today. They view it as akin to a life insurance policy: when you are living you cannot enjoy it; it is only effective after you die. Therefore, some people say: "Well, you believe in the Lord Jesus, and so you have eternal life. You are guaranteed to go to heaven, but that life is not available for today. You have to live by your old life and try to become better and better because eternal life does not operate today." What a huge mistake! Let us understand that eternal life begins to manifest itself today. This life we have been given is for us to live by today. Otherwise, life as a Christian has no meaning to it. Why would Christ come to live in us if He is not going to live *today* as our life? On the contrary, this life that has been given us is to grow into full maturity—that is to say, into the full image of Christ. It is like a seed that, having come into our spirit, grows and grows and grows until our whole being is glorified. Please bear in mind, however, that all this growing process occurs in our spirit.

SPIRITUAL LIFE

What do we mean by spiritual life? It does not mean that we have a healthy body or an intelligent mind. Spiritual life means that the life in our spirit is living, growing, maturing; that it is gradually being transformed and continually being conformed to the image of Christ. That is spiritual life. So there must be a growing process going on today deep down within us. That is the purpose of God, that is the way of God, and that is what we need to pay special attention to. When we exercise ourselves unto godliness, it is an exercise which occurs in our spirit. The more we exercise the better we grow and mature there. If we do not exercise our spirit, and even though it is there, the spirit remains dormant, and we are not profited by it. We will miss the whole purpose of God's salvation.

SPIRITUAL LIFE NEGLECTED

Sad to say, many Christians neglect their spirit and their spiritual life. As a result, they do not exercise the great gift of the spirit that God has renewed in them, and thus they do not grow in godliness as they should. This is a state of affairs which has bothered me greatly in recent days and has constantly puzzled me as I have been before the Lord in preparing for these messages. Why is it that though people have believed in the Lord Jesus and have had His life dwelling in them for many years there is so little growth? What is the reason? Where lies the problem? Perhaps the problem is, that they know how to exercise their body, and they even know how to exercise their soul—since from childhood they were sent off to school to learn, to study and to gather information from outside which would make them wise and intelligent—yet they do not know how to exercise their spirit.

ALL HAVE SINNED

In this connection, let me try to explain further how we are saved. The Bible tells us that we have sinned: "All have sinned and come short of the glory of God" (Romans 3:23). But if you tell people they have sinned and that they are sinners, will they receive such a word? Suppose I go to a person and say: "You are a sinner." What will he say? He may respond by saying: "I am not in jail for any reason! I am free. I am therefore not a sinner." Before we are saved we are in such darkness that we do not even know that we have sinned, nor do we recognize the seriousness of our sin even if we know.

Now from childhood I had been brought up in a Christian family. So by the time I was in high school, I was fairly well acquainted with the Bible and knew the plan of salvation, but I never believed. Why? It was not because I did not believe in God—mentally I did. It was not because I did not believe Jesus is the Savior of the world—I did. But I had no sense that I needed to be saved because I thought I was a good person. I was a good student and friendly with everybody. Hence, my thinking was that, yes, Jesus is the Savior of the world, and, yes, He came to save sinners; I thank God for that; but I myself did not think I needed Him. Little did I know that I was in total darkness, I not realizing that I, too, was a sinner.

What, though, happened when you and I began to realize we had sinned? We came to the realization that each of us was a great sinner, and that unless something significantly happened our hope of enjoying eternity was finished. Yet how did this realization first come to us?

Let us take note of what the Bible tells us happens to all people in the world. Jesus revealed to His disciples, as recorded in John 16:8 (ASV), what one of the primary responsibilities the Holy Spirit would begin to carry out when He came: He would convict all people of their guilt before God concerning sin (in that same verse we are told that He would convict them as well concerning their lack of righteousness and concerning God's coming judgment). But where in man does this convicting work of God's Spirit occur? It has to occur in that part of man which corresponds to the Spirit's nature—that is, in man's spirit. Yet, as was learned earlier, the spirit of all men in Adam became dead so far as it having any relationship with God was concerned, because, scientifically speaking, death is the cessation of communication with its proper environment. The proper environment of the human body, for example, is the world, and when one loses contact with the world, he is pronounced dead; for he cannot smell, he cannot feel, he cannot see, hear, or touch—he is therefore considered to be dead.

THE COMATOSE HUMAN SPIRIT

What, then, does it mean when it is said that the *spirit* of a person is dead? Answer: It has lost its contact or communication with its proper environment; and to explain a step further, the proper environment of the human spirit is God himself. Therefore, spiritually speaking, when people lose that contact, they are deemed to be dead. Let us understand, however, that the organ of man which we call his spirit is not annihilated; on the contrary, it is still there. How do we know this? Well, though people cannot contact God, they can certainly contact evil spirits as the Judeo-Christian Scriptures will abundantly attest. Therefore, this fact itself shows that the human organ we call spirit is there but it has lost its proper communication; and thus the spirit is dead to God. As far as the proper function of our spirit is concerned it had fallen into a comatose state. That is the best way I can describe it. But we know that sometimes people who are in a coma will suddenly wake up for a while, and that is what happens when a person is saved. Formerly, our spirit had become comatose, so far as its proper function was concerned, but it was awakened when we were saved.

Now in every person's life there are occasions when suddenly our conscience is awakened—perhaps, for a short while on each such occasion. And that happens when we find ourselves unexpectedly in some kind of danger. In this connection, I remember a true story of a missionary. One day he came across an atheist who was preaching that there was no God. Coincidentally, it just so happened that this man was one whom the missionary had rescued earlier when he was about to drown. The missionary had at that time heard him cry out: "God, save me!" And so he had gone into the water and had rescued the atheist. Nevertheless, this same man soon returned to preaching atheism again. So the missionary confronted him and said: "Why did you cry 'God, save me!' in your hour of desperation?" The Holy Spirit had convicted him of his guilt by having touched his spirit's conscience and intuition, thus momentarily awakening his spirit out of its comatose state; this was because intuitively he knew deep down in his being that there *is* a God. As a result, when he was in danger of drowning, he had immediately cried out to God for help. In Chinese we have a proverb that is apt here: "When a bird is dying, its cry is mournful. When a man is dying, his word is always good"—meaning that he will express some good things at such a time because he knows he is going to meet his Maker.

Is it not true that when you were saved, the Holy Spirit somehow touched your conscience? Your spirit had been in a coma—that is, you had not felt you were sinful, but suddenly you now realized you were. The famous Christian evangelist, Dwight L. Moody, once said that when a person is drowning, suddenly all his sins come rushing before him mentally. We today would liken it to a motion picture film being projected on a screen.

That happened to me. In a sudden moment of time the Holy Spirit revealed all my sins to me, and He also opened up my intuition by showing me that Jesus is the only Savior. I can still remember most vividly what happened to me when I was saved by the grace of God back in 1930. For at that moment my communion with God was resumed. I had gone to my room and opened up the Bible to II Peter, and the Scriptures finally began to speak to my heart. Now as mentioned earlier I had known the Bible before because I had read it from my childhood, but from the time I was saved and began to read it afresh, it was no longer a dead book. The Bible had at this moment become a living book and my heavenly Father was now speaking to me through His word.

THE HOLY SPIRIT WORKS IN OUR SPIRIT

Is it not true that when you were saved something wonderful happened in your spirit in that all of the functions of your spirit began to work? That is how you began your life with Christ. But what actually happened? God revealed to you that this inward way of the spirit is the way of life, and if you follow it and exercise it, you will be on the right path. Regrettably, very soon, we begin to be led astray by Christianity, for the latter begins to teach us many rules and regulations: "Now that you are saved, this is what you should do, and this is what you should not do." The result is we are brought back under law, and the Bible tells us that the letter of the law kills but the Spirit quickens into life (II Corinthians 3:6).

When we are first saved, the Holy Spirit begins to work in our spirit. He works in our conscience, illumines our intuition, and draws us into communion with God. These are the basic activities of the Holy Spirit. This is the inward way of life by which God wants us to live, and if we continue in that way we will grow spiritually. Instead of following that path, however, we begin to forget this inward way of life; therefore, we soon neglect it. Our conscience does continue to speak to us but we do not listen anymore. Light continually comes to us but we no longer obey. And so our communion with God becomes something outward—it no longer being something inward by the spirit. We try to commune with God with our emotion, with our mind, with our will—"will-worship" as the

Bible puts it (Colossians 2:23 AV, ASV). We even employ our physical posture by which to commune with God, but that, too, does not work. As a result of all this, our spirit is neglected; and hence, spiritual exercise is also neglected. This condition among Christians makes me cry.

Christianity is the culprit that has led us astray. We are not walking in the narrow way, the straight way, or the way which will lead to life. Instead, we are walking in the broad way which leads to destruction (Matthew 7:13-14). Is it not time that we should truly repent and return? The Christian way is the inward—not the outward—way. Christian life is the way of grace—not of law (Romans 6:14b). The Christian way is the way of the spirit—not of the body or of the soul. The question therefore to be asked is: Are we really walking according to this inward way of life?

What is the condition of your spiritual life today? Have you ever exercised your spirit? I believe the Holy Spirit is continually working upon our spirit, but are we cooperating with God's Spirit by exercising our spirit in order that we may grow spiritually?

EXERCISE

All of us who believe in the Lord have a spiritual life, and this life needs to grow in order for the will of God to be accomplished in us. Is that not what a Christian should be experiencing? If we are not experiencing this, are we really living a Christian life? A normal Christian life is one that lives in the spirit. If we live in the spirit daily, we will grow.

Moreover, your spirit needs to be exercised continually. If you exercise your spirit daily, your spiritual stature will quite naturally increase. With regard to our Christian life, I think there is nothing else more fundamental than this. If we do not even know this, nor pay attention to this, nor engage in spiritual exercise, then we cannot even talk about spiritual life as being a part of our Christian experience. We will only be living on the outside and not living before the presence of God. I believe that spiritual exercise is the necessary path of a normal Christian life.

What is exercise? Exercise is an activity of which we are conscious—it is not that which we engage in automatically. It is quite true, of course, that we are active every day in many ways, but such activity does not necessarily signify exercise. When we exercise, we are quite aware that what we are doing is indeed an exercise. It is something we do deliberately. It is something to which we apply ourselves. It is something we do regularly on a daily basis. It is something we do with purpose. And it is something we do with discipline. In some versions of the Bible the Greek word for exercise is translated into English as "train"—from which we can therefore infer that there is a need to have a trainer. And in the context of *spiritual* exercise the trainer is none other than the Holy Spirit. Therefore, this means that we do not exercise by ourselves, but we do so under the training of the Holy Spirit.

THE ANCIENT GREEK GYMNASIUM

In ancient days the Greeks paid much attention to their physical body. They wanted to develop a perfectly well-balanced body; and because of that, they eagerly and regularly went to the gymnasium. There they had trainers, and those trainers were considerably conversant with the science of physiology. They would study your particular body in order to discover what members of it were weak and which ones were too strong. They wanted to develop well-balanced bodies in their gymnasium. After they had studied your body they would tell you what kind of exercise you needed to go through to energize and develop your body into a well-balanced whole. Oh, how those who went to the gymnasium would work out and were most willing to sweat for it! Naturally, exercising involves a certain amount of pain, but they were willing to endure it and persevered in their various physical exercises. After they had engaged in these exercises for some time, gradually, they developed a beautiful, well-balanced, coordinated body. That is what the Greeks diligently sought after, but we Christians have something far better in view as our goal. They were being trained and were exercising just for time but we wish to do so for eternity; so we, too, need to go into the gymnasium—in our case, into the spiritual gymnasium of Christ.

Having said that, I do not wish to be understood here as advising you to go off to a school. Rather, I am advising you to go to the gymnasium. Now do not mistake what I mean. School, college or university is not an institution for training your body but for training your mind. Let us say, for instance, that you pay a fee to attend a university, and there the professors become your employees. *You* are the employer, and you go there to try to absorb all the professors' learning, knowledge and skills—and for nothing else. That, essentially, is what an educational institution is all about.

LET US ENTER THE GYMNASIUM OF CHRIST

We know that a gymnasium, however, is different from those educational institutions, because a person in a gym has to work out physically—causing much pain, agony and sweat in the process—in order to go through its regimen successfully. Interestingly, within the context of *spiritual* exercise, Paul declared that in the process of doing this he labored and suffered reproach. Likewise, we, too, must labor and suffer reproach if we are to arrive at our spiritual goal. The Holy Spirit may have to reproach us—in fact, He oftentimes does—yet not because He wants to but because of what we are. Can we endure it? Are we willing to suffer for it? "For this we labour and suffer reproach," wrote the apostle Paul; and he went on to say: "because we hope in a living God." And, he added, God is the "preserver of all men, specially of those who believe" (I Timothy 4:10).

I would hereby invite all of you to join with me in entering the gymnasium of Christ. By the grace of God we shall have, and must have, determination and perseverance. If we exercise once a day and neglect it for two days, such an exercise program will not be effectual. It must be a matter of persistency. It is that to which we have to apply ourselves daily.

God willing, over the next several weeks we will want to seek Him together in this area of our Christian lives of exercising our spirit; that is to say, we shall inquire as to how do we exercise our conscience? our intuition? our faculty of communion? What are the genuinely true exercises and what are the false ones? And by the grace of God, in our discussions together we will want to inquire into this entire matter not in terms of a scholastic approach but in terms of a practical, gymnastic one, as we look to God for His wisdom, strength and support.

Chapter 2

CONSCIENCE

I Timothy 1:19—Maintaining faith [i.e., holding fast the faith] and a good conscience; which last some, having put away, have made shipwreck as to faith.

I John 3:18-22—Children, let us not love with word, nor with tongue, but in deed and in truth. And hereby we shall know that we are of the truth, and shall persuade our hearts before him—that if our heart condemn us, God is greater than our heart and knows all things. Beloved, if our heart condemn us not, we have boldness towards God, and whatsoever we ask we receive from him, because we keep his commandments, and practise the things which are pleasing in his sight.

We want to focus our attention on this topic of spiritual exercise. We have already mentioned this subject of spiritual life. Every Christian is supposed to have a spiritual life. Yet, exactly what is spiritual life? It is a life *of* the spirit and a life *in* the spirit. Praise God, when He saves us, He quickens our dead spirit back into life, enabling us to communicate with Him, to know His mind and to do His will. He not only gives us His life but He also gives His Spirit to indwell within us. So when we are saved, we not only receive a new spirit, we also receive the life of God—which is Christ—in our new spirit, and we also have God's Spirit dwelling in our new spirit.

Why does God do this for us? It is because His purpose is that once He has given us His life He wants that life to grow into maturity. It is God's eternal will that each one of us who is saved will be transformed and conformed to the image of His beloved Son. In order to accomplish that goal He restores our spirit to life and puts His Spirit into that life. As a matter of fact, the Holy Spirit is there to be the custodian as well as the manager of that new life in us so that He may bring us into spiritual growth, maturity and conformity to the image of the Son of God's love. What a glorious salvation that is!

COOPERATE WITH GOD

In order for this spiritual life to grow within us and transform us into His likeness, there is something very important which we must do. God has provided everything for our spiritual life, but that does not mean that we automatically grow and are conformed to His image. God expects us to do something by His grace, and that is, to cooperate with Him. And in cooperating with Him we will learn how to exercise our spirit.

We have already mentioned that we know how to exercise our body because we know how important physical exercise is. We may eat well and sleep well, but if we do not exercise we will have health problems. That is why obesity is so prevailing in this country because people just eat and rest or sit and watch television or sit at the computer and do not exercise. And that naturally creates many physical problems.

In the same way, if we do not exercise our spirit that God has renewed in us, which is such a beautiful, wonderful gift of His, we will encounter a similar problem. Our spirit will become dull, insensitive and not able to cooperate with God. Hence, that is why it is so important that we exercise this great gift of our spirit which God has given us, and not allow it to lie inactive and unused—and thus, not growing. Otherwise, there will be spiritual sickness. We know how to exercise our body because it is made of matter. We can see and touch it, and we know how to make it exercise. But we do not see our spirit. Our spirit is not made of matter—it is spiritual, heavenly and unseen. Nevertheless, though it is not seen, it is real and it is there.

THE UNSEEN MORE IMPORTANT

In II Corinthians chapter 4 we are told that the seen is temporal—just for a time; but that the unseen is eternal—it is forever. In other words, the unseen is more important than the seen. Our spiritual life is more important than our physical life, for as the Bible explains: "Bodily exercise is profitable for a little, but exercise unto godliness is profitable for all things." Furthermore, spiritual exercise has the promise of eternal life because it is profitable not only for this life but also for the life to come (see again I Timothy 4:8). Yes, our spirit is unseen, but that does not mean it does not exist. It is there, and it is actually more real than our physical body, though it is not visible. Now how can we exercise this that is invisible?

I would like to ask a parallel question. Can we see electricity? It is true that electricity is something physical but even so, it is not seen. Nevertheless, everybody knows about electricity and how to use it. We know of it by its power, by its light and by its heat. Hence, we cannot deny the fact that there is electricity by claiming that because we cannot see it, it must not be there. That is a false statement. We all believe electricity is there and we all enjoy it. We enjoy its power, light and heat. When we had no electricity, how we trembled when it was so cold. I can well remember when we were in school in China and we had no heat, how we suffered much throughout the winter.

THE FUNCTIONS OF THE SPIRIT

How, then, do we exercise our invisible spirit? We do so by its functions. As we shall see, our spirit has three main ones. Similarly, our body has five senses or functions, while our soul has three: emotions—which are our feelings, thoughts—which include our opinions, and will—which includes the making of decisions. In summary, that is our soul, and it represents what we are.

Our spirit is known by its functions and it has three main ones which we can find mentioned or alluded to in the Bible. There is the function of conscience which God has given us; intuition, which is direct knowledge and revelation; and also communion, in order that we may commune with God since only spirit can commune with spirit. God is spirit; therefore, by His Spirit God gives us a spirit that we may communicate with Him, understand His mind, and do His will.

MAN'S SPIRIT

When God created man, he was entirely different from all other created beings because he not only had a body and a soul but he also had a spirit. The Bible tells us that when God created man, He breathed into man's nostrils; however, in the Chinese Bible there is a phrase which does not appear in the English Bible. The latter version merely states that after God breathed into that body, man became a living soul—a statement that is quite true. But in the Chinese Bible it reads that man "became a living soul with a spirit" and this is actually what happened (cf. Genesis 2:7). Man's spirit is produced directly from the breath of God and, therefore, our spirit can communicate with God because it is of the same nature. This is the highest gift in created man, and it makes him different from all other created beings and from all created things on earth. In other words, it is man's spirit that is the source for his dignity and nobility. If man loses the proper function of his spirit and becomes flesh, he thereby loses his dignity. So we see how important and how great a gift a man's spirit is!

After God created man and put him in the Garden of Eden (see Genesis 2:15 ff.), He came down from heaven and commenced communicating with him. Unfortunately, man had already sinned against God by doing that which He had forbidden. As a result of this sin, death entered into the world, which circumstance began with man's spirit; for the Bible tells us that God had said to man: "On the very day that you eat the forbidden fruit you shall die" (Genesis 2:17b). Now we know that after he had sinned, Adam lived on for hundreds of years more and begot children, which thus indicates that his body and soul were very much alive, though eventually Adam's body did die; but his spirit was what died on the very day he had sinned against God.

A WICKED CONSCIENCE

The spirit of a person who does not know the Lord Jesus is dead. Yet, though the spirit is dead, it does not mean that his spirit does not exist. Its death only signifies that it has lost its communication with its proper environment. Therefore, when a man sins and his spirit is dead, it simply means that he has lost his communication with God because God is the proper environment of his spirit. The functions of that spirit, as it were, went into a coma.

We will recall the Biblical story in Genesis 3 of Adam and Eve when they sinned and what happened to them. Upon their hearing the voice of God in the Garden of Eden, they had hid themselves because immediately after they had sinned they realized they were naked. So when God inquired: "Where are you? Why have you hidden yourselves?" they replied: "Because we are naked." What had happened? We know that every living being is clothed by God. You do not need to clothe your dog, as some people do. It is unnatural, for God has already given clothes to a dog. Every animal has clothes. Why at this moment in the Garden of Eden did man believe he was naked? I do not believe it was like that at the very beginning of man's creation, for I believe that God had clothed man with glory; but when man sinned, the glory disappeared and man became naked and ashamed before God.

Now who or what told Adam and Eve they were naked? It was their conscience; their conscience had accused them; in other words, they now had an uneasy conscience. Then when God asked Adam why he had eaten the forbidden fruit, Adam replied: "It is the fault of the woman You gave me." And Eve in turn said, "It is the snake's fault." In short, they both tried to put the blame on others. They attempted to cover and place the fault on others as a way to quench the voice of their conscience. Since then, man still has a conscience, but what kind of conscience is it? The Bible calls it "a wicked conscience" (Hebrews 10:22).

I often have people tell me, "I do everything according to my conscience. I have a good conscience." Now a robber can say that, a killer can say that, a cannibal, after eating a person, can say that; but what kind of conscience actually is that? The conscience of man is still there, and once in a great while it may suddenly wake up to realize that there is a God and that before Him he is naked. Throughout human history people have tried to bribe their conscience in order to have inner peace—but it is a false peace. They think that by doing something good it will cover their wicked conscience; unfortunately, it remains a wicked conscience.

Conscience can either accuse us or excuse us, but after a person has sinned, he is under accusation. He tries to excuse himself, but in times of danger it does not work: he only cheats himself. That is why when people are dying they try to say something good because their conscience bothers them. They know there is a reality which they have tried to cover up all their lives. How sad that is! But thank God, when He saves us, something wonderful happens. First of all, by the grace of God His Holy Spirit begins to reveal to us that we have sinned. Thinking that we have a good conscience, we have all tried to cover up our sins by making excuses for ourselves; but when the light of God comes and shines in us, we begin to see that we are real sinners—that from our head to our feet there is nothing good (Romans 7:18a). That was the way I myself felt when the Spirit of God convicted me of sin. I had to find the way of salvation, and thank God, I found it in Christ Jesus.

HEARTS SPRINKLED FROM AN EVIL CONSCIENCE

What happens when we believe in the Lord Jesus? The Bible tells us in Hebrews 10:22: "Let us approach with a true heart, in full assurance of faith, sprinkled as to our hearts from a wicked conscience, and washed as to our body with pure water."

When we are under conviction from God that we have a wicked conscience, we cannot face Him or eternity. But when we turn our eyes to Jesus, who is the Savior of the world, when we believe in Him as our personal Savior and as the Son of God, the Bible describes this event as follows: "We are sprinkled as to our hearts from a wicked conscience." In other words, the blood of the Lord Jesus that was shed on Calvary's cross has eternal power: His blood is sprinkled upon our hearts and we are delivered from a wicked conscience.

THREEFOLD EFFECT OF THE BLOOD

The precious blood of the Lord Jesus has a threefold effect. Number one, it is God-ward, for when we accept the blood of the Lord Jesus and it is sprinkled upon our heart, we are justified before God. He is a just God. He condemns everything that is unrighteous. But Christ Jesus who knew no sin was made sin for us (II Corinthians 5:21a), and if we believe in Him we shall be made the righteousness of God in Him (II Corinthians 5:21b) and are thus justified before God through faith (Romans 5:1). Jesus' shed blood is sprinkled upon our conscience (see Hebrews 9:13-14, cf. 10:22b). Blood has cleansed the way between us and God, and we are justified by His precious blood. Our sins are washed away and we are free. We will be judged no more. That is the preciousness of the blood of the Lord Jesus, and that is God-ward.

Number two in its effect, the blood of Jesus is us-ward. It is sprinkled upon our hearts inside a wicked conscience (see again Hebrews 10:22). At once our conscience is at peace. That is why when we are saved, there is such peace which comes into our lives. I felt this at the time when I trusted the Lord, and that peace is forever.

Number three, Jesus' blood is Satan-ward in its effect. The blood of the Lord Jesus shuts the mouth of our accuser who is Satan. He tries to accuse us, and sometimes his accusation is true. He has some basis for making the accusation. But most of the time Satan's accusations are not true; they are false ones. The blood of Jesus answers all the accusations and shuts the mouth of the accuser (see Revelation 12:10b-11a). How precious is the blood of the Lord Jesus! Throughout our Christian life we enjoy the efficacy of the power of His blood. Hence, a believer's wicked conscience is sprinkled with the blood of the Lord Jesus and is purged from all sin. This fact is given expression in Hebrews 10:2: "Since, would they not indeed have ceased being offered, on account of the worshippers once purged having no longer any conscience of sins?"

We who believe in the Lord Jesus have a cleansed, renewed, purged, sprinkled, and good conscience. That is what we receive at the time we are saved. How we do thank God for that! Many people can testify that the burden which was upon them fell away and there came great peace within. How precious that is!

CONSCIENCE: THE GUIDE TO OUR WALK

Now I would like to ask this question: Why did God save us and purge our conscience so that now we have a good conscience which no longer accuses us? What is the meaning behind it? What is the will and purpose of God in giving us a good conscience? It is more than just assuring us that one day we can see Him face to face and be with Him forever. That is true, but it is more than that. In our daily life He wants us to maintain a good conscience before Him because it is the guide to our walk. For us believers, our conscience is now the voice of God. The Holy Spirit who dwells in our spirit tells our conscience what is the right thing and what is the wrong thing before God. This is the way we can be guided in our daily walk. It is absolutely essential we keep a good conscience before God because if we do not, our faith will lose out. It is like being shipwrecked, as the Bible says (I Timothy 1:19). Therefore, maintaining a good conscience before God and man is the only way we can walk uprightly before them.

Before we were saved we could not depend upon our conscience because it had lost its standard. God was no longer its standard. On the contrary, our culture or our custom became the standard, and such a standard is no standard at all. It is a wicked conscience. A person cannot depend upon that wicked conscience and live rightly. But now, we believers in Christ have a good, clean and clear conscience. Henceforth, how do we walk out our Christian faith? How do we behave as Christians? It is not by somebody on earth telling us how, but by God himself. In our conscience He will show us the way to righteousness in order that we may live properly before God and man. So a Christian's conscience is God's wonderful provision for us to walk rightly before Him. It is absolutely essential that in our daily life we continually have a good conscience before God and man.

THE HOLY SPIRIT WORKS IN OUR CONSCIENCE

Who can maintain a good conscience? We ourselves are not able to do so, but the Holy Spirit is faithful. It is His job to instruct us. As we have said before, spiritual exercise needs a trainer or an instructor. You cannot go about exercising wildly, because if you do, you may hurt yourself—by overdoing it or by doing the opposite. Hence, we need to be under an instructor who knows our frame, and the Holy Spirit is the One who knows the spirit. He is the One who knows the life of Christ. He is there to increase Christ in us and to decrease us. He is an expert and is never wrong.

So the Holy Spirit will begin His work in our conscience. Of all the functions of our spirit, the conscience is the most active and sensitive one. Therefore, if we neglect our conscience, our spiritual life is finished. When the Holy Spirit begins to work in our conscience, He is so gentle. We often say the Holy Spirit is like a gentle dove (cf. John 1:3, Matthew 10:16b). When He speaks it is in a still small voice, and He will deal with us according to our measure—how much to which we are able to respond. He will never overwhelm us nor try to destroy or kill us. He knows us so well that He will gently but firmly touch our conscience, clear it and strengthen it so that we may walk rightly before God and man.

As I indicated earlier, we are not attending school but the gymnasium; and hence, I am not trying to give forth lots of teachings and doctrines. Instead, I would like to illustrate and prove by our experiences how to exercise our conscience. As a matter of fact, however, it is the Holy Spirit who exercises our conscience, and we are simply to respond by cooperating and working together with Him.

THE STILL SMALL VOICE OF THE HOLY SPIRIT

Do you remember the incident in Elijah's life that is recorded in I Kings 19? Elijah the prophet was very zealous, and he wanted to bring the whole nation of Israel back to God. But when Jezebel threatened him, he fled. When he was at Mt. Horeb, "a great and strong wind tore into the mountains and broke the rocks in pieces before the Lord; but the Lord was not in the wind. And after the wind, an earthquake; but the Lord was not in the earthquake. And after the earthquake, a fire; but the Lord was not in the fire. And after the fire, a still, small and gentle voice, saying: What are you doing here, Elijah?" (see vv. 11-14) When the Spirit of God speaks to our conscience, He speaks in a still and gentle voice.

Today, too many people cannot hear His voice from the inside because there is too much noise on the outside. When we try to listen to this and that, we will not be able to hear the voice within. We need to quiet ourselves before God, and only then can we hear this still, small and gentle voice. When the Holy Spirit speaks, it is very clear. It is not ambiguous and it is not confusing. He is not there to accuse us but to encourage and remind us. His speaking is not like a sudden strong wind to sweep us off our feet nor is His voice like a great earthquake or fire that frightens us. On the contrary, the Spirit within us is like a gentle, sensitive dove.

CONCLUDING OUR PAST

Thank God that after we are saved all our past sins have been forgiven. All our sins have been cleansed by the precious blood, and before God we are justified. We can approach Him with a clear conscience. That is the beauty of Christ in His redemption. After we are saved the Holy Spirit, so far as our experience is concerned, will be intent on encouraging and helping us to conclude our past. This does not mean that our past sins are not forgiven. They all are indeed forgiven, and before God there is no problem concerning them anymore. But we have to be cleared before man. Suppose that before I was saved I had stolen something. After I was saved God forgave my sins, but how about those things I had stolen? In the eyes of God we are justified, but in the eyes of the person offended we are not. We had no testimony before that person. So it does not mean that because God has forgiven us, all has been made right. No, some of our past has to be dealt with and cleared up. If, for example, we owe anything, let us pay it back with interest.

In the Old Testament period there was the trespass offering, which had two aspects or sides to it (Leviticus 6:1-8). We may sin against God only, but whenever we sin against our fellow man we are also sinning against God because that fellow man of ours has likewise been created by God. So with respect to the trespass offering which was offered up to God, we are told that there was the human side as well. On the divine side Christ is our trespass offering, but on the human side, if anyone had owed anybody anything, that person was required to pay the amount back and add one fifth as interest (Leviticus 6:5). That was what was required in the period of the Old Testament; nevertheless, the *principle* is there for us today to follow. Indeed, throughout church history, especially in the accounts of revival, and also in people's personal experience, this principle of restitution appears again and again.

After we are saved the Holy Spirit will remind us of something we did that offended or hurt people. God says, "Make it right." That is why we find many of God's people having to make restitution after they were saved. They have had to apologize. After I myself was saved I had to write many letters asking for forgiveness. I had wrongfully hurt the feelings of people and had to apologize.

Church history reveals that during the times of revival the post offices became unusually busy because of the considerable increase of letters—many of which were letters and packages of restitution. Things stolen were returned; funds owed were repaid. We need to ask ourselves: Have we done that? Could it be that one of the reasons Christians are so weak today is because they have never concluded their past? In the eyes of the world they are not Christians. It is true that when we need to apologize, it is shameful for us to have to do so; we as it were have to be humiliated; nevertheless, are we willing to humble ourselves and make matters right in order that we may have a good testimony before both God *and* man?

BAD HABITS ARE TO BE DEALT WITH

Many old bad habits have to be shed. Here are a few which come to mind.

Smoking

I had a friend who was a millionaire banker. He was also one of the best known fortune-tellers in China. I knew him intimately. He smoked seventy cigarettes a day with only one match. While he was eating his meal his servant would hold the cigarette for him. After he was saved, the cigarettes disappeared. His wife smoked opium, but after she was baptized, the opium also disappeared. It was a marvelous deliverance.

I have another friend who was a Christian medical doctor, Dr. Shih. He smoked but he knew it was not right. He tried to get rid of the habit but he was unable to give it up, so he smoked secretly. After he would smoke he would have to eat something in order to cover up the smell on his breath. But one day he finally saw the relevant spiritual truth, and said: "I cannot quit smoking, but He can." He turned his eyes upon the Lord and the habit was gone.

Drinking

On the subject of drinking, the Bible does say in I Corinthians 6:12a: "All things are lawful to me." After we are saved all things are lawful for us. We are not under bondage of any kind. We are free, but the passage goes on also to say that all things do not profit. Yes, all things are lawful: we can do it; but is a particular activity profitable? "All things are lawful for me, but I will not be brought under the power of any" (v. 12b AV). If any habit—such as drinking—has power over us, we have to overcome.

Movies

I was a pastor's son but I liked movies. That was my life before I was saved. After I was saved I still attended the movie theater but not on Sundays. All my young life I had only done so once on a Sunday, but my conscience pricked me. God was asking me: "Is it right for you to waste your money to support those who are ungodly?" Yet I could not overcome the habit. Sometimes I could go to the theater without paying anything because my friend's family owned the theater, and also I had other friends who sent me tickets. But my conscience bothered me, so I tried to overcome the practice.

For several months I did not attend any theater, but then the temptation appeared once again. Somebody had given our family tickets to a fancy theater for viewing a religious movie. I very much hated to give up that ticket. I tried to compromise with myself by saying: "It is a religious movie— "Noah's Ark"—what is wrong with that?" So I went to the theater. For two hours I sat there watching the movie, but there was a battle raging in my heart all along. When I walked out, praise God, He completely delivered me! Later on, my aunt said to me: "You are a young man. Why don't you enjoy yourself and go to the theater? I will give you the money for it." But from deep within my heart I replied: "You do not understand. I do not need it. I have something far more precious and satisfying than that."

Friendships

Then there is this area of friendships. A person's acceptance of Christ is why a Christian will usually change his friends. How can a believer continue having friendship with the world since that will mean enmity against God (James 4:4)?

Our Dress

Then there is the issue of our dress. Has the Lord ever touched your heart on the way you dress? Why are we dressed? It is to cover our nakedness and to keep us warm. But what is the meaning of dress today? I am speaking especially to sisters, though brothers are not exempt. We men can be guilty of the same thing. Now the love of beauty is a quite natural human inclination because God is a God of beauty. There is nothing wrong with beauty, but what is real beauty? The Bible teaches about our dress in I Timothy chapter 2: "In like manner also that the women in decent deportment and dress adorn themselves with modesty and discretion, not with plaited hair and gold, or pearls, or costly clothing, but, what becomes women making profession of the fear of God, by good works" (vv. 9-10).

Also, in I Peter we read this: "Having witnessed your pure conversation carried out in fear; whose adorning let it not be that outward one of tressing of hair, and wearing gold, or putting on apparel; but the hidden man of the heart, in the incorruptible ornament of a meek and quiet spirit, which in the sight of God is of great price" (3:2-4).

BEAR A GOOD TESTIMONY

There is no law here, it is simply grace. I believe that as we walk with the Lord He by His Spirit will touch our conscience and gradually deliver us from all things which control our lives so that we may be free to give ourselves totally to Him and bear a good testimony to the world. If we neglect our conscience we cannot walk uprightly before God and man. Most interestingly, towards the latter part of his life when the apostle Paul was brought before the entire ruling Jewish Sanhedrin Council and the chief priests, he was moved to declare the following opening statement: "I have walked before God in all good conscience up to this very day" (see Acts 22:30-23:1). And we are further told in the book of Acts that Paul subsequently made a similar declaration before the Roman governor Felix: "I exercise myself to live with a conscience without offense before both God and man" (see 24:16).

Are we able today to make such a declaration of conscience? What exactly is the character of our present walk before both God and man? Is the Holy Spirit touching our conscience? And are we cooperating with Him when He does? If not, our conscience will become harder and harder, growing more and more insensitive, until it will not bother us any longer. Let us, instead, yield each time to our conscience, for conscience is God's way to guide us into the way of righteousness, since He himself is the very standard of our conscience. If we are willing to exercise our spirit by cooperating with the Holy Spirit as He touches our conscience, we shall come to realize that there are many matters—even small ones—in our lives which God's Spirit will begin to clear up, as it were, by delivering us from being under the power of anything.

Now in concluding our discussion today, I would very much hope that none of us will feel in any way intimidated by what has been said here, and that we may all learn day by day to exercise our conscience. I hope, too, that as we daily go out from the gymnasium of Christ we can maintain before both God and man a good conscience without offense so that we may continually bear a testimony to the world. May God bless us.

Chapter 3

INTUITION

Ephesians 1:17—That the God of our Lord Jesus Christ, the Father of glory, would give you the spirit of wisdom and revelation in the full knowledge of him.

Hebrews 8:11—And they shall not teach each his fellow-citizen, and each his brother, saying, Know the Lord; because all shall know me in themselves, from the little one among them unto the great among them.

I John 1:5, 7—And this is the message which we have heard from him, and declare to you, that God is light, and in him is no darkness at all ... But if we walk in the light as he is in the light, we have fellowship with one another, and the blood of Jesus Christ his Son cleanses us from all sin.

I John 2:27—And ... the unction [anointing] which ye have received from him abides in you, and ye have not need that any one should teach you; but as the same unction [anointing] teaches you as to all things, and is true and is not a lie, and even as it has taught you, ye shall abide in him.

We have been burdened with this subject of spiritual growth. Since we have believed in the Lord Jesus, we have received His precious life, and we have God's Holy Spirit dwelling in our new spirit, and we ought, therefore, to grow in our spiritual life. This simply means there is a life in our new spirit which is according to the Holy Spirit of God. Why is it that we, who have believed in the Lord Jesus and have received all the precious promises and provisions which God has provided for us, do not grow as we ought? Why is it that we often remain as babes in Christ instead of being conformed to the image of Christ and growing into full maturity? This is our pressing problem, and this is also our quest: we want to learn how we can grow spiritually, be transformed, and conformed to the image of Christ.

Probably one reason for this lack in spiritual growth is that we do not know how to exercise our spirit. Thank God, when we believed in the Lord Jesus, the Holy Spirit came to us and quickened our dead spirit into a new spirit. Accordingly, every saved person has a new spirit within him or her. Why is that new spirit so important? Because God is spirit and there is no way to communicate with Him except in and through our spirit. As was mentioned earlier, we know that our spirit within us is not a material entity. Nevertheless, though it does not consist of matter, we cannot therefore say it is nonexistent. In fact, our spirit within us is as real as our body—and perhaps even more real than our body.

FUNCTIONS OF OUR SPIRIT

We had considered previously the question: How do we know that we have a spirit? We know by its function. We cannot see our spirit but we can experience it because it has three important functions. The first of these, as was discussed last time, is the faculty of conscience that has been cleansed by the blood of the Lord Jesus in order that we may live on this earth without any offense before God and man.

Conscience is a faculty within us which not only is awakened at the moment we are saved; it is also a law of life within our spiritual life which ought always to be operative within us. Accordingly, we need to exercise our conscience daily.

DIRECT KNOWLEDGE

We would next like to consider how to exercise the second main faculty of our spirit, which we would call intuition. This simply means direct knowledge; it is knowledge which comes directly from God himself. It comes not from the outside nor is it acquired by our human reasoning; rather, God speaks directly to our spirit. He tells us what is good and what is evil. There is a difference between what is right and wrong and what is good and evil. Good and evil in the Scriptures are terms possessing a deeper meaning than that of right and wrong. According to the scriptural meaning, good has to do with God's will. Whatever is God's will is good, and whatever is not His will is bad. It is not like the worldly concept. Therefore, our intuition will tell us what is good: the will of God, and what is bad: not the will of God. In our Christian life this is an important issue because we want to know what the will of God is in a certain matter or in a decision to be made or whether we should go this way or that. We want to know what God's will is so that we may obey and do His will. So how can we know it? We know it through intuition. If conscience is related to the righteousness of God, then intuition is related to the holiness of God.

What is the meaning of holy? Holy means we are separated to God. So how can we be holy as He is holy? It is through intuition. Accordingly, if we do not know how to exercise our intuition properly we will not know how to be holy. What we consider good may turn out to be bad, and what we consider bad is probably good and is the will of God. So intuition is very, very essential to our spiritual life. We need to exercise our intuition daily.

ACQUIRED KNOWLEDGE

There are two kinds of knowledge. One kind is called acquired knowledge. How do we gather it? When we are a little baby or a child we are innocent. And it is natural that as we grow up we begin to gather knowledge and information from outside. Such experience begins to give us human beings a certain kind of knowledge, and we store it, analyze it, and come to a conclusion as to what we think is good or what we think is bad. This way of gathering knowledge is from the outside and it is quite amazing how much information and data our little physical brain can collect and store. It can engage in a variety of activities such as thinking, analyzing and concluding. Our mind is indeed a marvelous thing. It is one of the faculties of the soul and can be exercised in the way of collecting information. So we call this information acquired knowledge, and such gives us the wisdom and cleverness by which to live, to behave, and to act as a human being.

INTUITIVE KNOWLEDGE

However, there is another and higher path to knowledge. That path we would call intuition, and the knowledge obtained we would call intuitive or revelational knowledge. We do not gather this information from outside because it is not affected by outer circumstances or data. This information comes directly from God to our spirit—not to our mind. It is the exercise of our spirit, showing us what the will of God is and what the will of God is not. It does not depend on outside circumstances or information.

THE TREES IN THE GARDEN OF EDEN

From Genesis we learn that before God had put man in the Garden of Eden, He had planted beautiful trees with all kinds of fruit for the needs of man's physical body. But in the midst of this garden He planted the Tree of Life and by its side the tree of the knowledge of good and evil (2:8-9). Now some people have assumed that the tree of the knowledge of good and evil is a bad tree. Not at all! In the Garden of Eden or in any garden of pleasure God would never plant a bad tree. As a matter of fact, the tree of the knowledge of good and evil is a better one than all the edible fruit trees there because though the latter are for our bodily needs, the tree of the knowledge of good and evil is for our soulical needs so that our mind may have the knowledge of good and evil. It is therefore a good tree. But in the midst of the Garden of Eden there is also the Tree of Life, and this tree is food for our spirit. Hence, there was provision made in the Garden of Eden for man's body, his soul, and his spirit.

THE TREE OF KNOWLEDGE VS. THE TREE OF LIFE

Why did God say, "Of all the trees in the garden you can freely eat except of the tree of the knowledge of good and evil, because on the day you eat thereof you shall surely die" (see Genesis 2:16-17)? It is because God loves us. He knows that without His life and just having knowledge in our soul would be death. The latter may seem wonderful because soulical knowledge makes us intelligent and makes us feel like somebody, even as Eve was tempted to eat of the tree of knowledge to make her like God. Knowing good and evil apart from the life of God brings death, because we know what is good but we cannot do it and we know what is bad but we do not have the life-power to resist it; and, therefore, it all brings forth death. As was indicated a moment ago, we can say that the tree of the knowledge of good and evil is for our soul. At that time back then sin was not in the world, so Adam and Eve might have been able to know what the will of God was and what was not; unfortunately, they did not have the life by which to obey the will of God and resist the evil. That is the reason God wanted to forewarn them and protect them from the tree of knowledge.

The Tree of Life, on the other hand, *has* the knowledge of God within it. Life gives us the knowledge of God himself. We often say, "You can know *about* God by searching, but if you want to know God himself, you have to receive His life." You can know that there should be a God somewhere, for where does the universe come from? So, by reasoning you can come to the point of saying: "Well, there must be a God. He must be mighty, He must be wise, He must be lovely," or whatever. You may have all this kind of knowledge but in the end it condemns you instead of saving you. Hence, if you really want to know God you have to receive His life, and when His life comes in, then you know Him directly and intimately—not indirectly.

Before you believed in the Lord Jesus you might have known about God, but there was no experience of Him. He, as it were, is billions and billions of miles away. And such distant separation is nothing less than condemnation because if you believe there is a God, then you are finished, for He is righteous and you are sinful. But praise God, the moment you believe in the Lord Jesus you can lift up your head and say, "Abba, Father" (Galatians 4:6, Romans 8:15). Immediately, you know Him—not simply know about Him—for He is now your Father. In so many words, I John 2:13b is actually saying this: "Little children, you know your Father." This is true. We may not know much about other things but we know our Father, and that gives us an intimate knowledge of God.

So we have these two different kinds of knowledge before us. Because of the sin of Adam all the knowledge which mankind acquires is from the tree of the knowledge of good and evil. Though man has gathered to himself all this information and has obtained all this wisdom, such knowledge will only result in death. But thank God, after we believe in the Lord Jesus, something quite remarkable happens: the inward knowledge of God gives life, and it is all in the intuitive faculty of our spirit. The knowledge which we acquire outwardly may help us in this world but the knowledge which comes from inward life will enable us to live before God and to please Him. That, according to the word of God, is the difference between these two different kinds of knowledge..

THE NEED FOR INTUITIVE KNOWLEDGE

Here we would like to concentrate on the intuitive knowledge. As a matter of fact, we Christians have all had that experience already. It is not something totally foreign to us because when we believed in the Lord Jesus something happened within us. Intuitively, we came to know God as our personal Father, but the problem for many of us is that instead of developing God's intuitive knowledge we are led back outside and into this acquired knowledge because that is what we knew before. So today I would like for us to know what are the characteristics of this intuitive knowledge.

KNOWLEDGE THROUGH REVELATION

Ephesians 1:17 gives us Paul's prayer for all believers. There he wrote: "That the God of our Lord Jesus Christ, the Father of glory, would give you [a] spirit of wisdom and revelation in the full knowledge of him." This passage unveils to us the first characteristic of intuitive or revelational knowledge.

This knowledge is that which is given by God—we ourselves do not have it. Indeed, we may recall how Peter had confessed to the Lord Jesus: "You are the Christ, the Son of the living God." This was a tremendous portion of knowledge, but from where did it come? The Lord Jesus replied: "Simon Peter, this is not what flesh and blood taught you. My Father in heaven revealed it to you" (see Matthew 16:16-17). So we can see from this that at the very beginning when we believed in the Lord Jesus, our ability to know God did not depend on acquired knowledge but on the revelational kind. Our knowledge of God did not come indirectly from outside—it came directly from God himself to our inner spirit. We could therefore say, "I know, I see."

Revelation means that something is revealed to us. Thankfully, He is the God of revelation, and if He will not reveal himself to us, none of us can know Him. He is the greatest mystery in the world. Whatever we know *of* God, in contrast to what we may come to know *about* God, comes from Him. He reveals himself to us in many ways, and such revelation always occurs in our spirit. It is there that we know Him. We may not be able to explain it but we know because He has revealed it to us. It pleases God, furthermore, to reveal His Son in us (Galatians 1:15-16)—that is, in our spirit. And that, too, is revelation.

Now as we consider this subject of revelation there may be some misunderstanding. We often regard revelation as generally being something tremendous and something which can only happen once or twice in our lifetime—that it is something which revolutionizes our life completely, and thus such revelation is drastic in its consequences. As a matter of fact, revelation can sometimes be that, but it can also be something far less dramatic and which we can receive daily. It may come to us as smaller light; nevertheless, it helps us to know Him further and to know His will on a daily basis, for we are in need of this every day. We want to know what the will of God is, for without knowing His will, how can we live or act as His followers? So the spirit of wisdom and revelation is given us through Christ Jesus. And hence, we should expect such revelation.

I remember brother Watchman Nee once saying this: "In your lifetime you may receive one or perhaps two great revelations. That is the extent of such kind of revelation you may ever obtain, and it is so drastic that it changes your whole being. On the other hand, God is also pleased to reveal His beloved Son to us daily."

"That [God] ... would give you [a] spirit of wisdom and revelation." What is wisdom? Wisdom and knowledge are different from each other. Knowledge acquired is only having information, but wisdom is having the ability to use that information. Some people have lots of knowledge but not much wisdom. In other words, they know many things or have much information but they cannot make use of such knowledge or data. They lack the wisdom. So we need both wisdom and revelation. Yet there are two different kinds of wisdom.

Two Kinds of Wisdom

James 3:15-18 declares: "This is not the wisdom which comes down from above, but earthly, natural, devilish. For where emulation and strife are, there is disorder and every evil thing. But the wisdom from above first is pure, then peaceful, gentle, yielding, full of mercy and good fruits, unquestioning, unfeigned. But the fruit of righteousness in peace is sown for them that make peace."

We see here two different kinds of wisdom: the wisdom from above and that from below. The wisdom from below will result in creating in our lives jealousy, envy, strife, disorder, and all kinds of evil things. It not only is earthly but also is natural, and even devilish. We will find a great deal of such wisdom in people around us in this world. These are people who think they are wise, but they are wise as serpents without being guileless as doves (see Matthew 10:16). Such is the wisdom from below. The wisdom from above, however, is pure, peaceful, gentle, yielding, full of mercy and good fruits, unquestioning, unfeigned. That is God's wisdom. We who are children of God need to have divine wisdom instead of the world's. People have much worldly wisdom but they are totally lacking in wisdom from above.

How can we live our spiritual life without the spirit of wisdom and revelation? We need to grow increasingly in this wisdom from above and live according to this revelational knowledge so that we may truly know God and His will.

John 17:3 says: "... this is the eternal life, that they should know thee, the only true God, and Jesus Christ whom thou hast sent." From this we conclude that eternal life has a kind of knowledge which is spiritual, and this is the knowledge we must grow in before the Lord. That will teach us how to live on this earth so as to glorify God, to live a holy life, and pursue a life of sanctification. That is the first characteristic of intuitive knowledge: that it is spiritual.

THE NEW COVENANT

The second characteristic is found in Hebrews 8:6-13 where we are told what the New Covenant is. We know that when we are breaking the bread and drinking the cup together at the Lord's Table, the cup is the New Covenant. The Lord said with respect to the contents of the cup: "This is the blood of the New Covenant; drink it, all of you, and remember Me" (see I Corinthians 11:25). Now as we have been doing that, we are constantly being reminded that we are not under the Old but under the New Covenant. God has made a contract with us, and it is sealed by the blood of the Lord Jesus. It cannot be changed or annulled.

What is in that New Covenant? In reading Hebrews 8:10-12 we see that it is actually quite simple. In the Old Covenant there are Ten Commandments but in the New Covenant there are but three articles. Let me explain.

There is one of these articles which is laid out for us in verse 10: "... this is the covenant that I will covenant to the house of Israel after those days, saith the Lord: Giving my laws into their mind, I will write them also upon their hearts; and I will be to them for God, and they shall be to me for people." Here we are told that in the New Covenant or Testament the law is not written on stone; it is written on human hearts.

God had originally said that if men would keep the Old Covenant's Ten Commandments, then they would be His people and He would be their God. But He later announced that He would write His new law or New Covenant upon men's hearts, and added: "I will be your God and you will be My people." In other words, God will now take upon himself all the responsibility—it is not what you or I do but what He does.

Then in verse 11 it says this: "And they shall not teach each his fellow-citizen, and each his brother, saying, Know the Lord; because all shall know me in themselves, from the little one among them unto the great among them."

Two Kinds of Knowledge

From this passage in Hebrews 8 we see that there are two kinds of knowledge. One kind results from the need for somebody to teach you: "Know the Lord," says this New Testament passage; and in Greek the word for know here conveys the idea that this knowing is objective knowledge. Because you do not know, somebody has to teach you to know the Lord. For example, the Old Covenant tells you that you should have only one God and besides Him there is none else. You had not known this, so a priest or a scribe would have to come and teach you that there is only one true God, and apart from Him you should not worship any other god. Under the Old Covenant that was the way a person gathered information or came into possession of a knowledge of God and His will.

But in this same passage we learn that God went on to say this: "You should not teach each his brother or his fellow citizen." Now we who believe are fellow citizens of the kingdom of God and we are brothers. God says, "You should not teach each saying, Know the Lord." But if nobody teaches us, how can we know? God has said, "All shall know Me"; and the "know" here is *oida* in Greek, which means "intimate knowledge." We know something intimately within ourselves. It is an experiential knowledge of God. We experience Him because there is knowledge within us which causes us to know God, and because we know Him we do not need anybody from outside to teach us. It is an inner knowledge.

And furthermore, God also declared that all under the New Covenant shall have this inner knowledge of Him—from the smallest one to the greatest among His people. In other words, as soon as we are born again we already have that knowledge within us. It naturally has to grow, but it is already there. Is that not wonderful? As soon as we are born again we know our Father, but we need to know Him more and more until we truly know the Father's heart—what His will is, and that we are able to share His responsibility. That is how we grow in the knowledge of God. Hence, we do not need anyone to teach us on how to know God—we know Him ourselves.

GOD IS LIGHT

I John 1 says: "God is light, and in him is no darkness at all" (v.5b). It does not say God's word is light, although that is a true statement. But here it says that God himself is light. To put it another way: God's very life sheds light. That is God.

In v. 7 it says: "if we walk in the light as he [God] is in the light, we have fellowship with one another, and the blood of Jesus Christ his Son cleanses us from all sin." We have an inner light within us. It shines upon our path, and by that light we know what is of God and what is not of God. And if we walk in that light in accordance with the degree to which we know God is in the light, we have fellowship. Whenever we disobey the extent of the light which we have within us at any given moment, our fellowship with God is interrupted. We need to confess our sins and be cleansed with the precious blood of the Lord in order that our communion with God may be recovered. So this kind of knowledge is inward—not from outside.

Let us say God is one hundred candles and you are only one candle because you have just been saved. Although you have just been saved, you already have the light. You know what is right and what is not pleasing to God. As you obey according to your current level of knowledge, you are walking in the light as God is in the light, and you are having fellowship with Him. When your conscience is clean, you can fellowship with God, and the blood of His Son Jesus Christ cleanses you from all your sins, because this light allows you to see what you could not see in the past.

If we submit and walk in the light, the blood of Jesus Christ cleanses us from our sins; thus we will be more like God. If we continue to walk in the light, it will grow brighter. If we obey completely the light we have within us, there will be no barrier between God and us. It does not mean that we are perfect. We are not perfect because only God is perfect. Nevertheless, God can have fellowship with us imperfect people because we obey and walk according to the light we receive. But if we do not obey, our conscience will accuse us, and our fellowship with God will run into problems. This is the path of spiritual growth for Christians.

THE INNER ANOINTING

We know this kind of knowledge is always true because I John also tells us: "you have the anointing abiding within you" (see 2:27). That anointing is the Holy Spirit. All of us Christians have the Holy Spirit in our spirits, and the anointing is there for the purpose of teaching us in all things—whether they be big or small matters. Oftentimes, in the big issues of life we want very much to seek the will of God, but in the small ones we think we can handle them ourselves. That is our problem. Yet the Holy Spirit will teach us in both big and small matters, in both great things and even the daily, mundane small things in our life. And whatever He teaches us is true and is not false. When man teaches, it may be incorrect; but when the Holy Spirit teaches, it is always correct or true. We need to listen to Him, and if we obey the anointing within us we abide in Christ.

How do we abide in Christ? How do we make our home in Christ? It is only by listening to the inner anointing, by experiencing the Holy Spirit every moment of every day. That is spiritual life; but if you ignore the inner anointing, you have no spiritual life at all. How vital this is!

SPIRITUAL LIFE AND SERVICE BASED UPON INNER TEACHING

Experiencing intuitive knowledge is the only way by which to have spiritual life and engage in spiritual service. If you want to see your spiritual life grow, that is the only way. It is not outside teaching that builds your spiritual life; rather, it is the inward teaching by the Holy Spirit. In I Corinthians 2 we are told that the natural man does not know the mind of God nor does he appreciate it; only the spiritual man knows all things (vv. 14-15; cf. Williams). So it is our spiritual life and our spiritual service that are accepted because we serve the living God, and we are to serve Him according to His will and not according to what we think is good for Him. We may call Him, "Lord, Lord," but if we disobey God's will, we cannot enter His kingdom. We may say to Him: "Lord, we preached in Your name, we have done miracles in Your name, we have even cast out demons in Your name." Yet the Lord's response will be: "I do not know you. Who are you? I do not acknowledge you. I do not accept you. I do not recommend you because you have not been doing My Father's will. You have been doing your own will" (see Matthew 7:21-23). Hence, we can see how necessary it is that we exercise our intuition.

EXERCISING OUR INTUITIVE FACULTY

How do we exercise our intuitive faculty? One day the disciples came to the Lord and asked Him a question: "Who is the greatest in the kingdom?" (see Matthew 18:1) Of course, this was a topic they had been arguing about among themselves all along, and their discussion was natural and earthly in character. In response the Lord gave them a demonstration. He placed a little child before His disciples and said, "Unless you are converted and become as a little child you cannot see the kingdom of God. Unless you humble yourself as this little child you cannot be the greatest in the kingdom" (see vv. 2-4). A little child, naturally speaking, has very little information or knowledge, so how can he or she live? Actually, a child lives by intuition. If you are sufficiently discerning, you will be amazed to see the way a child knows to be close to one person and to avoid another. Quite naturally, a child will find himself or herself drawing close to one individual with perfect faith in that person, whereas with another individual the child withdraws from that person. How does this happen? On what basis does it happen? It is intuition, and oftentimes it works. It is quite amazing!

As we grow up, however, we depend less and less on intuition and more and more on outside information. We as adult believers begin to live more and more on an outward basis instead of on an inward one. Our way of life has changed, and what God had provided we neglect. We gather more and more information from outside and think it makes us wise and knowledgeable. That is how we ultimately behave, and hence we cease using altogether our intuitive faculty which as children we had readily used. Though our child's intuitive faculty was there, it was not absolutely correct in all instances because there was lack of a standard. But, then, upon our being saved, the Holy Spirit commenced to teach us inwardly. Unfortunately, with the passage of time we neglect Him and instead depend on our mental exercise, logic, or reasoning. When we live by these means, we lose the use of our intuitive power.

In Chinese we have a proverb that is relevant to this issue. It is a little difficult to translate, but the essential meaning is this: "The more worldly-wise you are the deadlier is your inward sense or intuition." In short, if you are worldly-wise, the less will be your intuitive power.

In Matthew 11 we read how the Lord did many things while in the towns of Capernaum and Chorazin, yet the people there did not believe; so the Lord said by way of reaction: "Father, I thank You because You have hidden and kept these things from the wise and prudent but have revealed and given them to babes" (see v. 25). Is that not true? Unless we are converted as little children, we shall remain worldly-wise and depend only upon ourselves. We shall continue to use our logic or reasoning in deciding what we should do or what we should avoid, and the more worldly-wise we are the more pretentious we become. We are no longer true; we instead put on a façade. But little children do not have that. They are very genuine, open, and simple. We need to change and become like little children so that before God we are simply that—little children. We, of course, are not to be childish but are to be childlike. That is what we need to be. And the more childlike we are, the more humble we shall be and the less we shall depend upon ourselves or rely on our reasoning and logic. Then we will look up to God and allow Him to reveal His mind to us. That is the secret.

In the so-called Sermon on the Mount the Lord Jesus said the following: "Blessed are the poor in spirit for theirs is the kingdom of God. Blessed are the pure in heart, for they shall see God" (see Matthew 5:3, 8). We do not see Him because our heart is not pure. We have become complicated by our accumulated knowledge gained from the outside world. We are not pure before God, looking with our eyes fixed steadfastly upon Him. That is the reason we lose the power of intuition. But in order to regain that power we must learn the lesson of Matthew 11: "Take My yoke upon you and learn of Me. For I am meek and lowly in heart and you shall find rest in your souls" (see v. 29). In other words, the way to set our intuitive faculty free from bondage and allow ourselves to truly experience growth in the exercise of our intuition, we need to take up the cross. It is the cross which deals with and delivers us from our natural man and enables us to learn of Christ. That is the way. It is actually very simple.

So I often think intuition in our spirit may be the most mysterious faculty but it is not the most profound. As a matter of fact, it is the most simple. Yet we make it so complicated, and because of that, our intuitive faculty is not well developed.

Have you ever read a book entitled *My Utmost for His Highest* written by Oswald Chambers, who lived during the latter part of the twentieth century? He was not only an artist, he was also a philosopher and psychologist. He was a very intelligent British man. By God's grace, he was saved. Outwardly, he lived as a godly Christian; inwardly, however, he sensed darkness; therefore, he came before God in prayer. He felt he needed to be filled with the Holy Spirit but he did not experience this. One day he was reading in Luke 11: "If you then, being evil, know how to give good gifts to your children, how much more will your heavenly Father give the Holy Spirit to those who ask Him?" (see v. 13)

Suddenly he was enlightened. By simple faith like that of a child he received the word of God. He did not experience any special feelings, but from that day forward his life underwent a radical change. In all things—both large and small—he could now apply the faith of a child in trusting and relying on God. No difficulty was too great for him because he simply trusted and relied on God completely. As a result, he was greatly used by God in our generation. What does this tell us? If we have a heart which is pure like that of a child, God will reveal more and more of His will to us.

A WARNING

Finally, a warning needs to be issued: The soul and the spirit are so intertwined that it is very difficult to distinguish what is of the spirit and what is of the soul. In our soul there is the mind, and in our spirit there is intuition. These two faculties are so similar that, though their individual origin is earth and heaven apart, the experience of these two is so close and perhaps so similar-appearing in character that it is very difficult to distinguish what is of the mind and what is of the spirit's intuition. Extremely difficult! So in learning to distinguish, we tend to make mistakes. Sometimes we will have an impression in our mind and we take it as being an impression in our intuition. So we follow our mind's impression, but later on it is proven to have been wrong. In short, there may be mistakes, but we can learn from our mistakes.

Recently, I have been reading the two-volume biography of the greatest evangelist of the eighteenth century in England—George Whitefield. He launched out as an evangelist when he was very young—in his early twenties—and God greatly used him. But he made mistakes along the way because he sought guidance through impressions. He would sense an impression arising within him and, because he had such a nature, when an impression thus came to him, he could almost physically see it. So to Whitefield it seemed very much like a vision, and because he thought it was from God, he would accordingly act upon it. Consequently, he made mistakes. But thank God, he was humble enough that when people pointed out to him his mistake he would immediately acknowledge it, humble himself, and learn the lesson. Therefore, let us realize that it is very easy to mistake an impression as being from God which you sense within you that turns out later not to have been the case. This is a lesson we need to learn gradually.

Where, then, is the safeguard? We have previously learned from Scripture and have said that, fundamentally, you do not need anyone to teach you; but does this mean that you can refuse to have any teachers whatsoever, that you henceforth refuse to accept any help or correction from other people? In that case, you are in danger spiritually.

There is a very good reason why the Bible tells us the following in I John 2 when talking about this matter of the inward anointing: "Little children, you have no worldly knowledge yet, but the world is full of the spirit of antichrist and many antichrists are already here. Nevertheless, you have the anointing from the Holy One, and you know and can sense all things" (see vv. 18, 20, 26-27). How do we Christians—even the babes in Christ among us—know it is the antichrist? We all know it because we have the anointing within us. Even so, there is a place for receiving help or correction from others.

In this connection, I remember once when I was living in New York, there was a brother who was newly saved. He did not have any Scripture knowledge, and when he went to Boston and attended a church meeting of some kind, something was being taught in the sermon which he could not really explain. So as he listened to that sermon he increasingly sensed that something was wrong, although he could not put his finger on what it was which was wrong. When he returned to New York, we talked, and in the course of our conversation it was revealed how the thrust of the sermon was indeed wrong. The sermon said that we were gods just as Eve had wanted to be a god.

Returning, therefore, to the matter of having a safeguard, let it be said that in this same chapter 2 of I John we also read this: "... the word [from the beginning] which ye heard" (v. 7, cf. v. 24, wherein John is addressing the "little children"). In other words, the word of God is the vital safeguard. We need to check our impression with God's word. If it does not agree with the word of God it is wrong because the latter and the inward leading come from the same Spirit—God's Holy Spirit. He cannot say one thing in you or me and another thing in God's word. That is why we need His word. And we also need teachers; yet they are not to govern our lives: they are there to help—sometimes to correct, and also to confirm what the Lord is working in our life.

Hence, this is a warning which we need to take to heart very seriously. Just because you are a child of God having the anointing within you which teaches you all things does not mean you do not need any help nor need to hear what others might have to say. Whenever you have an impression, do not be so quick to conclude: That's it! Do be very careful, for we all need to be humble enough to be corrected, to learn, and, if need be, to repent. May the Lord help us all.

Chapter 4

COMMUNION

John 4:24—God is a spirit; and they who worship him must worship him in spirit and truth.

Romans 8:15-17—For ye have not received a spirit of bondage again for fear, but ye have received a spirit of adoption, whereby we cry, Abba, Father. The Spirit itself bears witness with our spirit, that we are children of God. And if children, heirs also: heirs of God, and Christ's joint heirs; if indeed we suffer with him, that we may also be glorified with him.

1 John 1:1-4—That which was from the beginning, that which we have heard, which we have seen with our eyes; that which we contemplated, and our hands handled, concerning the word of life; (and the life has been manifested, and we have seen, and bear witness, and report to you the eternal life, which was with the Father, and has been manifested to us:) that which we have seen and heard we report to you, that ye also may have fellowship with us; and our fellowship is indeed with the Father, and with his Son Jesus Christ. And these things write we to you that your joy may be full.

1 John 4:15-19—Whosoever shall confess that Jesus is the Son of God, God abides in him, and he in God. And we have known and have believed the love which God has to us. God is love, and he that abides in love abides in God, and God in him. Herein has love been

perfected with us that we may have boldness in the day of judgment, that even as he is, we also are in this world. There is no fear in love, but perfect love casts out fear; for fear has torment, and he that fears has not been made perfect in love. We love because he has first loved us.

We have been considering together this vital subject of spiritual exercise. I feel this is of tremendous significance because if there is no spiritual exercise, there can be no spiritual life. It is the will of God to give us His life in Christ Jesus and to put His Spirit into our spirit. These wonderful provisions of God are for one purpose—that we may have spiritual life. What is the use of this new spirit He has given us if it is not being used and exercised? Why is the Holy Spirit dwelling in our spirit if it is not for the purpose of seeing that the life of Christ is growing into fullness in us? I therefore believe it is extremely important and most fundamental that every believer should know how to exercise his or her spirit. Our spirit is not a material substance that we can see, but we can know the reality of it because of its functions or faculties. In our new spirit the Spirit of God dwells, and as we have noted before it has three main functions: two of which—that of conscience and of intuition—we have considered in our two previous discussions together.

COMMUNION: THE HIGHEST FUNCTION IN OUR SPIRIT

There is a third function operable in our spirit and it is communion. As a matter of fact, communion is the foundational function to the other functions of our spirit. If we are not in communion or in contact with God, not only our conscience will not function right but our intuition will not do so either. Communion is therefore the basic function in our spirit, and it is also the highest one. It is as Psalm 42 declares: "Deep calleth unto deep" (v. 7a). It is the depth of God calling to the depth of man's being. It is the depth of our being that responds to the depth of God. Indeed, it is through communion that we come into union with God in life. And it is that which fulfills His eternal purpose.

What is the eternal purpose of God concerning man? We are made in His very image, and therefore, we redeemed sinners are to be transformed and conformed to the image of God's beloved Son (see, e.g., II Corinthians 3:18, Romans 8:28b-29). This is the will and purpose of God for us. Yet how can this be fulfilled? In a word, it is through communion.

Communion also signifies fellowship. Oftentimes, when we speak of fellowship, we mean having interactive relationship with one another. When we speak of having fellowship with God or God fellowshiping with us, we call it communion. Actually, therefore, communion is a kind of fellowship. God opens himself up to us and we respond to Him. We open ourselves to God, and by such communication and communion we are gradually being transformed out of ourselves into Christ. Communion is the most basic and yet highest function of our spirit.

If, as we have pointed out before, conscience gives us the righteousness of God and intuition gives us the holiness of God, then communion gives us the glory of God which is love (II Corinthians 3:18; cf. I John 4:8b). This is how important communion is.

THE TREE THAT BRINGS LIFE

Let us again briefly retrace our human origin and early subsequent history according to Genesis chapters 1-3. After God created man in His image—that is, according to His likeness—He placed him in the Garden of Eden, which was a garden of pleasure. God planted all kinds of fruit trees as His food provision for man by which to sustain his human body. God also placed the Tree of Life in the midst of the garden, this particular tree symbolizing His very life. If man should eat the fruit of the Tree of Life, he would have God's life in him because this is what we were created for. When God created the universe and all the living creatures, none of them could receive God's life since they did not answer to His image. Only man was created in the image of God and that is the reason he can receive God's life and be united with Him in life. It is the highest blessing and purpose which God could have ordained for human beings.

THE TREE THAT BROUGHT DEATH

However, alongside the Tree of Life in the garden He placed the tree of the knowledge of good and evil which, it must again be emphasized, was not a bad tree. For God could never put anything bad in this garden of pleasure. In fact, it was a better tree than all of the fruit trees but it was not the best tree. It was by itself the knowledge of good and evil. Now if man should eat from this tree, he would be declaring independence from God and would make himself into a little god, he thinking he would now know everything because he would have the knowledge of good and evil just like God himself has. The result would be that he would know what is good but he would not have the power or the life to do the good. He would also know what is evil but he would not have the life or power to resist evil. Yet that is precisely what happened to mankind there in the Garden of Eden.

We must sadly acknowledge that our ancestors ended up eating from the wrong tree, and down through the millennia of human history that act has caused all human beings to be what they are. In other words, all human beings have lived ever since by the tree of the knowledge of good and evil because they do not have the life of God in them. For God had said to Adam: "If you eat of the tree of the knowledge of good and evil, on that day you shall surely die." So when Adam and Eve ate the forbidden fruit, it was their spirits that died. Let us be reminded that death in man signifies the cessation of communication with his spirit's proper environment; and the proper environment of man's spirit is God; but when man sinned against God, its communication with its proper environment—even God himself—was cut off. That is what it means to be dead spiritually. The spirit is still there, and even its operation is still there (this latter fact we know to be true because by their spirits deadened towards God people in the world have nonetheless been able to communicate with evil spirits); but man's spirit is no longer working properly anymore. Yes, worldly people can communicate with evil spirits but they cannot communicate with God. It requires the salvation of God to restore such communication.

SALVATION RESTORES COMMUNICATION WITH GOD

Salvation is not an external remedy. Some people deem the gospel of Jesus Christ to be the highest ethical teaching, but that is not a correct view of the gospel. Yes, Christ's gospel is indeed the highest ethical teaching in the world; but who can perform or carry out such a teaching? This highest ethical teaching condemns—it does not save. Thank God, though, that as a result of Christ Jesus dying on the cross for the sin of the world, He not only can cleanse our bad conscience so that we have a good conscience—a conscience without offense before God—but also He can enable us to live with a good conscience before both God and man. That in part is what salvation is. Salvation gives us a new spirit and restores to us the possibility and the capacity to communicate with God. It is the experience of all those who are saved. We may not know too much about the gospel, but we know that we have believed in Jesus as our Lord and Savior. And when we did that, something wonderful happened. Immediately, the heavens opened, and the invisible God, who is spirit, and our spirit began to be in touch with each other. Romans 8:15 tells us that we have received the spirit of sonship whereby we cried out to God: "Abba, Father." And as a consequence, we are now God's children. We now have His life in us and our communication with God has thus begun.

I was brought up in a devout Christian family and I can still remember quite vividly having a family altar experience every evening. My father would read from a big Bible, and after that we would kneel down and he would lead us in prayer. From kindergarten to college I was educated in Christian schools. When I was in middle school and high school, we were required to attend the Sunday church service. All the students would line up and march into the church building and listen to a sermon, which was given by the preacher, who happened to be my father. However, I the preacher's son had cleverly placed a novel behind the hymn book and was reading it throughout the sermon. I knew almost everything about Christianity and could speak to others about it. As a matter of fact, I had preached and led prayer meetings before I was ever saved. I knew *about* God; but I never knew Him. I read the Bible and knew what was in it, but it did not speak to me. It was to me a foreign book. Nevertheless, one day, when He saved me, something exceptional happened. I remember going to my room, opening the Bible, and it turned out to be II Peter chapter 1. When I read it, every word began to speak to my heart. It was as though my heavenly Father was writing a letter *to me*. The Bible was today so different from before. And now a communication between God and myself had begun.

This experience of mine can indicate to us that God wants to communicate with us and wants us to communicate with Him. He wants to have a life with us, and we must have a life with Him. That is the highest human destiny. But having begun in this way, are we continuing in this way? Do we grow in this way? Sadly, we find that Christianity has led us astray because its teaching imposes upon us a lot of rules and regulations: we should do this and not do that. If we obey the rules we will be deemed to be good Christians. And thus we are led into an outward way. When we do not know something, we ask, and a teacher will unhesitatingly tell us: "This is it. You do this and you will be all right. And if you do not do this, you will be wrong." Everything is from the outside. We ignore the fact that there is an *inner* way of life which God has ordained for us. Hence, communion is the one spiritual activity which we as believers must cultivate throughout our lives. If we neglect this experience of communion with God, we forfeit the basic foundation for fulfilling God's eternal purpose.

God is spirit. We cannot see Him with our naked eyes; but He is everywhere. The only way we can see Him is by our spirit. If the latter is living and active in us, then we can be in touch with God every moment of our lives. And such is genuine spiritual life. Are we, who are redeemed by the Lord, cultivating this communion life with God? Are we in living touch with Him every day? Are we living in His presence moment by moment? Such is what spiritual life truly is.

EXPRESSIONS OF COMMUNION

Worship

How can we commune with God? It is true that there are various expressions of communion. For instance, worship. Worship today is grossly misunderstood. We limit worship by time and space. On Sunday we go to worship, but it is actually to listen to a sermon. John 4 tells us of our Lord Jesus meeting a Samaritan woman and talking with her. Because of what the Lord told her she realized that she was talking to a person who must be a prophet of God. She discussed the issue of worship with Him, for at one point in the conversation she declared: "We Samaritans worship on Mt. Gerizim, but you Jews worship in Jerusalem. So please tell me where we should go to worship." In other words, worship was just a matter of where to go and when to worship; and other than those times, there was no other occasion for worship. If there was no other worship, what was she doing with her life? She was living an independent life. Therefore, she could previously have had five different husbands and was even now living with one who was not her husband. So the Lord Jesus said in reply to her: "It is neither in Jerusalem nor on Mt. Gerizim. The time is coming, and now is, that God is seeking for true worshipers to worship Him in spirit and in truth because God is spirit."

What is worship? In Old English this word worship actually was expressed as "worth-ship." We consider God as worthy, so we worship Him. Worship is putting God in His rightful place and ourselves in our proper place. So we can say that worship is an attitude—an expression of spirit. What God desires is a worshiping spirit that is neither restricted by time nor space. We will worship God everywhere and at any time because worship arises out of our spirit.

I recall one particular day when I was in the Philippines that I went to an island called Dagada. I saw a Catholic church, and when I went in, I saw what I took to be four white kneeling statues before the altar. When I approached closer, however, I discovered that they were actually four nuns dressed in white who were kneeling without moving in the slightest. My first reaction was to think how pious these nuns were. Then my second thought was: If the spirit is not there can this be said to be worship? Does one worship God with just one's posture? Is that worship? If the spirit is not there, and no matter how a person prostrates himself or herself, God is not being worshiped. Too often today we assume that worship is a matter of having the right physical posture. Now I am not saying here that real worship does not include the aspect of posture, but true worship does not originate from the physical body. No matter how pious we may appear physically, if our heart is not there, if our spirit is not being exercised, God is not being worshiped.

The Lord Jesus was quoted in Matthew 15 as saying: "You hypocrites, you Pharisees and scribes, you worship with your lips, but your heart is far from God" (see vv. 7-8). This is not worship. Worship is not only a mental activity. We may pray a beautiful prayer, just as can be found in a church's prayer book, but if it is only with our lips and our heart is not there, it is not worship. We may have high thoughts about God and may utter high-sounding words praising Him, but if our heart is not there, it is not worship. We may sing, but if we do not sing with our heart, and regardless how beautiful the sound may be, God does not hear it. Today, people will often sing highly soulical songs by which to try to stir up man's emotion and mind, they thinking that that is worship. No! Worship has to come from our spirit. Our spirits are to be bowed before God, and our hearts are to be opened to Him. In other words, our whole being is to be out towards Him. That is worship. It is placing God in His rightful place and putting ourselves in our proper place. And such is real worship. It is true that if worship is out from the spirit, it will indeed affect our mind and also even carry along our body; but we must discern the origin.

So the mistake we find in Christianity today centers around the origin of worship. Instead of allowing it to arise from the spirit, Christians too often try to work this activity up from outside in, but that is not God's way. Whenever God works, it is always from the inside and which then will touch the outside. (By contrast, whenever the enemy works, he always tries doing so from the outside so as to reach a person's inside.) Hence, what is true worship? Worship is communion with God, and out of that communion comes worship from the spirit.

Fellowship

Another expression of communion is fellowship. What is fellowship? We have mentioned before that we usually use the word fellowship as that which describes an activity occurring between or among believers. That is definitely an accurate and legitimate use of the word; but in I John 1 the apostle writes and adds a further dimension to this word. First he says the following: "That which was from the beginning, that which we have heard, which we have seen with our eyes; that which we contemplated, and our hands handled, concerning the word of life."

This is a description of Christ. He is the One who is from the beginning. We have heard Him who has been taught about to us by the prophets of old (cf. Hebrews 1:1). But now He has come into the world, and we have seen Him. Yet if we merely see Christ outwardly, we do not know Him. So we contemplate or meditate on Him, and we receive revelation. When we contemplate Christ, we see Him as having the glory of the only begotten with the Father. And He is the One whom the apostle John said he had touched and handled because when Christ was raised from the dead, He had declared to Thomas and the other disciples: "Touch My side and see the hole there. Touch My hands, and see the nail prints there" (see John 20:24-27). This is the Word of Life. It is Christ.

But John in his first epistle then introduces that further dimension surrounding the word fellowship alluded to a moment ago. Wrote the apostle: "And what we have seen and heard we report to you, so that you may have fellowship with us and our fellowship is indeed with the Father and the Son." Here, then, we learn the very origin of our fellowship. It originates from our fellowship with God. We who believe are all called into the fellowship of God's Son Jesus Christ. Therefore, it is His fellowship with the Father in the Spirit. So if you are not rich enough to join a prestigious fraternity or sorority, nevertheless, praise God, you are rich enough to be in the family of God. In fact, this is the most exclusive fellowship in the whole universe because it is the fellowship between the Father and the Son in the Spirit. And wonder of wonders, it has been opened to us believers as well!

So what is fellowship? Fellowship (in Greek, *koinonia*) means a sharing in common. God and His beloved Son share with us what is theirs in common. God does not withhold anything from us. Indeed, He shared His all with us when He shared His Son with us. What a rich and precious fellowship! Do we treasure this fellowship? Do we want to know Him more and more or do we think being saved is enough? An understanding of *this* fellowship ought to create within us a genuine desire for fellowship with God and with Christ and a desire to know both Father and Son more and more.

Now because God does not withhold anything from us, therefore, whatever we have received in fellowship with Him and His Son in the Spirit we ought to share with other Christian brothers and sisters. And that is true Christian fellowship.

Oftentimes we misunderstand this matter of fellowship and so we take social intercourse as being it. "Well," a believer may say, "let's have some fellowship." What does he mean? Too often it will merely mean having some chatting together and gossiping. Can we call that fellowship? On the contrary, Christian fellowship is based on us believers' fellowship with the Father and the Son. What we have received we report or share with our Christian brethren. That is a sharing in common. God has no desire to have a few spiritual giants and leave all the other believers as spiritual paupers. His desire is that we may all enter into the fullness of Christ, and the result will be that our joy shall be full (I John 1:4). Oftentimes we chat together and think we are having a good time. Yet what kind of joy is that compared with the joy of actually fellowshiping Christ? That is real joy.

I can never forget the story about a father and his daughter. Every evening after the father would come home and had eaten his supper, he would sit with his daughter and have a good time sharing. The father would tell the daughter what had happened during the day, and the daughter would tell the father what had happened to her. One day, after supper, the daughter told her father that she had something to do. She ran to her room and closed the door. The father did not know what had happened. For a month, perhaps even longer, the daughter acted strangely in this manner, and the father suffered greatly as a result. One day it was his birthday, and the daughter presented her father with a pair of slippers which she had made with her hands in her room. She said, "Father, I made these for you." The father said, "Daughter, I do appreciate this, but you do not know how much I have missed you." Now this is what our heavenly

Father feels. We are busy, perhaps even busy in doing something *for Him*, but He would far more treasure our presence with Him. More than anything else, He would desire our fellowshipping with Him, opening our hearts to Him and listening to Him. That is communion. How much time have we spent in our heavenly Father's presence?

Prayer

Prayer is another form or expression of communion. Some Christians believe prayer is simply petition. They have a need so they tell the Lord their need and fully expect Him to supply it. Yes, that is prayer; but let us realize that the basis of prayer is communion. So what is prayer? Prayer is having a heart-to-heart talk with the Lord. We open our hearts to Him and let Him open His heart to us. And when we have such communion with Him, then out of that communion will come forth petition, intercession, and other forms of prayer. Such is true prayer.

We often say that Christians should have a time of morning devotion. That is, when we arise in the morning, we should not just rush out into the world and do whatever we have set ourselves to do that day. If that be our daily routine, how can we live as Christians? We all realize that the first activity in the morning should be that we draw near to God and have our morning devotion: that we have a time of prayer and reading the Bible. In other words, we should have a short period with the Lord. It will then give us strength to go out into the world and be witnesses for Him. I often point out that modern life is not conducive to Christian living. We are too busy. If we sleep late, we have no time for communion.

We too often, as it were, simply say to the Lord, "Good morning" and "goodbye." Then we rush out.

Yet, how do we pray in prayer? Do we merely offer up a few hasty words and then depart, not even remembering what we have said? How *do* we pray in our private prayer? Do we draw near to God first and make that contact with Him, being sure that our spirit is open to the Spirit of God, and that we are entering into His very presence? Then out from our heart we start to pour out to Him? If so, then I would consider that to be true prayer.

Do we draw near to God in prayer so that He may draw near to us? In this connection, I often recall this hymn:

Nothing between, Lord, nothing between;
Let me Thy glory see,
Draw my soul close to Thee,
Then speak in love to me—Nothing between.

That hymn was written by Evan Hopkins. He was the theologian for the Keswick convention, and he lived a very close life with the Lord. He wanted there to be nothing between him and the Lord which would hinder him from drawing near to Him and listening to what He had to say. That was his life and continual testimony. I was greatly helped by him.

In the morning that hymn's text is often my prayer: "Nothing between, Lord, nothing between. Show Thy glory to me. Draw me close to Thee, let me see Thy face, and let me hear Thy voice." In such a circumstance as this there will be a communion. If you and I commune with God, He will commune with us. What a blessed time! And as a result of such communion, when we go out into the world, His presence goes with us. Now that is prayer.

Bible Reading

We should all read the Bible and know what is to be found there. George Mueller (anglicized form of Müller), who was from Prussia (now part of Germany) and later lived in England, read the Bible a hundred times from Genesis to Revelation. Brother Mueller (1805-98) was a very methodical person and wrote down everything, keeping a record of all which happened to him. God used him to establish many orphanages in England—places of refuge for literally thousands of orphans. Yet it all came about by prayer. Throughout his life he had offered up some ten million prayers which God answered. We know this because brother Mueller had kept a record of them. What did he do daily in the morning? The first thing he did was to approach God, and, taking one verse in the Bible, he would read it, meditate upon it, and then he would start to pray. Sometimes what he read would cause him to confess and repent before God. At other times what he read would make him joyful, he breaking out with praise and worship of the Lord. Thus did brother Mueller conduct himself every morning for a very short period each time: reading a Bible verse, meditating on it, and then turning it into prayer.

I myself had found it very helpful in my early days to select a book in the Bible that is more conducive to meditation; and so, every morning I would read a verse from it a few times, meditate upon what it said to me, and then turn it into prayer. Such a spiritual exercise became for me a form of communion. Such can be spiritual food for our daily life. If we read the Bible only for knowledge, that is not enough when it comes to this matter of communion. It is only when we actually meditate on the Scriptures before God and turn it into prayer that we have food for the day. I can testify that it is a wonderful spiritual experience.

Breaking of Bread

The breaking of bread (or, Lord's Table, Communion, Last Supper, Eucharist) as described in I Corinthians 11 is an act of remembrance. Remembrance is a recalling the past and bringing it to the present for one's contemplation. And through what we remember and contemplate upon, we are touched, and so we worship and give thanks.

In I Corinthians we also read: "I speak as to intelligent persons: do ye judge what I say. The cup of blessing which we bless, is it not the communion of the blood of the Christ? The bread which we break, is it not the communion of the body of the Christ? Because we, being many, are one loaf, one body; for we all partake of that one loaf" (10:15-17).

Let us not view the Lord's Table as but a remembering of the *past*. Yes, it *is* that, but it is also a *present* reality. Christian communion is always a present activity: it never becomes the past nor is it in the future: it is always a present reality. When we drink from the cup, we are in fellowship with His blood. When we are partaking of the loaf, we are in fellowship with His life in our spirit—not in our physical body. In our spirit we are in fellowship with His blood, which cleanses us; we are also in fellowship with His life which gives us the energy and the strength to proceed to face another week. What a communion that is! It is not simply an objective act, but especially a very subjective experience. Let us therefore ask ourselves: When we are participating in the Lord's Table, are we truly experiencing communion with the Lord Jesus?

Thanksgiving and Praise

Another expression of communion is offering up thanksgiving and praises. "Praise waiteth for Thee, O God" (see Psalm 65:1a). "Whoso offereth praise glorifieth me" (Psalm 50:23a).

We ought to come to God and offer up the sacrifice of praise, which is the sacrifice of our lips. Let us also give thanks in all things. These, too, are expressions of communion. The Bible tells us that Daniel prayed three times a day (Daniel 6:10). One of the psalmists confided that he praised God seven times a day (Psalm 119:164). That is truly a life of communion. And that is what God wants us to enter into because out of that communion experience comes forth union. Out of such communion comes forth our transformation and our being conformed to the image of Christ.

PRACTICAL HINTS ON COMMUNION

Spend Time with the Lord

Give time to the Lord. We should not be so busy that we do not have time for Him. I remember a dear Christian sister who was the wife of my principal in high school. She had several children. She greatly wanted to have time with the Lord, but she was so busy. What did she do? She got up at 4 a.m. while others in the family were still sleeping and spent time with the Lord; then she went back to sleep. In this way she made time for her Lord. How can we say that we have no time for the Lord? He certainly has time for us. Indeed, He is patiently waiting.

We need to spend time with the Lord. But let us not overdo it. If we do, we cannot continue. Let us be before the Lord to see how much time we can actually spend before Him. And then let us pursue it faithfully.

Exercise Your Spirit

When you are spending time with the Lord, learn to exercise your spirit. Do not spend the time by simply saying your prayers and reading your Bible. That is what I did when I was first saved. I was usually the first one up in the family. So I would go to a room, shut myself in, and have my morning time with the Lord. I would sing a song and kneel before Him. I was told if I read four chapters a day I could cover the entire Bible in one year. Therefore, I would read four chapters three times, think over it and then pray. This was my daily devotional routine. But if afterward you were to ask me what I had read, I would already have forgotten it. In short, I spent time, but I did not spend it well.

Spend your time with the Lord himself. Approach Him and draw near to Him. Wait upon Him. Abide in Him. Make your home in Him so that you can be in His presence. In the Bible there are so many different devotional descriptions. But basically, you must spend time with Him himself by using your spirit—that is to say, by exercising your spirit.

Listen to One's Conscience

When we exercise our spirit in communion with God, if there is any problem, our conscience will speak to us. When we approach the Lord intuitively and detect in our conscience some sin which has not been confessed, we are to confess it and claim the blood of the Lord Jesus for forgiveness and cleansing. It is thus a time of repentance. Intuitively, the Lord will show us some area of our life in which we have not obeyed. And hence, whenever we come into the presence of God, He will remind us if there is anything amiss; and that is the time when we need to surrender and obey. So we soon come to realize that these three functions—conscience, intuition, and communion—cannot be separated. They can be distinguished, but not separated.

Hence, every morning is the time that we offer up, as it were, our burnt offering. Each morning we put ourselves on the altar as a burnt offering for the Lord and we renew it every evening (see Leviticus 6:8-13). With that kind of communion life, we will find that we have strength for the day.

Confess Sin Right Away

During the day, do not allow any sin to remain. Confess it right away. Do not wait until the evening to confess; rather, do so immediately in order that your communion with God may not be adversely affected. Maintain a clear account with Him throughout the day.

Reminding Ourselves of God's Presence

Now at the beginning of our Christian walk with the Lord the presence of God with us is usually maintained by our memory. In other words, when we remember, then we are in God's presence. But when we are busy with other things, we are no longer in His presence. So we must try to remember and recall from time to time. Perhaps we need to simply lift up our hearts and say, "Thank You, Lord, You are here." This will help to maintain us in God's presence. That, however, is but the beginning of our Christian experience, not the end. It is only as we learn the lesson of the breaking of the outward man that we can truly begin to live in His presence.

These are but a few suggestions. Hopefully they will help us in our experience of communion with God. Even as the apostle Paul informs us: "we all, looking on the glory of the Lord, with unveiled face, are [being] transformed according to the same image from glory to glory, even as by the Lord the Spirit" (II Corinthians 3:18). Now that is what communion really is and should be for each one of us.

PART TWO:
SPIRITUAL EXERCISE OF
THE SOUL AND THE BODY

Chapter 5

EMOTION

I Timothy 4:7b-10—Exercise thyself unto [godliness]; for bodily exercise is profitable for a little, but [godliness] is profitable for everything, having promise of life, of the present one, and of that to come. The word is faithful and worthy of all acceptation; for, for this we labour and suffer reproach, because we hope in a living God, who is preserver of all men, specially of those that believe.

I Thessalonians 5:23-24—Now the God of peace himself sanctify you wholly: and your whole spirit, and soul, and body be preserved blameless at the coming of our Lord Jesus Christ. He is faithful who calls you, who will also perform it.

Matthew 10:34-39—Do not think that I have come to send peace upon the earth: I have not come to send peace, but a sword. For I have come to set a man at variance with his father, and the daughter with her mother, and the daughter-in-law with her mother-in-law; and they of his household shall be a man's enemies. He who loves father or mother above me is not worthy of me; and he who loves son or daughter above me is not worthy of me. And he who does not take up his cross and follow after me is not worthy of me. He that finds his life [i.e., his soul-life] shall lose it, and he who has lost his life [soul-life] for my sake shall find it.

With regard to this subject of spiritual exercise, we previously have said that it is like being in the gymnasium of Christ. After hearing about spiritual exercise we should be exercising our spirit, allowing it to be led by the Holy Spirit. And if so, we shall find that the conscience within us is working, being clean, clear, and alert. The intuition in our life shall also be working, and thus we shall be able to receive revelation and light from God and His word. So, too, our communion shall be deepening, and hence our daily life with the Lord shall be increasing. The only way to make progress in our spiritual life is through spiritual exercise. If we do not engage in such exercise, we may undoubtedly be able to accumulate much Biblical knowledge, but it does us little or no good. There is no growth in spiritual life unless we exercise our spirit under the management of the Holy Spirit.

SPIRITUAL EXERCISE IMPACTS UPON OUR WHOLE BEING

Let us now take this subject a step further. We know that spiritual exercise profits our spirit because the Bible has told us that exercise unto godliness is profitable for all things, it having the promise of life eternal, not only for this age but also for the age to come. So we see that spiritual exercise is profitable for everything—not only will it increase our spiritual life but it will impact upon our whole being.

We know that God made us with a spirit, a soul, and a body; therefore, spiritual exercise will not only purify and sanctify our spirit, it will also touch our soul and affect our body. Hence, in these next few messages we will center our attention on how spiritual exercise affects our soul and also our body.

MAN BECAME A LIVING SOUL

As was mentioned previously, when God created man, He took some soil from the ground and formed the body and then breathed (or Spirit-breathed) into the nostrils of that body (Genesis 2:7a). The Bible immediately says thereafter that man became a living soul (v. 7b). In other words, in creating man God made him into a tripartite being: he has a spirit—enabling him to have God-consciousness; he also has a soul—making it possible for man to have self-consciousness; and, finally, he has a body—thus man can have world-consciousness. According to God's divine order, the spirit should occupy and exercise the primary function in man because by the spirit we human beings can be in touch with the All-Sovereign God the Spirit. The soul, on the other hand, is the center of man's being, or to put it another way, this is where man's personality dwells—it is I myself. And, finally, the body of man is enabled to be in touch with the world around him.

So let us understand that of man's entire tripartite being, the soul occupies the very center. Sometimes the Bible uses the terms soul and man interchangeably. For instance, it states that seventy *souls* went down into Egypt (Genesis 46:27); that is to say, that seventy *men* of Jacob's lineage went down to Egypt (Exodus 1:1mgn Darby, 5). Hence, we men and women, boys and girls—all human beings—are living souls.

God created us with a soul, but the soul itself is invisible because it is not made up of matter or of physical material. Then how do we know we have a soul? We know this fact by observing its functions or faculties. According to God's word, the soul has three main ones. One is emotion—this involves feeling. Another is mind—such is marked by thinking. And a third is will—the exercise of volition. By these three functions we human beings are able to express ourselves.

EMOTION IS A GIFT OF GOD

Now we would like today to focus our discussion upon the function of emotion, and learn how spiritual exercise will purify our emotion. Let us be clear at the outset that emotion or feeling is a gift of God. If we have no emotion, then we can have no feeling of any kind. In that case, what kind of life would we live? For emotion is the very spice of life; but sadly, it can also bring on the bitterness of life. God created us with feeling. We feel good or we feel bad. We express laughter and we also express sadness and anger. All of us are unquestionably emotional beings. Some people may be more emotional than others, that is true; even so, we all have emotions. And we thank God for that! Nevertheless, we discover that in our emotion there is something amiss, a matter which I want us to consider together shortly.

Now when we were saved, what happened to us? Formerly, we were dead in sins and transgressions, having no hope of any kind and heading towards eternal death. But praise God, He saved us. Yet what does it mean by our having been saved? First of all, our dead spirit was quickened with new life. Christ came into our life and became the life of our new spirit. And then the Holy Spirit came and dwelt in our new spirit. When all this happened, we were saved. That which is born of the Spirit is spirit (John 3:6b). And being born of the Holy Spirit we now have a new spirit and thus we are able to communicate with God. The life of our spirit is Christ:

it is "Christ in you, the hope of glory" (Colossians 1:27b). The Holy Spirit dwells in our spirit in order to see to it that the new life of Christ in us will grow into maturity so that we may be conformed to the image of Christ. All that is what happened when we were saved.

SALVATION OF THE SOUL

As we consider the soul and the body, we might ask ourselves this question: Was our soul saved at the time we were born again and was our body redeemed at that same time? In one sense we do experience something happening in our soul and body at the time we are saved. For instance, the Bible tells us to repent, and believe in the Lord Jesus (see, e.g., Acts 2:38; 3:19 with 20, 26). In other words, had we not repented we would never have believed in the Lord Jesus because repentance is a change of mind, and that was an action which happened in our soul. In having saved us God by the Holy Spirit worked upon us and brought us to a sense of sinfulness (see, e.g., John 16:8-9). Formerly, we may have thought we were perfect, or almost perfect—better than anyone else. However, when the Holy Spirit touched our conscience, He brought us into a deep conviction and, having sensed such a burden of sin upon ourselves, we repented and turned to the Lord Jesus. As a consequence His blood cleansed our conscience, and we were saved. In short, when we were saved, our soul was being touched and impacted upon. There was indeed a change, but let us realize that it was only superficial.

Basically, our soul remains the same. The one who dwells in our soul is still our old, natural, Adamic life—our very self.

Even though Christ dwells in our spirit and is the life of our spirit, self is still the life of our soul. The old man in us is still using our soul to express *himself* instead of Christ. That is why after we are saved we begin to discern that there are two persons dwelling within us. Deep within our spirit Christ is talking to us and telling us what is right and what is wrong, what is good and what is evil. He is attempting to lead us into a life of holiness and victory. But then we discover in our soul that our self is still there: we continue to have our own ideas, ways, and opinions. Accordingly, there appears to be a civil war going on in our lives. It is a conflict between the life of Christ in our spirit and the self-life or the flesh. It is a conflict between the Holy Spirit on the one hand and our soul or flesh on the other. I believe we all—if we have been truly saved—have gone through such experiences.

What, though, with regard to our body? I have often commented that before we were saved we had a long face, but after we are saved, our face becomes rounded. Is that not wonderful? Yet is our body transformed from a mortal to an immortal body? No, we still have a mortal body. It has not changed, it simply needs to be redeemed.

When we were saved, our spirit was saved, in that we received a new spirit, but our soul and body have remained the same old entities. Nevertheless, we can thank God that His salvation is a full one. He will not abandon our body and soul but will save them as well. Briefly stated, He wants to save our whole being. That is what Paul tells us in II Corinthians 1:10: We *were* delivered from so great a death, we *are being* delivered, and we *shall be* delivered. In other words, deliverance is threefold in nature. In the past we were delivered from a great death because our *spirit* was saved.

Moreover, presently we are being delivered, which is our daily experience once we are saved, and this is the salvation of our *soul*. But even further, we are yet to be delivered in the future, and that will constitute the redemption of our *body* when this physical frame of ours will be changed into a spiritual body at the second coming of the Lord Jesus. That is why we can declare that God's salvation is a full one. And this thought is also expressed in I Thessalonians 5:23 where Paul writes: "Now the God of peace himself sanctify you wholly: and your whole spirit, and soul, and body be preserved blameless at the coming of our Lord Jesus Christ."

Our soul needs to be saved and that is, or should be, taking place today—day after day after day. As long as we shall remain alive after we are saved this process of the salvation of the soul will go on daily until that day when we shall see the Lord Jesus face to face. This, then, is a present salvation which is most important. That is the reason the Bible tells us that there is such a spiritual reality as the salvation of the soul (I Peter 1:9).

Yet can we save our soul by exercising our soul? Take, for instance, the soul's faculty of volition or the will. Once a brother told me that he had a weak will, and he asked me how he could strengthen it. I explained to him that the more he tried to strengthen his will, the worse it would become. The salvation of the will lies not in exercising it by one's soulish effort. The secret is in exercising our spirit. As our renewed spirit grows stronger, the will of our soul is overcome by the life of Christ residing in our spirit.

THE SOUL'S DELIVERANCE THROUGH JESUS CHRIST

Hence, the way of the soul's deliverance lies not in soulical or mental exercise. The more we exercise our soul, the greater our soul will become until it becomes a monster, beyond our control. The only way we can be delivered in our soul is through Jesus Christ who is resident in our spirit. This is most graphically borne out in Romans 7 where the apostle Paul described his personal struggle over this very issue of the soul versus the spirit: What he wanted to do, he could not; what he did not want to do, that he did; he even declared: "It is not I, but the sin that dwells in me. Who can deliver me from this body of death? Thank God, through Jesus Christ" (see vv. 20, 24-25). The more we try to save our soul, the lower we shall sink. But as we continually yield and give ourselves over to Christ Jesus, He is able to save us to the uttermost—that is, completely and forever.

Accordingly, the means by which the salvation of the entire soul with its various faculties comes about is not through any effort of ours but through the grace of God. We may be able, for instance, to suppress and hold back our emotion, but it is still bubbling up within us. Outwardly we may be calm, but for how long? Eventually our emotion will explode some day. We may also be able to hide our mind's thinking and act differently, but that makes us a hypocrite. We may even be able to hide our will, but it is there, nonetheless, and never changes.

Hence, the salvation of our soul can only be realized through spiritual exercise. The Holy Spirit will reveal to us in our spirit where the manifestation of our various soulical faculties are wrong, and then He will arrange our circumstances to bring us to a point that on any given issue we have to choose between Christ and self. That is the work of the Holy Spirit.

WHO CONTROLS OUR EMOTION?

Now in our further discussion on the salvation of the entire soul we will first focus upon the function or faculty of emotion. It is the most apparent, the most active, the most volatile of all the faculties of the soul. In fact, we may say that man's emotion is the clearest and most frequent manifestation of the self-life in the soul. Our emotion reveals and expresses us. In brief, it tells who we truly are. Moreover, I believe that emotion is a most wonderful human faculty: indeed, it is the gift of God; indeed, how could we human beings live if we did not have emotion?

Unfortunately, however, there is something wrong in man's soul—even in redeemed man's soul. This is because the one who uses our emotion is that old self of ours or what is termed the fallen man. As long as our emotion is used and controlled by the old self, that which is expressed through our emotion will be our old self and not the life nor the beauty of Christ. The problem lies not in emotion itself but in the one who uses or controls the emotion. The basic question to be answered, then, is this: Who is being expressed through our emotion—Christ or that old self of ours? This is why our emotion needs to be saved.

Have we ever realized that our emotion needs to be purified? Has the Holy Spirit ever convicted any of us that what is being expressed by our emotion is not Christ but is still our old self? If it is still the latter, we need to consider how it can be delivered. But first, some background from the Bible can perhaps be helpful here.

"WITHOUT NATURAL AFFECTION" AND "PAST ALL FEELING"

Romans 1 tells us how we have fallen and sinned. We find there a whole list of sins which mankind has committed ever since the fall, and when we come to verse 31 we find listed this particular sin having to do with man's emotion: "without natural affection, unmerciful." Here we glean the fact that there is something wrong with the emotion of fallen man: it is without natural affection and is unmerciful. Now the phrase natural affection here refers to the affection which God has given us. However, what we today call natural affection is *un*natural, for it is no longer controlled by God but is controlled by me myself. In Ephesians 4 we are given a short description of how the unbelieving Gentiles live and walk; one characteristic of which is this: that they are "past feeling" (AV) or are "void of all feelings [i.e., they do not care]" (Darby) (v. 19a).

Therefore, not only in the Scriptures do we learn that there is something not right with our emotion, but also, even we ourselves, I believe, have discerned from our life experiences the same sense of there being something amiss in our emotion: what we should love, we hate; what we should hate, we love. In sum, we do not like the will of God but we very much like the world. We sense that the way we express our emotion after we are saved is not pure, and hence we struggle over it. What then ensues is a battle or conflict within, which ultimately compels us to choose between the Lord and our self—or soul-life.

THE BATTLE IN OUR EMOTION

This choosing is what we read about in Matthew 10. The Lord Jesus is recorded there as declaring: "Do not think that I have come to send peace upon the earth." This, by the way, sounds very contradictory to the whole Christian notion of eventual peace on earth and glory to God. The coming Messiah (who of course is Jesus) is called in Isaiah 9:6 the Prince of Peace, and yet here Jesus himself says, "Do not think that I have come to send peace upon the earth" because the world—being so upside down and thus unable to enjoy any peace—needs to have the sword applied to it first in order to clear the way for peace. Jesus therefore declares: "I have not come to send peace but a sword"; He went on to declare the following as recorded in that same chapter: "Anyone who loves father or mother more than Me is not worthy of Me. Anyone who loves his son or daughter more than Me is not worthy of Me. Whoever does not take up his cross and follow after Me is also not worthy of Me. And whoever finds his soul-life shall lose it, and whoever loses his soul-life for My sake shall find it."

What does all this mean? Let us thank the Lord that He knows so well where we may fail. Accordingly, He has made every provision for delivering us. As was indicated earlier, after we are saved we begin to discern and experience some kind of conflict or battle occurring in our emotion. As a matter of fact, we are being challenged by the Lord—not by man. He will raise up circumstances in our life through the demand of the ones we love naturally which is obviously in conflict with His demand. When such a development occurs in our lives, we begin to struggle over whether we shall uphold our soul-life or allow the Christ-life in our spirit to be in ascendancy, that is, over whether we shall obey the Lord rather than ourselves. If we deny ourselves, it will be painful because, above all else, we want to satisfy and gratify ourselves. Whenever self is being challenged, automatically our feeling or emotion is going to be challenged over whether we love the Lord or ourselves. Where does our love come from? And is it pure? If not, then we are in trouble. I believe we all have encountered such emotional conflicts in our lives. And the issue really comes down to this: if we obey ourselves, we disobey God; If we obey God, we put our self-life to death. Now this latter "if" is the way of salvation.

THE EMOTION OF THE LORD JESUS

If we contemplate the life and character of the Lord Jesus to any extent, we shall readily see that He is the most compassionate person in the whole world. We often read in the New Testament that He looked upon the multitude and had great compassion towards them—yet not only for the welfare of their body but also for that of their soul. Nevertheless, as we carefully read through the Gospels, we find that He sometimes appeared to act insensitively, harshly, even cruelly. For instance, once while Jesus was speaking to a crowd, His mother and His brothers appeared on the scene wanting to speak to Him. What did the Lord Jesus do or say in response? Looking at the people who were around Him, He said this: "Who is my mother, my brother and sister?

Whoever does the will of My Father is my mother, brother and sister" (see Matthew 12:46-50). Does that not seem most cruel? Jesus has a soul, as do we, but unlike ours His was sinless. Yes, indeed, He had emotion and feeling and was given to weeping at times. Yet while on earth His emotion and feeling were pure and were not controlled by His soul but by His Father's will. Did that circumstance thus make Him out to be harsh and insensitive towards His mother? It may have appeared that way to others. But not so; for when Jesus was suffering and dying on the cross, He beheld His mother and compassionately provided for her: He looked down at His mother and said, "Your son" and turned to His disciple John and said, "Your mother." From that moment forward John took Mary to his house and treated her as his own mother (John 19:25-27). What pure love Jesus displayed here!

A further instance of the Lord's pure compassion and love, though at first seemingly unloving, cruel and insensitive, is related in John 11. There we learn how He was being denied and persecuted by the unbelieving Jewish world. In response to this Jesus crossed over the river Jordan and stayed there for awhile. And while there, news came to Him that His friend Lazarus had become deathly ill. Now the Bible record here tells us that Jesus loved Lazarus and his two sisters, Martha and Mary (v.5). Let us be clear that the Greek word for love employed here is not *phileo*—friendship love—but *agape*—divine love. He loved them with the love of God—that is to say, it was absolute and unconditional. Now Martha, Mary and Lazarus loved the Lord, but the Greek word which might be employed for their love would be *phileo*: they felt good about Christ and had a close friendship with Him. The two sisters no doubt believed that if they sent an urgent message to Christ, He would immediately rush over to their home, lay His hands upon Lazarus, and heal him out of His love and concern for His friend. Yet, when the Lord received the news, He remained where He was for two more days, waiting until Lazarus was indisputably dead. What a disappointment to these two sisters! Their thoughts in response to Jesus' inaction may have been these: "What kind of Lord is He? Master, You do not any longer love us, because in our time of crisis You neglected and ignored us completely." Yet was this the case? Not at all. Jesus eventually went to where they were, Lazarus having now already been in the tomb for four days. Upon observing the entire scene, Jesus wept (v. 35). Then He miraculously brought His dear friend Lazarus back to life, and declared: "I am the resurrection and the life."

Here we see that the Lord was quite emotional but was under the perfect control of God His Father. Moreover, there is not a hint of himself but only a manifestation of the best of himself. Was that easy for the Lord Jesus to do? People may unthinkingly believe such; but no, He is human as well as divine. And thus by His conduct shown here, Jesus demonstrated to man that humanity must sometimes suffer greatly because it is so natural for us human beings to rush in to solve a given problem or to offer immediate help in a time of crisis.

PETER—THE MOST EMOTIONAL DISCIPLE

Let us also briefly consider Peter. I think of all the twelve disciples of the Lord Jesus, Peter was the most emotional. His temperament was one of being impetuous, brave, outspoken, and fearless. Without a doubt he was a highly emotional person. When Jesus told His disciples that He, the Shepherd of their souls (I Peter 2:25), would be killed and that because of this they would all be offended, fall away and be scattered but that after He would rise from death He would go ahead of them into Galilee, Peter blurted out bravely with: "The other disciples may fail You, Lord, but I will not. I will follow You even to death" (see Mark 14:27-31; cf. with John 13:36-37). And at that moment he meant it. But when later a little maid questioned him about his relationship with Jesus, he trembled in fear (Mark 14:66-68). Moreover, he would deny his association with the Lord three times (Mark 14:72).

Now that was the man Peter. Nonetheless, thank God that on one occasion the Lord would say to His impetuous disciple: "Simon, Simon, behold, the enemy is trying to get hold of you. You will be sifted like wheat and only what is of God will remain but what is not of God will drop away. I have prayed for you that after you have recovered, you will strengthen your brothers" (see Luke 22:31-32). And on still another occasion the Lord said to Peter: "When you were young, you went your own way, but when you grow old, others will lead you away." By this latter comment Jesus was alluding to the kind of death Peter would experience in bringing glory to God (see John 21:18-19). What a change came over Peter! And this would be the one who would later write the epistle of I Peter which deals primarily with the salvation of the soul in all its faculties. Peter tells us therein how our soul —even our emotion, mind and will—can be saved so that we may come under the management of the Shepherd and Overseer of our soul, the Lord Jesus (1:9, 2:25).

This is the salvific process we all have to go through. If we try to avoid it, if we neglect so great a salvation, it is to our hurt. If, however, we are willing to lose our soul-life, take up our cross and follow Him, we shall save our soul-life— including especially our emotion—unto eternity.

THE EXPERIENCE OF WATCHMAN NEE

Brother Watchman Nee was saved in 1920. By 1922 there was already a group of mostly young believers, including brother Nee himself, meeting together who would go out to preach the gospel. He was at that time still a college student. He told us that one day he was going to speak, so he searched the Scriptures for the topic of his sermon. He came to Psalm 73 where the psalmist inquires of himself: "Whom do I have in heaven but Thee, whom do I desire on earth but Thee" (see v. 25). He wanted to use that text as the basis for his sermon, but frankly he felt he could not utter this. He might have been able to say, "Whom do I have in *heaven* but Thee?" That was easy to say. But at that moment he could not bring himself to assert in total honesty: "Whom do I desire on *earth* except Thee," for he was in love with a young lady. They had been together for ten years and had even grown up together. They were seemingly meant for each other. Then, after he was saved, he tried to bring this lady to Christ, but he found that he was able to talk with her on any subject except Christ. She would not listen to any discussion about Jesus, and so he struggled much over this issue in his conscience but without any spiritual resolution to it. Nevertheless, he went ahead and preached the sermon anyway. We find, do we not, many preachers today who are preaching against their conscience.

After some time, brother Nee was again going to speak, and this very same verse came to him. He once more sought to avoid the issue by asking the Lord, "Will you change Your mind and not require that I give her up?" The Lord, however, would not do so. Then he began to promise the Lord, "If you allow me to have this lady, I will go to Tibet and preach the gospel." The Lord once more refused to negotiate. Still unyielding towards the Lord, brother Nee delivered the same sermon that morning; but in the afternoon, upon returning to his room, he prayed: "Lord, fill me with Your love. I am willing to give her up." Whereupon the Lord answered by filling brother Nee's heart with His love. It was at this time that he bade farewell to the world, he doing so by changing his dress, taking some gospel posters out to the street, and paving the street with these posters. He even wrote a poem about this crucial event in his life, which can be found in the hymn book entitled: *How Vast, Immense, and Measureless*. The world was now behind brother Nee, and Christ became everything to him.

THE EXPERIENCE OF ALLAN YUAN

Recently I was reading a biography of brother Allan Yuan (1914-2005), and I noticed that when in 1943 he was about thirty years old, he felt the call of God to go to the country places of China to preach the gospel. He was actually at a crossroads in his life because he knew that his parents had high hopes for him in the future to become rich and take care of them. That was his duty which was traditionally expected of a son in China, and for two months he struggled over this matter.

Two verses in the Bible were given to him by God. One was Matthew 10:37: "He who loves father or mother above me is not worthy of me." The other one was Luke 14:26 and in the Greek original it reads, as translated into English, as follows: "Unless you hate your father and mother, your wife, your children, your brothers and sisters, and your own life, you cannot be my disciple."

Before proceeding further with this brother's story, I would here interject and say again that there is nothing wrong with love and hate. These are simply expressions of our emotion. The problem, though, comes down to this: Do we love what we should love and hate what we should hate? If we hate what we should love and love what we should hate, then there is something drastically wrong.

Now when these two verses were given to brother Yuan by the Lord, he felt that the Lord was asking him the following: "Alan Yuan, I have spoken to you with these words. How will you react? Are you willing to take up your cross and follow Me? Are you willing to live a life that may be nameless, profitless, misunderstood, and unknown to others? What is your response?" And brother Yuan was so touched by the love of Christ that he surrendered. It was not an easy way for him. Indeed, it was the way of the cross; but praise God, the Lord purified his soul and henceforth used him as a precious vessel. Brother Yuan would later become one of the pastoral leaders of the Chinese house churches.

This is just one of many illustrations which could be presented. I believe that in this area of emotion, God must have already dealt with, or be in the process of dealing with, each one of us. This is because He loves us so much. Unless our emotion is being saved, our way before the Lord will not be straight. Emotion is not a facet of our self-life which is to be dealt with in and by our soul; to the contrary, its resolution has to begin with spiritual exercise. In fact, it is our life with Christ in our spirit which will save our emotion.

THIS CONFLICT PRODUCES SUFFERING

This is not a special experience for special people. No, every true believer must go through this experience. Our love, our hate, our other feelings—our entire emotional life— needs to be sanctified. Unless it is Christ who—willingly on our part—is in charge of our feelings, we will abuse our emotion. Our emotion needs to be delivered, but not in such manner as to make us emotionless or without natural affection. For does not the Bible command us to honor our father and mother? This is the fifth of the Ten Commandments and the only one with a promise. This is not only found in the Old Testament, it is likewise repeated in the New Testament—both the Lord himself and the apostles having spoken of this (see Exodus 20:12, and see also, e.g., Matthew 15:4, 19:19; Ephesians 6:2-3). We should therefore honor our father and mother. Why, then, does the Lord say, "If you love your father and mother more than Me, you are not worthy of Me"? It is not because, in the first instance, He wants to be the first but because He wants to purify and save our soul's emotional life.

Do you want to have your emotion saved? Are you listening to the still, small voice of the Holy Spirit? When you are in conflict over this issue of emotion, do you uphold your self-life to make yourself feel comfortable or great, or do you yield to the Lord in your spirit and suffer reproach for having done so for His sake? May God have mercy upon us!

Chapter 6

MIND

Matthew 16:21-26—From that time Jesus began to shew to his disciples that he must go away to Jerusalem, and suffer many things from the elders and chief priests and scribes, and be killed, and the third day be raised. And Peter taking him to him began to rebuke him, saying, God be favourable to thee, Lord; this shall in no wise be unto thee. But turning round, he said to Peter, Get away behind me, Satan; thou art an offence to me, for thy mind is not on the things that are of God, but on the things that are of men.

Then Jesus said to his disciples, If any one desires to come after me, let him deny himself and take up his cross and follow me. For whosoever shall desire to save his life [soul-life] shall lose it; but whosoever shall lose his life [soul-life] for my sake shall find it. For what does a man profit, if he should gain the whole world and suffer the loss of his soul? or what shall a man give in exchange for his soul?

Romans 12:1-2—I beseech you therefore, brethren, by the compassions of God, to present your bodies a living sacrifice, holy, acceptable to God, which is your intelligent service. And be not conformed to this world, but be transformed by the renewing of your mind, that ye may prove what is the good and acceptable and perfect will of God.

Philippians 2:1-11—If then there be any comfort in Christ, if any consolation of love, if any fellowship of the Spirit, if any bowels and compassions, fulfil my joy, that ye may think the same thing, having the same love, joined in soul, thinking one thing; let nothing be in the spirit of strife or vain glory, but, in lowliness of mind, each esteeming the other as more excellent than themselves; regarding not each his own qualities, but each those of others also. For let this mind be in you which was also in Christ Jesus; who, subsisting in the form of God, did not esteem it an object of rapine to be on an equality with God; but emptied himself, taking a bondman's form, taking his place in the likeness of men; and having been found in figure as a man, humbled himself, becoming obedient even unto death, and that the death of the cross. Wherefore also God highly exalted him, and granted him a name, that which is above every name, that at the name of Jesus every knee should bow, of heavenly and earthly and infernal beings, and every tongue confess that Jesus Christ is Lord to God the Father's glory.

I would remind ourselves that we are still in the gymnasium of Christ, but I wonder how many of us are actually exercising in His gymnasium. It is not of any use if you and I visit the gymnasium but are not involved in its various exercises. What we are going to share today will not profit us in any way unless we are willing to participate in the exercises of Christ's gymnasium. It may cost us in terms of some sweat and some hardship, even some pain, agony and suffering, but it is worth all of that.

Today we shall be considering together how spiritual exercise can and will affect our mind for our good and for fulfilling God's purpose. The Lord God is omniscient—He knows everything. As the apostle Paul was concluding the section in Romans 11 dealing with the marvelous salvation which God has prepared for us, he suddenly broke forth to exclaim: "O depth of riches both of the wisdom and knowledge of God! how unsearchable his judgments, and untraceable his ways! For who has known the mind of the Lord, or who has been his counsellor? or who has first given to him, and it shall be rendered to him? For of him, and through him, and for him are all things: to him be glory for ever. Amen." That is a tremendous description of the wisdom of God and the mind of God, for the Sovereign God is the greatest mind in the entire universe.

THE MIND IS A PRECIOUS GIFT

When God created man, He created him after His own image and according to His likeness. As such, He created man with a wonderful mind. What if we had to exist without a mind? Our lives would count for nothing because they could not accomplish anything whatsoever. Thank God, however, He created us with a marvelous mind that could do so many things. We are now in the computer age, but I for one am allergic to computers and know little or nothing about them. But one thing about them I do know is that the computer can do so many things which I cannot. It is a mystery to me how such a device can accomplish so much! However, let us never forget that it is the human mind that created the computer. Our mind is far more marvelous even than the computer.

God has given us a wonderful mind. It is a precious gift of His to us. Even so, can anyone believe that God would give us such a great gift without there being any purpose behind it? He is a God of purpose, and He accomplishes everything according to His purpose. Has any one of us ever considered why God created us with a mind? What was His purpose in doing so? I believe this is a most fundamental question which we need to ask ourselves, because no matter how dull I am, this mind of mine is nonetheless most wonderful. Why, indeed, did God create me with such a marvelous faculty? Was it simply done so I could earn a good living, or did He have something more important and more glorious behind its creation because He has such a mind himself? I believe God gave us a mind in order that we might serve His purpose, that we might learn to understand and know Him, and that we might be able to serve Him according to His will. All that, I firmly believe, is why God created us with a mind; for without it, man could not serve Him at all.

TWO TREES IN THE GARDEN

As we have often noted in the past, God is the supreme will in the universe, and He—having himself a free will—created us with a free will also. Accordingly, what purpose would free will serve if there were no choice associated with its creation? Therefore, after God created man He set up a choice by planting two trees in the center of the Garden of Eden—the Tree of Life and the tree of the knowledge of good and evil. And let us be reminded again that God would never plant nor did He plant any bad tree in the Garden of Eden because it was a garden of pleasure.

Now the Tree of Life was the best tree to be found in the garden because it signified that God wanted His life to be possessed by the man whom He had created. It signified that God was offering His life to man—offering not only a brilliant mind and a free will but His very own life. Let us ponder that for a moment! God never ever offered His life to the angels or to the animals or to any other created being. But He did offer it to man.

Simultaneously with the Tree of Life God planted another tree beside it—the tree of the knowledge of good and evil. Do any of us think that was a bad tree? If so, we would be terribly mistaken! For what knowledge is better than that of good and evil? Scientific knowledge or philosophical knowledge cannot be compared with ethical knowledge, moral knowledge, or the knowledge of knowing what is good and what is evil. Such is the highest knowledge the world can ever possess aside from knowing God himself. I would declare it to be a better tree than all the other trees in the Garden of Eden, but it was not the *best* one. All the other trees were, and are, for our physical needs. Yet, whereas the tree of the knowledge of good and evil was meant to provide the food of the soul, far above and beyond that good tree God gave to man His life that it might be the food of our spirit. If man were to eat of the Tree of Life, he would possess a knowledge even better than that of good and evil because man would have the knowledge of God himself. For did not the Lord Jesus declare that to know God and to know the One whom He has sent is eternal life (John 17:3)? *That* is the highest knowledge.

There are those who say, and most likely it is true, that God purposely placed these two specific trees in the center of the garden as His way of confronting man with a choice. Regrettably, our ancestors made the wrong choice. When they were tempted by the enemy, they began to think on this wise: "If I eat of the tree of the knowledge of good and evil, my mind will be highly developed. I will be as God, and I can live independently. I do not need to depend upon God because I am God myself. My knowledge makes me God; why, then, should I take the life of God and be dependent on Him? Why should I not myself be God?" Man chose the tree of the knowledge of good and evil instead of the Tree of Life. He and the woman God gave him would rather be gods and be great in themselves and be independent than submit themselves to their Creator and live life on the highest plane. Sadly for them and for us that was what our ancestors back then in the Garden of Eden chose for themselves.

What happened to man after he chose the tree of the knowledge of good and evil? God had forewarned by saying: "Of all the trees in the garden you may freely eat except the tree of the knowledge of good and evil. On the day that you eat of that tree, you shall surely die" (see Genesis 2:16-17). Was God jealous of man as the enemy had suggested? Or did He forbid man from eating of that tree because He knew what would happen if man became independent of Him? Despite God's warning, our ancestors ate of the forbidden tree anyway, and they immediately discovered that they were naked (Genesis 3:7a). The glory with which they had been clothed left them. They therefore tried to make aprons from some of the garden's fig leaves by which to cover themselves, but the weather had now changed; for when the wind blew, all their nakedness was quickly exposed: the leaves proved to be useless. So when God came into the garden, they hid themselves among the trees because they did not dare face Him (Genesis 3:7b-10).

MAN'S INHERITANCE FROM ADAM

Now Adam was the name given to the first man, and all who have come out of Adam since then have inherited his nature. Adam had become selfish and self-centered; therefore, all who are born of Adam are born with a fallen nature. We are born as men and women of flesh. We live by our soul and body because our spirit is dead towards God (Romans 5:12 ff.; cf. Psalm 51:5). The life within our soul is a fallen self-life—it is self-centered, self-interested, and self-exalting.

As a result of man's fall, what happened to his mind? When he fell, his mind also fell—yet not in the sense that all the abilities of his mind were forfeited but that all his moral sense was now lost. That is the reason why the writer of Romans 1 was moved to list all the sins which man had begun to commit; and then, in summation, he wrote that because mankind did not want to know God, He "gave them up to a reprobate mind to practice unseemly things" (v. 28). Here we learn what over time eventually happened to the mind of man: it became a reprobate mind. The word reprobate simply means "void of moral discernment." Hence, fallen men are able to discern everything except what is really of God. They have put Him out of their mind; therefore, in all their consideration, God is not present. The supreme standard of morality is no longer there; everything is now relative; nothing is absolute. People with a reprobate mind do all kinds of unseemly things and commit all kinds of sins. And the source of it all is a reprobate mind.

Do not assume your mind to be all right. Do not think that you have so brilliant a mind that you can therefore depend upon it for living your life successfully. No matter how brilliant you may be, your mind—like all fallen minds—is a reprobate one. It has lost its moral standard and its moral discernment. For that is what we all have inherited from our fallen ancestors.

THE MIND OF THE FLESH IS DEATH

There are many places in the Bible which tell us what happened to our mind in our fallen state. For example, Romans 8 says, "The mind of the flesh is death but the mind of the Spirit is life and peace" (see v. 6). If your mind functions according to your flesh or according to the life of your soul, it will result in death. Only when you obey the Holy Spirit within your spirit can you have life and peace. The mind of the flesh is at enmity with God, which signifies that our natural mind is an enemy of God (v. 7b). It cannot obey God because it does not understand Him. And thus it becomes His enemy. Hence, that is what you find throughout the world today. There is brilliance on every side, but when the mind is confronted with the subject of God, it draws a blank. In short, man's mind has become vain.

Fallen man's understanding of God and the things of God has become darkened because he has been alienated from God's life (Ephesians 4:17-18). Indeed, fallen man has become high-minded and trusts in uncertain riches rather than in God (I Timothy 6:17). Not only that, he has become double-minded and unstable in all his ways (James 1:8). That is the condition of his reprobate mind. Whether fallen man acknowledges it or not, whether he knows it or not, is not the question. Oh, how alienated human beings do boast of their mind! The more they exercise their mind the sharper and keener, as it were, their mind will become—but in what area? The sharpness and brilliance of their mind will be centered around self: self-interest, self-pride, self-exaltation. As a matter of fact, nearly everything which fallen man's mind may express is but a manifestation of what his self is. And the consequence of it all is spiritual death.

NEW LIFE BUT OLD MIND

Thank God, however, that the Bible tells us who are believers that He has delivered us from so great a death (II Corinthians 1:10a; cf. Romans 7:24-25a). By His Spirit, God has birthed anew our spirit and placed His life in us. Our spirit was quickened from the dead and by the blood of Jesus was cleansed from an evil conscience. And we, therefore, who have believed in the Lord Jesus were saved. His life has thus become the life of our spirit. And this makes it possible for the Holy Spirit who dwells in our spirit to teach us how to have the life of Christ in us grow into maturity. Every provision is there.

Next, though, the Bible tells us that the believer—even his or her soul with all its faculties—is being delivered (II Corinthians 1:10). This means that for us who believe in the Lord Jesus, even our soul's reprobate mind is included in that deliverance. That in fact is what should be taking place in us continually today. We were instructed by the Scriptures to "repent and believe in the Lord Jesus." And this is what we did, for how could anyone believe in the Lord Jesus without repenting?

Yet let us not think that our reprobate mind can repent in and of itself; not so. Now it is true that we can express regret: If I do something which brings an adverse or evil effect upon me, of course I will regret it because I know I will suffer for it: I may even change my mind, but even then, it is still an act taken for my personal profit or well-being: so no matter if I change my mind, it still falls within that original scope or parameter of a reprobate mind that is totally void of moral and ethical discernment. Let us therefore realize that it is only the Holy Spirit who can fundamentally change our reprobate mind.

We readily acknowledge that the Holy Spirit is the one who convicted our conscience which had previously lain in a comatose state. For when the Holy Spirit touched our conscience, a sense of repentance began to dawn upon us and thus moved by God's Spirit we repented. But He likewise touched our intuition which had also lain in a comatose state, and as a result we began to see by revelation what we had never seen before; namely, that Christ Jesus is the only Savior, and that He died for us. Then we believed.

So, yes, our repentance is indeed a change of mind, but let us understand that such act of repentance is only superficial in its effect and is just for a time; for, basically, our reprobate mind has not been renewed in any significant way because the life which directs that mind is still of the flesh; it is of the self and has therefore not yet been delivered.

Let us pursue this matter further. After you were saved, did you realize that though you now have a new heart you still have an old mind? Your mind has not been renewed yet. Being renewed in mind simply means that the life which directs your mind has changed. It is changing from your self-life being in charge of your mind to the Christ-life in your spirit being so. It will constitute—when fully realized and matured in you—an exchanged life, and that is an experience which hopefully is going to happen in every Christian life.

Let me use an example from Scripture here. We are told in Matthew 16 of how Simon Peter received a tremendous revelation from God the Father. The Lord Jesus had asked His disciples: "Who do you say I am?" And Simon Peter was the one who responded. In so many words he said the following: "You are the Christ, the Son of the living God. So far as Your person is concerned, You are the only begotten Son of God. So far as Your mission is concerned, You are the Christ—the anointed One of God—sent with a mission from Him to save us." And to all that the Lord Jesus replied by saying, again in so many words, the following: "Simon Bar-jona, you are blessed of God because no human being could have told you this. It is my Father in heaven who has revealed it to you. You are Peter, and you are a little stone—from dust you have become a stone. A new life—with a new character and a new nature—has come into you. I will build my church upon this massive rock and the gates of Hades shall not prevail against it" (see vv. 13-18).

Immediately after Peter and the others had received this immense revelation, the Lord Jesus began to share with them that He must go to Jerusalem, must suffer and die, but that on the third day He would be raised from the dead. Upon hearing this, Peter, without hesitating a moment, physically laid hold of the Lord. I can almost imagine that he took hold of Jesus' two hands and began to shake Him most vigorously while at the same time saying to his Master, "Lord, never! You do not need to do that. You can have the kingdom without having to suffer and die!" (see vv. 21-22) On the one hand, Peter at this moment manifested a beneficent—even, perhaps, a noble—mind. Can there be anyone who could not appreciate what Peter did? For if Peter had done that to me, I would most certainly have appreciated it very much and would have said to Peter, "You really do love me, for I see that you truly want to save me from death." On the other hand, though, the Scriptures make it quite clear that Peter was not aware that Satan was using him here to try to persuade Christ from going to the cross. Indeed, were Peter to be successful in his persuasion, there could not and would not be any salvation for mankind. Jesus, however, had spiritual discernment; for He turned around and said to His ignorant disciple: "Get behind me, Satan. It is not you, Peter, but Satan in you who is attempting to do this because you were being mindful of the things of man and not the things of God" (see v. 23).

We can glean from this event that within a person who is newly awakened, having only recently received a new life and a new spirit, the old reprobate mind is still in charge of his or her life. Do you think Peter really loved the Lord so much? The truth of the matter is that behind his declared love and concern for his Master there was more love and concern for himself; for Peter probably harbored in his mind this thought: "If the Master is to suffer and die, what about me? Can He not have the kingdom without dying? Surely He can, and so can I." But the Lord Jesus now said to Peter and the other disciples: "If you are willing to lose your soul-life, you will gain it; you will save your soul. If, though, you try to save your soul-life today, you will lose it. What does it profit you if you gain the whole world but lose your soul?" (see vv. 25-26a)

Here, then, is a very clear example for us who have been enlightened and saved but in whom our old mind is still maintaining its grip on us. Do we believe we are able to live a Christian life by means of an old mind? Such is impossible! What is the reason we cannot live a true Christian life? To many of us it seems so hard to do so. Actually, though, it is very simple if we understand and have a true picture of ourselves. Within the soul there is still the fallen Adam with his old mind. He is continually trying to assert his authority over you and me. He is using our fallen mind to keep us away from the mind and things of God. I do believe this is what is happening to every one of us. Is it not true that upon our first believing in the Lord Jesus, it often appears to us as though we are walking in the clouds; for when we look around ourselves, everything is blue and the birds are chirping and singing sweeter than ever. At that moment of first love there is nothing we are not able to offer up to the Lord. That, however, does not last long. Gradually, the old Adam with his fallen mind begins to raise his head. He has been in charge for so long and wants to keep it that way. And thus begins the so-called battle for the mind.

THE BATTLE FOR THE MIND

Many people have read John Bunyan's *Pilgrim's Progress* but there is another book of his called *The Holy War* and in it he writes that our mind is a battlefield and our will is a citadel or castle fortress. The enemy of our souls is always trying to occupy our mind. He is attempting to keep at bay Emmanuel (i.e., "God with us") who is intent upon capturing that castle fortress himself—yet not by force but by His love. Let us never forget, though, that in this conflict the mind is actually the place of battle.

In our *awakened* mind we know what is right, but somehow we find another power in our soul that is resisting. It is the conflict between an awakened mind and the flesh. The last verse in Romans 7 has Paul declaring: "I thank God, through Jesus Christ our Lord. So then I myself with the mind serve God's law; but with the flesh, sin's law" (see v. 25). Here we find a battle between an awakened, enlightened mind and the flesh. And it is during each battle that we begin to learn some very important lessons.

If you do not love the Lord, if you do not care, you will not sense the fierceness which often marks such battle. Instead, you can live an easygoing life, living against your conscience. You can live contrary to what God has revealed to you—and void of any sweet communion with your Father God. In short, you can return to living your old life. Yes, you can do that, but I believe that that is not what you really want to do. For is it not true that after you were saved you somehow wanted to please God because there is now a life within you which continually tells you about God? Is it not true to say that you began to sense something you had never sensed before? Even in the matter of your speech you in the past may have exaggerated everything in what you spoke, but that made you feel good; today, however, in exaggerating your words once again, somehow you now find a check within you: you ask yourself, "Is what I just now uttered actually true?" Yet you had gone ahead and said it anyway;

but after saying it, you felt bad. In fact, that very evening, when you tried to pray to God, you realized you had to confess first, otherwise there could not and would not be any contact with Him.

This experience, and others like it, is but a reflection of the fact that you as a young Christian are confronted with the recurring question of what is God's will in this situation or that; and such question comes to you on almost a daily basis. Previously, you always knew what you wanted to do or say or where you wanted to go without there being any check within; indeed, you were never concerned with, or never even thought about, the will of God. Now, however, having experienced God's salvation, His will is what you inwardly care about, for today it often seems you do not know what you may do or not do or where you may go or not go; and hence, you find yourself repeatedly asking yourself: "What is the will of God" in this instance or that?

Moreover, so concerned are you about this matter that you may even seek out an older brother or sister and inquire of him or her: "May I do this?" "May I go there?" "What is the will of God for me in this situation?" Do realize that you have this question because you now have the life of Christ dwelling in you and that it is from your spirit that that question arises. On the other hand, do realize that in your asking an older believer—"What shall I do?" "Where may I go?" "May I do this or not?"—that older Christian now becomes your teacher and will respond to your inquiries by saying: "Yes, you may do this" or "No, you may not do that" or "You may go here but not go there." And if you are obedient to that older believer, you will abide by what he or she has instructed you;

nevertheless, you shall discover that you are now under law and in bondage.

I well remember that when I was first saved, I was told that I had to observe Sunday as a holy day. On that day I was not allowed to study. So I was always in fear that if any examination should be scheduled on a Monday, I would not be permitted to touch my school books on the Sunday before. Instead, therefore, I spent my Sundays playing ball. I also never dared to go to a movie theater on Sunday because, again, it was considered a holy day. (I did so only once.) Consequently, I was in bondage. Outwardly I was a good Christian, but my life was all under law with no experience of true Christian freedom.

Let us be very clear here that there is a battle being waged for the control of our mind. On the one hand, God wants to save our mind; on the other hand, the enemy desires to keep our mind under his control. It is just as the apostle Paul once wrote: that the enemy of our souls has built strongholds or walls in our mind that are high-minded and full of arguments and reasonings contrary to the mind and will of God. Such a mentality has been built up through the years in our mind. It tells us that we are all right, that we are on the right path, that we should just be ourselves. These strong walls need to be pulled down through the word of God and through prayer (see II Corinthians 10:4-5).

Ultimately, therefore, our mind needs to be renewed; we who have believed and are saved cannot live any longer by our old reprobate mind. Yet how can our mind be renewed? Thank God, He has made every provision for us for the renewing of our minds, but there is one action we must take, and that is to consecrate ourselves to God. This spiritual exercise is found described for us in Romans 12.

CONSECRATION

Leading up to that particular chapter in the letter of Paul to the Romans we learn in chapters 1-11 that God has made every provision for our full salvation. But then Paul writes the following exhortation: "Brethren, I beseech you, by the compassions of God (may "the love of Christ constrain" you— cf. II Corinthians 5:14a), to present your bodies as living sacrifices, holy, acceptable to God, and that is your reasonable service. Be not conformed to the world ("love not the world"—cf. I John 2:15a), but be transformed by the renewing of your mind so that you may prove what is the good, acceptable, and perfect will of God" (see 12:1-2).

Our mind naturally gravitates towards the fashion of this world. We desire to be conformed to the world because we do not want to be considered by others as out of fashion or old-fashioned. To put it another way, we want to be at one with the world. That is only natural. By contrast, we look upon the will of God as something hard, harsh, and difficult to follow. That, too, is natural. How, then, can we despise the world and love the will of God? We in and of ourselves cannot do it, but there is one spiritual exercise which we can and must engage in, yet it can only be accomplished by the grace and love of God. As we are being constrained by Christ's love we are willing to offer ourselves as a living sacrifice to God. This simply signifies that you wish to hand over yourself to Him and to say to Him: "Lord, I cannot save myself. I today place myself in Your hand; I am Yours and You have the right to do whatever You wish with me." That is true consecration.

Why should we consecrate? And how can we consecrate? We cannot give ourselves as living sacrifices unless we are constrained by the love of Christ to do so. He loves us so much that we are willing to give up our right to ourselves and let Him have the right over us. As a matter of fact, that is what we should be doing. But God is so gracious towards us that He never forces us to do anything without our consent. It is as though God would say to each one of us: "If you give your consent, I Myself will do the work to save your soul to the uttermost." If you really present yourself to God and say, "Lord I am Yours; I permit You to do anything You like with me," strangely the Holy Spirit shall begin to work by renewing your mind. Renewing one's mind simply means that He can change your mind in a true way. You will find that the life of Christ will come into your mind, causing you to begin to see and think about things differently. For instance, you begin to see that the world is trash; and contrariwise you begin to view God's will as perfect and precious. In fact, it becomes easy for you to lay aside your own mind and allow the mind of Christ to function through you.

I recall that many years ago I was once in Albuquerque in the western American state of New Mexico. A few of us were in our host's sitting room talking. In the center of the room there was a table with a bowl full of candies sitting there. While we were talking, a little boy came in, and he began to wander around the room. As he circled the room one could observe that the boy was moving closer and closer until he reached the table. He quickly picked up one of the candies, ate it, and went away. He came into the room several times more and engaged in the same routine. He would go round and round until he reached the table and then picked up a piece of candy and put it in his mouth. He finally sheepishly acknowledged to us who were there: "I know I should not do it, but I love candy so much." Here I saw a picture of myself as I once was—a young Christian whose mind had not yet been renewed. It was awakened but not renewed because it was the same old flesh that was still in control of my mind. How we all very much need an exchanged life. An exchanged life means that the life of Christ becomes the life of our soul— including the life of our mind—instead of our old Adamic life being so.

RECALLING OUR PAST LIFE

How true it is that in recalling our past life, we can remember many crises which we have gone through. One crisis after another arose in the form of a cross to confront us—God's mind versus our mind: God wanting one thing and our mind wanting another (cf. Romans 7:15-23). And so there was a conflict, with the Spirit lusting or setting its desire against the fleshly mind and the fleshly mind lusting or setting its desire against the Spirit (cf. Galatians 5:17).

Even today in our Christian walk the Spirit and the mind are in conflict, wherein there is a battle for the mind. And the issue is, who will have control over the mind? There is Christ and there is Satan, and you are caught in between. This battle is very real. Yet the more you consecrate yourself, the more your entire viewpoint towards things will change. What you had deemed as being very precious in your life before will now become dross to you. What you had previously considered to be something hard and terrible will now become your treasure.

This very experience happened to the apostle Paul. In Philippians 3 he tells us that he had reason to boast of his life and accomplishments more than most anyone else had because he was such a brilliant, religious, moral, and zealous young man. He had wanted to make a name for himself in Judaism. But when Christ met him on the road to Damascus, the Lord changed him. Now it so happened that when he wrote this Philippian letter he was languishing in a Roman jail for the sake of the gospel. Yet he could declare to the Philippians such sentiments as these: "What I considered as treasure before, I now look upon as rubbish. I am willing to count all things as refuse for the excellency of the knowledge of Jesus Christ" (see vv. 7-8). With Paul it had not been a mindset forced upon him; rather, it was something supernaturally natural which had occurred in him because his mind had been so renewed that he henceforth looked at all things through the prism of heaven and no longer through the prism of the earth.

TAKING ON THE MIND OF CHRIST

Why is it that we lay emphasis on consecration so much? It is because the repeated act of consecration will give God the opportunity to complete His deliverance of our soul in all its faculties. As we willingly continue to lose our self-life and allow the life of Christ to be seated on the throne of our soul we shall gradually take on the mind of Christ. What was the mind of Christ when He was on earth? It was simply this as stated by Paul in his letter to the Philippians chapter 2: He emptied himself, then humbled himself, and finally gave himself up in obedience to the Father—even offering up himself to death on a cross (vv. 6-8). To describe it another way, it was an absolute surrender, He having given himself up completely. Throughout His earthly life Jesus never once considered what would happen to Him nor how something might affect Him—for good or ill—because His life was governed totally by the will of God. As a result, what a salvation Jesus has accomplished for us! He is now glorified and now has a Name that is above every name; so much so that to that Name every knee shall bow and every tongue shall confess that Jesus is Lord to the glory of God the Father (again, in Philippians chapter 2, vv. 9-11).

What all of us today need is the mind of Christ. If we have His mind, then as was the case with Paul, this is what will happen, even as he wrote to these same Philippian believers: "If then there be any comfort in Christ, if any consolation of love, if any fellowship of the Spirit, if any bowels and compassions, fulfil my joy" (2:1). If we truly want to be of service to our Christian brothers and sisters, then we all must begin to take on the mind of Christ, resulting in our "having the same love, joined in soul, thinking one thing; [and] letting nothing be in the spirit of strife or vain glory, but, in lowliness of mind, each esteeming the other as more excellent than themselves; regarding not each his own qualities, but each those of others also" (2:2-4).

Why is it that we cannot be one with our Christian brethren? Why do we think so differently from each other? It is because we all think of ourselves too highly, with each one holding onto his or her way. And the result is that we cannot be one. But if we have the mind of Christ, we shall not think of ourselves as being better or superior but are willing to yield to our brothers and sisters; and eventually, we will have the same mind—but only in Christ. Outside of Christ we shall always have different minds. Therefore, having the mind of Christ is our only hope. Nevertheless, thank God, I do believe the Lord is working with some success among us in that very direction.

LADY POWERSCOURT

I would like to share a true story about a young woman who was born in the nineteenth century. When she was nineteen years old, she came to the Lord. She was later married to a member of the British nobility, Viscount Powerscourt (who died a little over a year after they were married), and thus she inherited the title of Lady Powerscourt. She also inherited a beautiful palace in Ireland with its Powerscourt Garden being one of the largest and most beautiful private gardens to be found in Europe and is still today world-famous. We ourselves have visited there.

After she was saved she very much gave herself to the Lord. She was quite pious and accomplished many good works for the Lord. At that time interest in the subject of prophecy in the Bible was being revived and people were discussing about it a great deal. And it so happened that Lady Powerscourt opened up her palace for holding special gatherings to which famous preachers were able to come for fellowship and have discussions about this very topic of prophecy. By this means she came into contact with the prominent Plymouth Brethren Bible scholar and teacher, J. N.

Darby; and they soon fell in love. In fact, they became engaged; but, then, Darby's Christian brethren in Dublin expressed the opinion that because God was beginning to use him so marvelously, they felt he should not be tied down with a family. They shared their feeling with brother Darby, and this development became known to Lady Powerscourt. Now we do not know for certain what actually happened, but some people have said that the letters of these two lovers about this matter crossed each other in the mail. For the sake of the Lord, both were willing to lay their lives down for whatever God wished. Darby's letter to Lady Powerscourt expressed the feeling that he could not continue his relationship with her because he must give himself totally to the Lord and His work. Lady Powerscourt, in her letter to Darby, expressed a similar sentiment: she felt she had to lay aside her own life's wish and give up brother Darby.

It turned out that Lady Powerscourt only lived to be thirty-six years old. Some people have asserted that she died of a broken heart. Others who have spoken of her have noted that she was always looking down instead of looking up because, they explained, she had constantly lived a life in the heavenlies and was therefore always looking down upon the earth. Indeed, they observed, it seemed as though her feet barely ever touched the earth, she having been such a heavenly-minded person. One could readily compare Lady Powerscourt to what is taught in Colossians: "Seek not the things on the earth, but seek the things above where Christ is seated" (see 3:1). In other words, Christ is to be one's very life. She literally lived out her life like a most heavenly-minded person. We often hear or utter the adage that if you are so heavenly-minded, you will not be of any earthly good.

That was not true of Lady Powerscourt: God used her to do so many good works in His service.

T. AUSTIN-SPARKS

Then, when I recall our brother T. Austin-Sparks in England, I sense the same trait about him. His mind always appeared to be so occupied with the heavenlies that his feet never seemed to touch the earth. He felt that whatever touched the earth changed the nature of it—for the worse and not the better. In my contact with him he seemed to constantly be hesitant to touch the things of the earth. What marvelous revelation God had given him concerning the spiritual, heavenly nature of the church and the ascendancy of Christ!

A GREAT MIND TO SERVE A GREAT GOD

Finally, I would caution all of us not to go to the extreme of thinking that our mind is supreme and therefore does not need to be saved. But neither let us go to the other extreme that teaches the false notion that our mind is not to be used. There are people who teach that we are "never to use the mind." We must reject such teaching, for the mind is a great gift of God, and He wants to purify and sanctify it that it may be used for Him in His service. We should strive to have a great mind that is to be used for serving a great God. And if that be the case, then that will be the salvation of our mind.

Chapter 7

WILL

Romans 7:15-25—For that which I do, I do not own: for not what I will, this I do; but what I hate, this I practise. But if what I do not will, this I practise, I consent to the law that it is right. Now then it is no longer I that do it, but the sin that dwells in me. For I know that in me, that is, in my flesh, good does not dwell: for to will is there with me, but to do right I find not. For I do not practise the good that I will; but the evil I do not will, that I do. But if what I do not will, this I practise, it is no longer I that do it, but the sin that dwells in me. I find then the law upon me who will to practise what is right, that with me evil is there. For I delight in the law of God according to the inward man: but I see another law in my members, warring in opposition to the law of my mind, and bringing me into captivity to the law of sin which exists in my members. O wretched man that I am! who shall deliver me out of this body of death? I thank God, through Jesus Christ our Lord. So then I myself with the mind serve God's law; but with the flesh sin's law.

John 12:24-28—Verily, verily, I say unto you, Except the grain of wheat falling into the ground die, it abides alone; but if it die, it bears much fruit. He that loves his life [soul-life] shall lose it, and he that hates his life [soul-life] in this world shall keep it to life eternal. If any one serve me, let him follow me; and where I am, there also shall be my servant. And if any one serve me, him shall the Father honour. Now is my soul troubled, and what shall I say? Father, save me from this hour. But on account of this have I come to this hour. Father, glorify thy name. There came therefore a voice out of heaven, I both have glorified and will glorify it again.

Matthew 26:36-46—Then Jesus comes with them to a place called Gethsemane, and says to the disciples, Sit here until I go away and pray yonder. And taking with him Peter and the two sons of Zebedee, he began to be sorrowful and deeply depressed. Then he says to them, My soul is very sorrowful even unto death; remain here and watch with me. And going forward a little he fell upon his face, praying and saying, My Father, if it be possible let this cup pass from me; but not as I will, but as thou wilt. And he comes to the disciples and finds them sleeping, and says to Peter, Thus ye have not been able to watch one hour with me? Watch and pray, that ye enter not into temptation: the spirit indeed is ready, but the flesh weak. Again going away a second time he prayed saying, My Father, if this cannot pass from me unless I drink it, thy will be done. And coming he found them again sleeping, for their eyes were heavy. And leaving them, he went away again and prayed the third time, saying the same thing. Then he comes to the disciples and says to them, Sleep on now and take your rest; behold, the hour has drawn nigh, and the Son of man is delivered up into the hands of sinners. Arise, let us go; behold, he that delivers me up has drawn nigh.

As we have reminded ourselves again and again, spiritual exercise, or exercise unto godliness, is profitable for everything. It has the promise of eternal life—not only for this present age but also for the age to come. I therefore hope that none of us will miss this marvelous promise which our Lord has granted us.

We have been fellowshiping together concerning this matter of how spiritual exercise saves our soul; indeed, the end or outcome of our faith, as the apostle Peter has declared, is the salvation of our soul (I Peter 1:9). We have indicated previously that according to the Scriptures God not only *has* delivered us from so great a death—even our spiritual death—but He also is *currently* delivering us, and He will *yet* deliver us (II Corinthians 1:10). Moreover, not only does He want to save our spirit; He also wants to save our soul and our body because His salvation is full and complete. And to remind ourselves still further, we are saved when our dead spirit is quickened into new life. Christ comes into our spirit to dwell and to be our life there. Then the Holy Spirit comes into our spirit to manage that life of Christ in us in order that day after day it may unceasingly grow into full maturity so that we may be totally conformed to the image of Christ. Let us see, therefore, that the salvation of the soul is to be an ongoing present reality in our lives. Yes, we have been saved, thank God for that; but we need to be saved daily so far as our soul is concerned.

Our soul needs to be delivered from ourselves—from the old life. It needs to be replaced by the life of Christ so that He may be in charge of our soul as well as our spirit. To put it another way, our feeling, thinking and deciding will be increasingly brought under the control of the life of Christ instead of their being controlled and then expressed by our natural, fallen, self-life—that is to say, by our flesh. Now that is the salvation of our souls which we have been exploring together in these first few messages of this series.

And today we would like to focus our attention on how our will is to be delivered. We pointed out earlier that our emotion or feeling is the most active of all the faculties of the soul. Our emotion is highly volatile and is therefore changeable all the time; and consequently, it is very much in evidence in our daily experience. On the other hand, our mind is deep and the most influential of all the soul's faculties. What, though, can be said about the will in man? It is the deciding element of our being. We have noted before that in John Bunyan's *Holy War* volume, he has pictured for us our mind as being a battlefield and our will as a citadel or castle fortress. The enemy does battle in our mind as his means of reaching to our will. For he realizes that the will is actually the most important part of man's soul. In fact, it is what gives man his dignity.

Let us be reminded again that God is the supreme will of the universe. Indeed, His is the only free will, and because of this, He does everything according to His good pleasure. Furthermore, God does not need to ask permission from us to do whatever He wishes to us or with us: He is free and able to do anything He wishes because His will is supreme.

MAN CHOOSES HOW HE WILL LIVE

Let us never forget that it was God's good pleasure to create man, and He created him according to His image and after His likeness. This means that God, having a free will himself, gave man a free will as well; thus signifying that originally he could exercise his will in complete freedom without any restriction and decide whatever he wished. Man thus had the privilege and the capacity of choosing one way or the other. In brief, man was his own master. Now if it be true—and it is—that God gave man a free will, what kind of free will would that be if He did not provide man with the opportunity to choose? That is why we find in the book of Genesis that after God created man, He placed him in the Garden of Eden where He had planted two name-identified trees—the Tree of Life and the tree of the knowledge of good and evil—and had done so in order to give man an opportunity of making a free choice. In other words, God gave man the opportunity to make a choice as to how he wished to live his life. The issue therefore became: Does man want to maintain his existence by the life of God, which would involve his eating of the Tree of Life? Does he wish to live a life depending upon God, doing His will, and living for His glory? That was surely one way man could have chosen for living out his life.

Yet there was another way he could choose. He could decide to live by eating of the tree of the knowledge of good and evil. Again, we must observe here that this was not a bad tree. To repeat what was said earlier, this tree was better than all the other trees God had planted in the Garden of Eden. Even so, it was not as good a one as the Tree of Life— yes, indeed, it was a better tree, but not the best one. Eating of the tree of the knowledge of good and evil would mean that man would have the knowledge of knowing what is good and what is bad. That is the highest knowledge which man can have in this world. It is higher than scientific knowledge and even philosophical knowledge, for the fruit of this tree would provide man with moral or ethical knowledge which is the highest earthly knowledge. By choosing to have this knowledge man could determine for himself what is good and what is bad and thus be independent from God: indeed, man himself would be as god.

So from all this we see that there were two ways of life placed before the free will of man: either choosing to live by the life of God—which would be a dependent life but nonetheless a glorious one—or else deciding to live a life governed by his own knowledge and thus choosing to be his own master independent of God and hence, because of God's explicit forewarning, it would be a life whose end must surely be death.

Unfortunately, our ancient forefather Adam chose a life of independence. He wanted to be his own master, always deciding the issues of existence according to his own knowledge. Not needing God, man simply wanted to be his own god. Today we all know too well the tragic consequence of man's choice. Since he had decided to live according to the tree of knowledge, God declared to man in the garden: "You are dead. Your spirit has died, and you do not need Me anymore." The spirit of man which could give him God-consciousness had ceased its communication with Him.

MAN'S WILL IS IN A CAPTURED CONDITION

All who have been born of Adam throughout the centuries have inherited his fallen life (see again Romans 5:12, 19a). We who are Adam's descendants are no longer born with a free will. People make a tremendous mistake in thinking that we descendants of Adam have a free will and can decide everything by ourselves. Not so! According to the word of God, Adam was created with a free will but all we who have come after fallen Adam are born with a captured will. We have been captured by the enemy of God and are under the bondage of the law of sin and death (cf. Romans 8:2b). None of us is free. Even though the world does not recognize this fact, as believers we need to realize that our will is not free anymore. It is under bondage and in a captured condition. No matter what in our volitional capacity we will to do or not do, such willing falls within certain parameters which are outside the boundary of the will of God.

I Corinthians 2:14 makes clear that "the natural man does not receive the things of the Spirit of God, for they are folly to him; and he cannot know them because they are spiritually discerned." This Biblical term "the natural man" refers to all those who have been or will be born of Adam. This means that we are all born as natural men and therefore cannot receive the things of the Spirit of God because they are foolishness to us. Those who have not been born anew of God's Spirit cannot know the things of the Spirit because they had died to God. All the things of the Spirit must therefore be—and can only be—understood spiritually.

FREE WILL OR DIVINE ELECTION?

Romans 8 tells us that "the mind of the flesh is enmity against God: for it is not subject to the law of God; for neither indeed can it be: and they that are in [the] flesh cannot please God" (vv. 7-8).

The mind of the flesh—or the natural mind—is at enmity with God. It is God's enemy and not subject to His law. Even if we fallen human beings wanted to subject ourselves to the word and law of God, we could not because our will has been in bondage, has been in captivity; and, therefore, those who are in the flesh cannot please God. Do you believe that or will you question it? Do you think you are not in that condition?

Interestingly, the great Protestant Reformer Martin Luther wrote a thick book called *The Bondage of the Will*. In it he claimed that man's will is under bondage. John Calvin, another Protestant Reformer, taught the doctrine of divine election which holds that none of us can choose our eternal destiny (see e.g., Romans 8:28-30). On the contrary, everything is determined by the sovereignty of God because fallen man does not have a free will to choose. Can you or do you accept that? On the other hand, the founder of Methodism, John Wesley, claimed that we *have* free will, he citing Scripture which states that whosoever will can come and accept Jesus Christ as the Savior (see, e.g., John 3:16, Acts 2:21). Then, too, the famous Christian evangelist, D. L. Moody, once held a special ministry session arranged for only atheists and agnostics to attend. The hall was packed with these exclusive attendees, to whom this famed evangelist preached a most powerful gospel message. After he had finished, someone in the audience stood up and said, "I cannot believe." To which Moody replied: "It is not because you cannot, it is because you will not." So regarding this issue of free will and divine election we see that there has been a contradiction of opinion among various men of God.

If we fallen human beings do not possess free will to choose, how could we have chosen Christ as Savior and Lord?

If prior to our salvation our will had been in bondage and at enmity with God, how could we have subsequently believed in the Lord Jesus and been saved? In Christianity, the debate between these two opposing schools of thought has been fought out ever since the sixteenth century and the issue has never been settled. Even today, for example, Baptists believe in divine election whereas Methodists believe in free will. How are we going to reconcile these two schools of thinking?

Ironically, the Bible teaches both. These two notions can be found side-by-side in Scripture. The letter to the Romans chapter 9 teaches the sovereignty of God: Everything is by God's election, for He chooses this way or that way; therefore, this chapter argues, who are we to question Him? On the other hand, the very next chapter, chapter 10, tells us that the word of God is not far from any of us, that it is in our mouth and in our heart; consequently, this chapter goes on to say, if we believe in our heart that God raised Jesus from the dead, and if we confess Him with our mouth, then we certainly shall be saved. Is that not free will?

Let us realize and humbly acknowledge that there is no way for man to reconcile these two opposite principles. God—not man—is the only One who is able to resolve this issue and to work with *both* principles. Though we fallen people no longer possess a free will, God is able to reach out to us by His grace and somehow choose us and bring us into eternal life. Is that not marvelous?

The best illustration for helping us to understand this seemingly insoluble conundrum is what Moody had often shared in his preaching. He observed that when someone comes to the gate of salvation, that one will see written thereon: "Whosoever will, enter in, and drink of the water of life" (cf. Rev. 22:17). At this point Moody would comment as follows: Had it been that only this particular person's name had been written there and not the general word "whosoever," then that would mean that only that person could have entered in. But "whosoever," Moody would go on to say, includes you, me, and everybody else. So no one is excluded but all human beings are qualified to accept this divine invitation to be saved. Then Moody would continue with his illustration: This individual did accept the invitation and went through the gate; but when he looked back, he saw written on the back of the gate: "Blessed are you, for you have been chosen by God" (cf. I Peter 2:4,9; Rev. 17:14).

Let us not try to reconcile in our mind these two seemingly contrary principles. None of us can reconcile them; for in attempting to do so, either we shall strengthen the one or else weaken the other. Yet God is above all such considerations. His way of salvation is so marvelous that by His grace He reaches even out to us whose will was under immense bondage and by His sovereignty has chosen even us from before the foundation of the world. And this makes our salvation most sure.

AN AWAKENED WILL

What is the condition of your will now? You have believed in the Lord Jesus, and you are saved, but what is the current state of your will? Is it still in bondage and captured by the enemy? No, the Lord has done something to your will. You today have what can be called an awakened will; it is awakened to God. How do you know this? Well, after you are saved, is it not true that you will to do the will of God? You want to do His will. Before that, you had no desire at all for God's will. Rather, you wanted to carry out *your* will or whatever was according to the will or fashion of the world. But no longer; you know that you are the Lord's and you want to please Him. You want to do what is right in *His* eyes and not yours.

Now the content of Romans chapter 7 is actually the experience of an awakened will because early on in its narration Paul writes: "I will to do the will of God, but I cannot. I hate sin, but I do it." Is that not our experience as Christians? This autobiographical statement of Paul's points up the difference between Christians and unbelievers. Unbelievers do not even will to do the will of God or want to please Him. They only engage their will to please themselves. As a sign, then, of our being a true believer, and even though we may have a weak will, in our awakened heart we now want to do God's will and please Him. Therefore, it really hurts us when you and I will to do the right thing but we do not do it. We do not have the strength or power in ourselves to do it. The things which we do not want to do, these we do because we are still under a contrary force or compulsion in our flesh: there is a law of sin and death operating in us which is still very strong (Romans 7:25). Nevertheless, according to our inner man, we love the word of God and want to please Him. On the other hand, our outer man argues, "No; you should please yourself and the world." That is our condition.

"WHO SHALL DELIVER ME?"

Do we cry out as did the apostle Paul—"O wretched man that I am! who shall deliver me out of this body of death?"?

Can you? Can I? Nobody can except the One named by Paul: "Thank God, through Jesus Christ." This means that the salvation of our will is through the Lord Jesus. He is able to strengthen our will and make it a submissive, sanctified will so that we may live a life pleasing to Him. How is all this to be accomplished in us? On the one hand, God has made every provision for the deliverance of our will; for when the Lord Jesus was crucified on the cross, He not only bore our sins in His body but also put our old Adamic man away. So far as the work of Christ on the cross is concerned, our old man is dead. When Christ died, old Adam died in Him, even as the apostle Paul wrote: "Knowing this, that our old man is crucified with him [Christ]" (Romans 6:6a). Paul can therefore also declare: "I am crucified with Christ, and no longer live, I, but Christ lives in me; but I still live in the flesh, so I shall live by faith and not by sight—even by the faith of the Son of God, who loves me and gave himself for me" (see Galatians 2:20).

So we see that God has already made provision for us to have a will that shall both will and do His will. That provision is Christ himself. He is the only One who is able to do that; and Christ does this by living in us as our life. He is able to live through us in perfect obedience to God. But it must be this: "not I, but Christ." If we totally cast ourselves on Christ, He will do it because it was for this reason, among others, that He was sent by the Father.

CONSECRATION

Yet how do we enter into this provision God has made for us in Christ? The secret is once again to be found in Romans 12. After we have come to know all that Christ has done for us, we are to respond in the following way: "I beseech you therefore, brethren, by the compassions of God, to present your bodies a living sacrifice, holy, acceptable to God, which is your intelligent service. And be not conformed to this world, but be transformed by the renewing of your mind, that ye may prove what is the good and acceptable and perfect will of God" (vv. 1-2).

Of all our Christian experiences consecration should be the very first one following our new birth in Christ. Upon our believing in the Lord Jesus, the first spiritual exercise we are to do is to present our bodies—our whole being—to God and express the following from the heart: "Lord, I do not want to live by myself anymore. I give myself to You. You live in me. It is no longer I but Christ. I am Yours." As we give ourselves to God, something most positive happens: the Holy Spirit renews our mind. Once we thought the world so lovely; but now, something has happened to change our attitude: we now see the world as ugly and count all things in it as dross. If that be true, who wants to collect and retain any longer such refuse? It must be thrown out. By contrast, therefore, to our former way of thinking and living, we now consider the knowledge of Jesus Christ as the most excellent and precious possession we could ever obtain. We love to do the will of God, and somehow the strength to do so is there. Not only the understanding is there, even the power to follow through is there. What you could not do before you now are able to do; yet not you, it is Christ in you, the hope of glory (Colossians 1:27b).

For an awakened will to be strengthened there has to be a consecrated will because God respects our will. If we do not want a strengthened will, God will not force the issue: you are free to go your way as you like. The reason the life and power of God is not as evident as it should be today in our Christian life is not because His life is weak but because we do not allow Him to live in us. We want to struggle forward by ourselves. I think the Lord would say in response, "Fine, you go ahead and struggle to your death." If we simply let Him have His way in us, He will see to it that the power of God is there to do what He wishes because He is faithful.

F. B. MEYER AND CONSECRATION

I find the following story of F. B. Meyer most helpful regarding this issue of consecration. He was a very famous preacher of a church in Leicester, Scotland, and when he was young, he was already very eloquent. He very much loved the Lord. One day, another young man visited him—C. T. Studd, *the* cricketer of that time in England. His name was well known to everyone, but God soon laid hold of him for His service: he gave up everything to go to China to be a missionary. Shortly before he went off to the mission field he traveled about and visited different places in Britain. One of those places was the home of F. B. Meyer where he stayed for a time. It was in November and Leicester was very chilly. Early the next morning, brother Meyer noticed that there was a light in C. T. Studd's room. As the host, he was a little bit concerned. He dared not go and knock on the door because it was too early. So he waited, but the light continued to burn. Finally, he went to the door and knocked. When brother Studd said to come in, he went in and saw his guest wrapped in a rug—because it was so cold—and reading the Bible. At this sight Meyer remarked, "My, you are up early." In response brother Studd explained as follows: "I love my Lord, and I am searching the Bible to find His commands so that I may do them."

Is not that a wonderful statement? When we Christians of today read the Bible, we are usually searching for promises. In fact, we have become so lazy that we even have what is called a promise box so that we can simply pick one out for the day without searching. Moreover, who wants to search the Scriptures for *commands*? We shy away from such. C. T. Studd, however, searched the Scriptures for God's commands because he loved the Lord so very much.

Now F. B. Meyer sensed that there was something in his guest which he did not have. So he asked him, "What is your secret? How can I have what you have?" So C. T. Studd asked his host, "Have you consecrated yourself to the Lord?" Was that not somewhat ludicrous to ask that of a famous Christian preacher? "Of course," replied brother Meyer, "I have." "No, you must go before the Lord and hand over to Him everything in your life, one by one," explained brother Studd. Whereupon Meyer acknowledged to his guest, "I have never done that." "Then you must go and do it," Studd said.

And so, while brother Meyer was praying and handing over to the Lord everything he could think of in his life, it seemed to him as though he saw in a vision the Lord coming towards him with His hands outstretched and with brother Meyer appearing to be giving the Lord a large bundle of keys to every room in his life—keys to large rooms and to small ones. But also in this visionary scenario of brother Meyer's he was seen to be keeping back a key to a small room. In response to such action the Lord shook his head and said, "If I am not the Lord of *all*, then I am not Lord *at all*." Brother

Meyer pleaded with the Lord to allow him to keep this one key for himself. "If so," he said, "then I am willing to serve You with double effort." At this response the Lord immediately began to turn away. In his desperation Meyer cried out, "Lord, make me willing to be willing." The Lord came back and took the bundle of keys which now included the key to that small room in his life. Therefore, on the basis of this initial consecration, the Lord began to search every room of F. B. Meyer's life, cleaning each one and filling it with himself and His Spirit, and thus God used him mightily thereafter.

To have an awakened will is not enough. As a matter of fact, it is almost worse to have only that. Formerly, we had no consciousness of ourselves; but now we are conscious. Thank God, He does not want us to remain in that situation. He is able to deliver us if only we are willing to consecrate and surrender our will to Him. But please note that this is to be a lifelong experience, not a one-time spiritual exercise. As we are continually willing and standing on the ground of an ongoing consecration, we shall discover that our will is gradually being sanctified. Ultimately, we shall have a completely sanctified will that only wills the will of God.

"NOT MY WILL, THY WILL BE DONE"

Let us consider the life of the Lord Jesus. He came into this world to be and live as a man. Yes, He is God, but when He took upon himself the flesh of a man, He also had the soul of a man in all its faculties and functions. For example, He had feeling and was the most compassionate of men. He also had a mind with thoughts of all kinds coming forth like any other man's mind would. He likewise had a will. Throughout His earthly life Jesus never did or said anything or go anywhere according to His will; rather, the one consideration which governed His entire life was this: "What is the Father's will for Me?" That was the one dominating concern throughout His life. Did Jesus experience any temptation? Yes indeed. Let us recall how after His final entry into Jerusalem, it seemed as though for the first time in His life that the whole world was wanting to follow after Him. Even Grecian gentiles wanted to see and converse with Him. Some Bible commentators have noted that this was undoubtedly the glory time for Jesus in His life on earth. At this very moment even Jesus himself had acknowledged and commented that "the time of glory has now come"; but the glory He saw in His mind's eye and sensed was far different. Yes, this man Jesus was tempted, but He did not succumb to the world's pursuit of Him and the glory which would be His if He did so; for Jesus recognized its true nature—a *fading* glory.

Let us read carefully Jesus' words of reaction to this tempting hour of earthly glory: "Verily, verily, I say unto you, unless the grain of wheat falling into the ground dies, it abides alone; but if it dies, it bears much fruit. I am a grain of wheat. I have fallen into the ground not just to live but to die, and unless I die I cannot bear any fruit. He that loves his soul-life shall lose it, and he that hates his soul-life in this world shall keep it to life eternal. If anyone would serve Me, let him follow Me and be where I am. But now is My soul troubled: 'Father, I have come for this very hour—the hour of death; glorify Your name'" (see John 12:24-28a). And there immediately came a voice from heaven that declared: "I have both glorified it and will glorify it again" (v. 28b).

Let us inquire further into this matter. Do any of us believe that the hour of temptation had now ceased for this man Jesus? That the issue of His dying like a fallen grain of wheat had now been settled in Jesus' mind, heart and will? No, not so; for we know that the fiercest struggle over this issue still awaited Him in the Garden of Gethsemane. Jesus was aware that this personal crisis in His life was of cosmic significance and was about to be played out to its final end in Gethsemane's garden, to where He and His disciples had now gone. The entire universe, as it were, was in breathless suspense, awaiting the outcome of this very hour in the life of this man Jesus. His burden was becoming increasingly heavy and His soul was now deeply depressed.

In the garden He left most of His disciples behind and took only three of them with Him a short distance away. He asked them to wait for Him and pray with Him for an hour. Then He went forth a further short distance, prostrated himself and prayed, "Father, if it be possible, remove this cup from Me; yet not My will but Thy will be done." Can we sense the heavy burden of that hour? The whole world was in suspense waiting to see how this man Jesus' personal crisis would turn out. In order to save the world, He who knew no sin had to be made sin for us (II Corinthians 5:21a). This divine fact and its implications for Jesus was unbearable to His soul. He in himself could not bring himself to go through with it. It was too much. He prayed and He struggled. In the end, however, Jesus laid down *His* will, accepted His Father's will, and peace returned to Him (Matthew 26:36-39, 42, 44).

Let me ask if this has ever happened to you in a small way? For our experience can never be compared to what the Lord went through. He went through such experience for the whole world. He did it for mankind. The struggle was most fierce. When He prayed there in the garden, His sweat fell to the ground as drops of blood (Luke 22:44). He was so exhausted from the ordeal that an angel had to come and sustain Him (Luke 22:43). Such is what the fight unto death can be for the will of God, and the man Jesus won the battle on behalf of God's will. He as a real man fulfilled the prophecy of Psalm 40 concerning himself: "I come to do Thy will, O my God" (see vv. 7-8; cf. Hebrews 10:5-7). Are we, too, going through this purifying of the will? Are we willing to take up our cross and follow the Lord?

MISS MARGARET BARBER

I had never met Miss Margaret Barber, a close friend and fellow-believer in Christ of Watchman Nee's, because she lived slightly before my time. I heard that she had been a very strong-willed woman. Let me add, however, that had she not been a strong-willed woman, how could she have gone through everything which happened in her life? When a young man, brother Nee quickly became aware just how strong her will was. Oftentimes he went to Miss Barber to complain about his Christian brothers, but she always responded with: "You are the younger brother, so you will have to submit to them." Now Miss Barber was not naturally a person who could easily yield her will to God. She often struggled in her life over the issue of her will. Once, the Lord was demanding something in her life, and she could not and would not hand it over to Him. We would think such a spiritual person as she was would have had no problems, but she had bigger problems, ones far more serious than we have. Yet listen to her prayer: "Lord, do not give up on me. Wait until I turn around." Thank God, she did turn around.

A WILL SANCTIFIED THROUGH SPIRITUAL EXERCISE

Consider the condition of your will. Are you really surrendered? Can you truthfully say, "Not my will but Thine be done?" How many of us today have a sanctified will? By which I mean, do you will nothing but the will of God in spite of your will? That is how our will is sanctified through spiritual exercise. A sanctified will never comes easy nor does it come naturally. It can only come through spiritual exercise. May the Lord help each one of us.

Chapter 8

BODY

I Corinthians 6:19-20—Do ye not know that your body is the temple of the Holy Spirit which is in you, which ye have of God; and ye are not your own? for ye have been bought with a price: glorify now then God in your body.

Romans 12:1—I beseech you therefore, brethren, by the compassions of God, to present your bodies a living sacrifice, holy, acceptable to God, which is your intelligent service.

I Corinthians 9:27—But I buffet my body, and lead it captive, lest after having preached to others I should be myself rejected.

Romans 8:11—But if the Spirit of him that has raised up Jesus from among the dead dwell in you, he that has raised up Christ from among the dead shall quicken your mortal bodies also on account of his Spirit which dwells in you.

Romans 8:23—And not only that, but even we ourselves, who have the first-fruits of the Spirit, we also ourselves groan in ourselves, awaiting adoption [or, sonship], that is the redemption of our body.

As we continue further in our discussion together on this important subject of spiritual exercise, I have been wondering if we are still in the gymnasium of Christ and are continuing to engage in these exercises of the spirit. If you only desire to receive some words or teachings, that will not help. If you are truly, actively cooperating with the Lord and, according to His word are exercising your spirit before the Lord, then it will bring great profit to you—not only in this life but in the life to come. Here today we will focus our attention on the topic of how spiritual exercise can sanctify our bodies.

THE BODY FORMED WITH RED EARTH

Interestingly enough, there is but one short verse which tells us how our body was formed: it is found in Genesis 2:7. There we learn that the Lord God formed man's body with the soil of the earth. That is the meager extent we have in explaining it! The elements in our body today are no different from the elements of the red earth from which it was made back then in the time of Genesis. Yet that is why our bodies provide us with world-consciousness: by means of our bodies we are in touch with the world around us. It may be difficult for us to imagine what a marvel our body is when realizing that it has been formed by God with the dust of the ground. Yet, in the hands of God the skillful Potter, He was able to make this body—a mere vessel of clay, of earth—into such a wonderful entity.

This is why the psalmist David, upon considering the body which God had himself created, was deeply moved to declare in Psalm 139:14: "I will praise thee, for I am fearfully, wonderfully made. Marvelous are thy works; and that my soul knoweth right well."

How awesome is our God that He can take up the ordinary soil of the ground and make out of it the wonder that is the human body. For it is indeed fearfully and wonderfully made. The more we study our body, the more marvelous it becomes. Even today, after so long a time in which the physiologists have studied the human body, these scientists still do not fully know all there is to know about the body. They must acknowledge and confess that this body of ours is surely most fearfully and wonderfully made! "Marvelous are Thy works, and that my soul knoweth right well."

THE PURPOSE OF THE BODY

Why does God give us a body? Is it that by means of this incredible creation of His we may simply live to eat, drink, and be merry—and then tomorrow we die? Or is there some purpose God had in mind for having used such cheap, ordinary material to make such an extraordinary creation? Can any of us imagine that the Creator of the entire universe would make something without there being some purpose behind it? Clearly, our God is One of purpose. Even before the foundation of the world He had purposed a purpose in His heart in accordance with His good pleasure, and that included the human body. What, then, is God's purpose in having created a body for us? For that is a question we should definitely ask of ourselves and search out the answer. Otherwise, we shall not know how to use our body properly and how to live in it, out of our ignorance as to why it has been given to us. Hence, I believe it is a matter of first importance that we know the purpose of God in His having created man with such a fearful and wonderful outer vessel. Do you know the answer?

I think the answer is very clear from what we learn in the New Testament book of Hebrews. There in its chapter 10 and speaking about the coming of Jesus into this world to become a man, we are specifically told what He said to God the Father: "Wherefore coming into the world he says, Sacrifice and offering thou willedst not; but thou hast prepared me a body. Thou tookest no pleasure in burnt-offerings and sacrifices for sin. Then I said, Lo, I come (in the roll of the book it is written of me) to do, O God, thy will" (vv. 5-7).

Here, then, is the revealed secret. This revelation from God's word tells us why He has given us a body. He created it for us for but one reason—to do the will of God. Now if it was true with the Lord Jesus—for is He not the true Man, the Man whom God had in mind when He created mankind?—then it must certainly be true with all of us. What, therefore, is the purpose of God in having created such a fearfully-and-wonderfully-made vessel for us? Simply put, it is that we may live to do God's will. Anything short of that fails the purpose of God concerning our body. It has been created purposefully; for with a living, breathing body, we are able to live for God, do His will, and fulfill His eternal purpose. What a glorious purpose that is for the human body!

Sad to say, our ancestors in the Garden of Eden made a wrong choice for how they would live out their lives in the bodies God had created for them. God gave man a free will to choose one way or the other how he was going to use his body. Our ancestors could choose to live by the life of God—as they could do by eating of the Tree of Life—depend upon Him alone, and by His grace proceed to live in their bodies to glorify God. Or they could eat the fruit of the tree of the knowledge of good and evil, develop their self-life, live for themselves, be their own gods, and reduce their wonderfully-made bodies to be vessels of sin and death. Regrettably, they made the wrong decision not only for themselves but for us as well. And hence, though we each were born with a wonderful body which God had created, sad to say, this outer vessel of ours was henceforth sunk in bondage to the law of sin and death (Romans 7:24, 25c; 8:2b).

THE BODY BECAME A BODY OF SIN AND DEATH

What is the nature of this mortal body of ours today? Romans 6:6 tells us that it has become a body of sin. It lives for nothing but to sin and sin again. It is unable to do God's will because it is in bondage. It is under the control of the enemy of God, and it is also governed by fallen sinful man, the flesh, even that self of ours. This body of ours, instead of serving God's purpose, is a body of sin that serves God's enemy. It exists for nothing except to sin against God.

In addition, Romans 7:24 tells us that this mortal body of ours is also a body of death. To sin is to do what we should not do, and death is to not do what we should do. When we look at the world today, we see millions and billions of bodies. What are these bodies doing? They do nothing but sin and are therefore under the law of death (Romans 8:2b). One day, as Scripture tells us, dust shall return to dust (Genesis 3:19b, c).

We need to have a very clear understanding of what happened to our body by virtue of Adam having failed. Thank God, the Lord Jesus has come to the rescue by having purchased our body with a great price—even with His blood. That is why, week after week, we come together to participate together in the Lord's Table in order to remember the death of the Lord Jesus. We must never forget what an enormous price He paid to ransom us from the bondage of sin and death when He purchased us back to God. That is why Paul writes in I Corinthians 6 that we have been bought with a price and have been set free to glorify God in our body (v. 20).

A SLAVE GIRL SET FREE

I can never forget a true incident which occurred long ago when America still had slaves. One day somewhere in America's Southland there was to be a public auction held to sell slaves, and at one point in the proceedings a girl who was chained was brought forth and placed on the auction block. A group of people gathered around to bid for this girl, who was now beginning to weep. Secretly, she glanced about to see who these people were who wanted to buy her; but when she looked at them, she lost all hope: they were all so cruel- and harsh-looking! Suddenly, a man not of this group entered into the bidding. Having, in the end, put in the highest bid, this man purchased the girl. To the surprise of all the people who had gathered around, he asked someone to step forth and break the chains which bound her. Once the chains were broken, the man told the girl: "I bought you to set you free. You may now go." And having said that he turned around to leave. The girl was so stunned that she did not know what to do. Then she raised her arms and ran after the man and shouted: "Please take me, sir; I wish to serve you for life!"

OUR BODY'S OWNERSHIP CHANGED

Now having once believed in the Lord Jesus and been saved, did any of us find that our physical body had changed? Not really. So far as our body's constitutional makeup is concerned, it has not changed. Our body is still a mortal entity. Yes, superficially speaking, there may be some change: for instance, our long face has become a round face! But so far as our physical frame is concerned, it remains the same. Positionally, however, there did occur a change for our body—a most significant change. What was that? In brief, the ownership of our body changed. Before we were saved our body belonged to God's enemy—even Satan. He used our fallen self as his means to extend his management even over our body. Which explains why in our fallen state we lived to sin and lived to die. Praise God, though, that upon our being saved, a great change came over our body. This body of ours is today no longer under the bondage of God's enemy; rather, it belongs to God now because He purchased us with a great price—even the spilt blood of His only begotten Son. Thus we today have a ransomed body. Its ownership has changed because God regained us and became our Owner. Therefore, He has the right to use our body as He sees fit because our body's position *vis-à-vis* the owner has changed.

CONSECRATION

Legally, therefore, we are God's possession, and hence, we have no right to live for ourselves. But God does not deal with us according to legality. He always deals with us in love, and out of His love He set us free. Nevertheless, if after we have been bought with such a great price we still insist on living for ourselves, we can do so. But is that what any of us would really want? If, though, we have been constrained by the love of Christ, what will we do? We will gladly enter into the experience of that former slave girl; like her with the man who had unchained her and set her free, we shall most willingly give ourselves to the Lord who has set us free and serve Him all our life (see II Corinthians 5:14-15). Now that is consecration.

Let us explore further the meaning and implications for the Christian of this spiritual exercise we call consecration. Because our body has been ransomed by God, it belongs legally to Him; nevertheless, we are free—free to choose whether we still wish to continue to live out that old life of ours, which would continue to be a life of sin and death, or whether we wish to live for the glory of God. All we need to do, as the Scripture in Romans 12 tells us, is to present our body a living sacrifice. Yet a sacrifice is usually *killed* first and then offered up, but this which is spoken of here in Romans is to be a *living* sacrifice: thus signifying that as long as a consecrated Christian lives on earth he gives himself to the Lord who is his new Owner and Master and allows the Lord to live out His life in and through him; and that, according to Romans 12, please note, is the Christian's reasonable service. Are you as a believer in Christ doing that today in obedience to your new Owner and Master?

A RENEWED AND RETRAINED MIND

Consecration, then, is a presenting of our body as a living sacrifice to our body's new Owner and Master, the Lord

Jesus; after which He will renew our mind, for only with a renewed mind can we do the things of the Spirit and no longer the things of the flesh. After He has bought us and we have consecrated ourselves to the Lord, it requires some time for the mind to be reset and retrained. That process is what is taking place in our mind today. If He has bought us and we do not present our bodies as a living sacrifice, then there can be no retraining and, therefore, we shall continue to use our body in the same old way as before. Unfortunately, that is what is occurring in the lives of many so-called Christians.

We have been constrained by the love of Christ. As a result of this love, we have presented our body to Him as a living sacrifice. We are willing to serve our new Master. We are willing to live a new kind of life, and this will be a life not of sinning but of glorifying God. We need to have our minds trained in a new way.

This brings us back, does it not, to the gymnasium of Christ and to a further need to engage in spiritual exercise. If given the opportunity through our having consecrated our bodies to our new Owner and Master, the Lord Jesus, the Holy Spirit will begin to work in our lives. Whenever we encounter what we used to do formerly, He will say to us: "No more." Whenever we are encouraged by the Lord to do what we could not do before, the Spirit will say, "Do it now, because this is what I Myself will to do." In essence, therefore, we are enrolled in a retraining course that is part of our various spiritual exercises and whose Course Instructor is God's Spirit. We need to learn to listen to the Holy Spirit who dwells in us and is instructing us in a new way of life. Is this theory? No, this is everyday life. Every day we are experiencing this process of renewal in our minds.

OUR BODY BELONGS TO THE LORD

Once there was a group of soldiers who were on a train going to the battlefront. Some of the soldiers decided to play cards, but there were only three of them and they needed a fourth player. They turned to another soldier who was sitting nearby and said, "Come, join us and play cards." The soldier, who was a Christian, said, "Sorry. I have no hands." They looked at him in surprise and said, "But you do have hands. How can you say you have no hands?" The soldier replied and explained: "Sorry, these are not my hands. They belong to my Lord."

Do we have such an attitude of mind? When you are about to do certain things which may be questionable, do you have a sense that these hands do not belong to you and that you therefore have no right to use them to do those things? Those hands of yours now belong to the Lord. Do you realize that your feet are not your own and hence you cannot just go anywhere you wish to? Rather, you only can go to where He sends you. Do you realize that you cannot speak anything you would like? that your mouth does not belong to you, it belongs to the Lord? Do you realize and acknowledge that your life is no longer yours; that it is His? Let us understand that with a heart attitude like that there will be much spiritual exercise taking place in our lives. Unfortunately, many Christians neglect this; in fact, their bodies are not being used for the glory of God but for their own selfish purposes.

When we are truly consecrated, our body becomes a living sacrifice. This is a daily matter, and it involves not only big things. In fact, life is mostly composed of small matters. If we are not faithful in the small things of the day, we cannot be faithful in the larger issues of life. All details of our lives accumulate and add up over time. It is in our daily life that we are to learn how to allow the Lord to use our body. Our body is for the Lord and the Lord is for the body (I Corinthians 6:13b). Even in those more ordinary activities of our lives—such as eating and drinking, the way we spend our time, the places we go to, and the company we keep—this body is not ours, it is the Lord's: this body is not for gratifying ourselves: this consecrated body is solely to glorify the Lord. And how glorious, indeed, that is!

In I Thessalonians 5:23 we read: "Now the God of peace himself sanctify you wholly: and your whole spirit, and soul, and body be preserved blameless at the coming of our Lord Jesus Christ." Our body has been ransomed, and it now needs to be consecrated. But, further, our consecrated body needs to be sanctified by means of the process of which we have been speaking. Romans 12:1 says, "Present your body a living sacrifice." What kind of body is that? Is it your fallen body—the body of sin and death? God will not accept a sacrifice like that. It must be a consecrated body. Then God will accept it. And after God accepts it, His Holy Spirit who dwells in us will begin the process by which the body can ultimately be fully sanctified. Even so, for this process to be successful, we must be in the gymnasium of Christ on a daily basis and be willingly engaged in spiritual exercises of all kinds.

BUFFET THE BODY

Let us be aware, however, that this process will continually be marked by two distinct sets of experiences. One is what Paul has described in I Corinthians: "I buffet my body, and lead it captive, lest after having preached to others

I should be myself rejected" (9:27). When you truly consecrate your body to the Lord, the Holy Spirit will begin to work in you, leading you into spiritual exercise of a certain kind. For instance, suppose you like to sleep late. That is a common desire because even the book of Proverbs has remarked about it (6:9-10, 10:5, 19:15, 20:13). The reason you sleep late is to gratify your lazy body. Consequently, upon finally arising from bed, you see that there is no time for you to go before the Lord and have a quiet time—reading the Bible, praying, and having sweet communion with the Lord. One Christian sister has noted: "Our problem is a conflict between the bed and the Lord." In other words, who or what do you cherish more—God or your bed? This means that you as a consecrated believer will have to buffet your body, which means dealing with the body in such manner in order that it be brought into proper submission for the sake of the Lord and His purpose. In employing the term, "buffet the body," Paul was speaking it in relation to using his body to serve him instead of his being controlled or governed by his bodily requirements. Your body wants to be your master, but because Christ is now your Master, there arises a conflict. You therefore must be strict with your body in order that in a time of spiritual need it will not be gratified but that you may lead it captive. In other words, your body should be under your control or, as I would say, under Spirit-control: it should not control you; instead, your spirit should be in control of your body for the Lord's sake.

Eating may seem to be such a small matter. Yet we each should inquire, Why do I eat? Can I be gluttonous and indulge myself? Who actually is my master—this body of mine or Christ? These are very practical questions to be asking ourselves. There is nothing theoretical about such conflicts, and they are to be resolved in a supernaturally natural way. Here is another body issue which may be present in your life: tension and/or nervousness. We are not to be tense and become so nervous in our body, for God surely does not want us in that state; and such is also to be resolved in a supernaturally natural manner. Such challenges and crises will most certainly manifest themselves, but these are opportunities for you to buffet your body and lead it captive.

That, then, is one set of experiences which will frequently be a part of this sanctifying process of the Christian's consecrated body. But before proceeding to identify the other set of experiences in this process, we need to take note of the difference there is between "buffeting the body" and "ill-treating the body." The difference between these two is as vast as that which exists between heaven and earth. Briefly stated, "ill-treating one's body" has its source in the self-life whereas the "buffeting of one's body" has as its source the instruction and guidance of the Holy Spirit.

If we have consecrated our body to the Lord, God's Holy Spirit will work in our spirit. And as you and I are in communion with God, He by His Spirit will reveal His mind to us. He will tell us what we should do in the use of our body. But when in any given instance He tells us how we should use our body, more often than not our old master—that old self of ours—will come back and tell us that that is too hard, that there is a better way: we should just indulge ourselves. Whenever this happens, however, we will find that if we are to overcome we will need to bear the cross and by God's grace follow the Lord.

THE QUICKENING OF THE MORTAL BODY

Let us come, now, and consider that other, and most wonderful, set of experiences the consecrated believer will encounter in the process of sanctifying the body. This side of the process is explained for us in Romans 8:11: "if the Spirit of him that has raised up Jesus from among the dead dwell in you, he that has raised up Christ from among the dead shall quicken your mortal bodies also on account of his Spirit which dwells in you."

As we have seen, on the one hand, you will experience the buffeting of your body in order to lead it captive for the Lord's sake. On the other hand, you will begin to experience the quickening of your mortal body by the Holy Spirit. As you are led by the Lord to undertake something for Him, your body will at times not seem to be able to respond sufficiently as is called for. In such a circumstance, what can you do? The solution is that as you look to the Lord for the enabling power, you will experience a quickening of your mortal body by the Holy Spirit.

Let us observe what we can learn in this regard from II Corinthians 12. There we are told what the apostle Paul experienced when he had what he called a thorn in his flesh (v. 7b). Now different people have put forth different interpretations as to what this might have been; but most likely it was a physical ailment of some kind. We know, for example, that Paul had traveled through some areas where the possibility of catching malaria existed, and perhaps he may have contracted this disease. And we know that malaria can adversely affect one's eyesight, a malady which we are fairly certain the apostle had contracted, causing him to have to write some of his letters in very large script. This he had

172

himself acknowledged, for in one of his epistles he had commented thusly: "See with how large letters I write" (Galatians 6:11 ASV). It is also true that if a person has come down with malaria, that person's body will sometimes exhibit the phenomenon of shaking or trembling. This problem, too, Paul had written about: "I came to you in weakness, and in fear, and in much trembling" (see I Corinthians 2:3). So perhaps both these physical ailments of his were due to a case of malaria; but we do not know for sure.

Nevertheless, because God wished to give His servant-apostle a great revelation but at the same time keep him humble, He allowed Satan to place a thorn in Paul's body (II Corinthians 12:7). Yet we know, from the apostle's account of this event, that it was not a little thorn but, as it were, a continuing troublesome stake—and all for the purpose of preventing pride from arising in the heart of God's servant. Let us understand and realize that certain things happen to us because God has a purpose. Now because of this thorn in his flesh, Paul felt extremely uncomfortable physically; even so, through it all he never thought of himself; he only thought of the glory of God and the negative impact his physical ailment could have upon God's glory. For as he was preaching among the people, he could very well have thought that with such a defect in his body causing it to shake and tremble, it could adversely affect the testimony for the Lord when, as was often the case, he would be preaching that God is the God of resurrection. Would people not therefore mockingly say, "Look at his weak and frail and shaking body; where is the testimony of God's resurrection power in him?!?" So for the Lord's sake and not for his own sake, Paul beseeched the Lord on three separate occasions to remove this profoundly troublesome stake in his flesh. In response, however, the Lord said to His faithful servant: "My grace is sufficient for you; for see, My power is perfected in your weakness." Upon hearing this from the Lord, Paul immediately changed his attitude towards his bodily ailment and declared this: "I will therefore boast in all my weaknesses because His power is perfected in them" (see II Corinthians 12:8-10). Though this episode in Paul's life, arranged by God himself, was humbling to him, it enabled Christ to be manifested and magnified. This is what the Spirit's quickening can and will accomplish. Here we learn what Paul could do with such a weak body through his experiencing the quickening of his mortal body; and this we all can experience as well. We all, I believe, have experienced something of this to a greater or lesser degree at some point in our Christian life. On those occasions how we have felt so insufficient—as though even the Lord himself was insufficient to meet the need of the hour. But when God begins to speak in you, then you shall discover and experience the all-sufficiency in Christ Jesus that is needed.

In the early days of Watchman Nee's ministry for the Lord his body was quite weak. We are told that when he would walk from one place to another, he often had to stop at all the electric power posts along the way and wrap himself around them in order to rest awhile. Then he would walk on. Oftentimes in those same early days of ministry he would lie in bed in great physical agony until the hour arrived for him to minister. Then he would arise and minister for two long hours. What was our brother experiencing in these difficult circumstances? It was nothing less than the quickening of his mortal body. You, too, will begin to experience—even in this life—the resurrection power of Christ in your mortal body.

And so, by means of spiritual exercise these two sets of experiences—the buffeting of the body and the Spirit's quickening of the body—will take place continuously in the process of sanctifying the believer's consecrated body. Even so, thank God, that is not yet the end.

THE REDEMPTION OF THE BODY

Romans 8 tells us: "we ourselves, who have the first-fruits of the Spirit, we also ourselves groan in ourselves, awaiting adoption [or, sonship], that is the redemption of our body" (v. 23).

One day, at the return coming of the Lord—and let us thank God that that day is near—this mortal body will be fully redeemed. From this mortal body, we shall take up an immortal one. From this corruptible body we shall take up an incorruptible one. From this physical body we shall take up a spiritual one. At that time death will have been conquered (see I Corinthians 15:42-54). We have a blessed hope; namely, that this body of ours will be fully redeemed and sanctified just as the Lord Jesus had experienced. Let us recall that after His mortal body was placed in the tomb and was then resurrected, He took upon himself a spiritual body—but a body, nonetheless (see John 20:19-28). One day, we, like Jesus, will be relieved of this mortal frame. Let us praise God that we will have an immortal, incorruptible, spiritual body. And in that body we will be able to serve without bounds, restrictions or limitations of any kind. How wonderful! And such, we may add, is the full salvation God has promised. In view of such a hope, what should we be doing today?

D. L. Moody, the famous evangelist, was a large man of two hundred and eighty pounds. When he was young, he heard someone say, "God is still waiting to find a man who will wholly surrender himself to Him. What can God not do in and through that man?" When Moody heard that, he responded with the following words: "That person did not say God is waiting for a great man or a small man, a learned man or an unlearned man. He is simply waiting to find a man—any man—who will totally offer himself up to Him. I am that man. I am willing to yield myself totally to God. Every ounce of my two-hundred-and-eighty-pound body belongs to Him." Oh, what God can do with such a consecrated body as that!

The Lord Jesus with that mortal body of His lived only thirty-three years. And He only ministered some three years. And yet, the apostle John was moved to write this comment at the conclusion of his Gospel: "If I were going to write down all the things which the Lord Jesus said and did, even the world could not contain all the books which would need to be written." How much, indeed, the Lord accomplished through His mortal body while on earth!

In I Corinthians we read: "ye are not your own, for ye have been bought with a price: glorify now then God in your body" (6:20). That is the message God wants us to hear and to obey today.

PART THREE:
HOW SPIRITUAL EXERCISE AFFECTS PRESENT LIFE

Chapter 9

PERSONAL LIFE

I Timothy 4:7b-10—Exercise thyself unto piety [godliness]; for bodily exercise is profitable for a little, but piety [godliness] is profitable for everything, having promise of life, of the present one, and of that to come. The word is faithful and worthy of all acceptation; for, for this we labour and suffer reproach, because we hope in a living God, who is preserver of all men, specially of those that believe.

Philippians 1:21a—For for me to live is Christ.

Galatians 2:20—I am crucified with Christ, and no longer live, I, but Christ lives in me; but in that I now live in flesh, I live by faith, the faith of the Son of God, who has loved me and given himself for me.

I hope that you are not tired of hearing the words spiritual exercise. But the more I meditate on them, the more I feel the importance of it. "Exercise thyself unto godliness." If we want to be like God—and that is His purpose for us—the only way is for us to exercise ourselves unto godliness. If we do not do so, godliness will not be our portion. This verse says that exercising ourselves unto godliness is profitable for everything. This word everything means what it says: every single thing in our lives is touched and impacted upon by such exercise. By exercising our spirit we have the promise of eternal life. In other words, the issue is, how can we release the life of Christ in us?—and the Biblical answer is, that it is through spiritual exercise. Moreover, let us take note that this verse goes on to say, "for the present day." That is the here and now. Hence, by this we can discern the importance of spiritual exercise. And furthermore, I believe that this holds the key to unlocking and the maturing of our spiritual life. If we do not exercise our spirit, we will not have spiritual life because the life of Christ will be imprisoned within us. Therefore, His life needs to be released in order for it to live and express itself through us.

We need to consider how spiritual exercise affects our daily life, and this daily life of ours consists of four major areas: we experience personal life, family life, church life, and social life. It is in these four areas that we live out our lives daily. Thus, we want to understand how spiritual exercise stands as the key to our successfully living out our Christian life in all these areas. So, to begin with, we will want to discover how spiritual exercise affects our personal life.

THE ADAMIC LIFE

When we were born into this world, we began our existence as human beings. Yet how did we conduct our daily life before we believed in the Lord Jesus? We may have lived twenty, forty, or sixty years; but by what life were we living? From the Scriptures we learned that we lived by the Adamic life within us because we who were born of Adam belonged to Adam. We received his life and that is what we lived by.

What exactly is Adamic life? When God created the first man Adam, He breathed into his nostrils, and that man became a living soul. Adam lived by this soul-life. And let us be clear that when he was created, his soul-life was initially pure, or, may I say, it was neutral—it being neither holy nor sinful. Therefore, as was discussed earlier, being born with a free will, Adam would need to decide how he was going to live: would he follow the path of holiness or that of sin. Hence, this explains why it was that God placed man before two specifically identified trees in the Garden of Eden. In the center of the garden was the Tree of Life, and by its side was the tree of the knowledge of good and evil.

God put these two named trees before Adam and allowed him to freely choose by what source of life he would live out his existence. Would he wish to live by the life of God or would he want to live by enhancing his soul-life? Were he to choose the latter, he would obtain the knowledge of good and evil and would thus not need God: he would henceforth live an independent life by his developed soul-life. On the other hand, were Adam to opt for living a life dependent upon God, he would submit himself to God and allow His life—to be gained by eating of the Tree of Life—to live in him.

So here we see in the Edenic garden these two distinctively different ways of life placed before man from which he was to choose. Unfortunately, for him as well as for us, our ancestor Adam chose the way of the soul. He decided to live by developing and enhancing his soul-life, thereby choosing to live independently of God and, not realizing by his having done so, that his life would fall into sin and suffer death—for God had forewarned Adam: "If you eat of the tree of the knowledge of good and evil, you shall surely die."

When, therefore, we ourselves were born into this world, every one of us was automatically caused to live by the Adamic life—a fallen, sinful life—within us all. Ever since the fall, each one of us born into the world has been compelled to live by that life throughout many years, all of us being by nature self-centered and wanting to be independent. Having neither God nor hope, death would be our final destiny.

But let us be thankful to God that when we believed in the Lord Jesus, something drastic and far-reaching in its implications for us happened. Not only was our dead spirit renewed and the life of God in Christ began living in us, the Holy Spirit began dwelling in us as well. In short, God enabled us to live by a different life instead of by the Adamic life.

LIVING A LIFE DIFFERENT FROM THE WORLD

We do not need anyone to tell us we are saved, because we have the sense within us that we are now the children of God. We cannot live any longer in accordance with the way we lived before. Today, we should live as God's children— even as Christians, the Christ-ones. The Lord Jesus himself has told us, as recorded in Matthew 5:17-48, that He expects us to be *extra*-ordinary. For has He not said, "You should be perfect as your heavenly Father is perfect" (see v. 48)? In other words, having saved us and given us His life, He now expects us to live extra-ordinary lives; that is, lives different from what we were living before and different from the world.

I Peter 2:9 informs us that we are now a chosen race, a kingly priesthood, a holy nation, a people for God's possession; and the purpose, we are told there, is to declare and set forth the excellencies of our God who has called us out of darkness into His marvelous light. Having believed in the Lord Jesus and having received His salvation, we know inwardly that henceforth we are to live differently. We are expecting to be—not simply ordinary but—extra-ordinary. We are expecting to be perfect in love even as God is perfect. We are here with a purpose: to proclaim the perfections and praises of God who has delivered us out of darkness and brought us into His wonderful light. Everyone who has believed in the Lord Jesus has known immediately that from that day forward he or she needs to be different. We are to live differently because we cannot live as we were living before. So how can we live differently? How can we be those who show forth the excellencies and wonderful deeds of God?

LIVING BY THE NATURAL LIFE

Two distinct choices—two distinct ways—for living lie before every believer. One is the human or natural way, which is the wrong way. That way is to try to live religiously as best as one can. Formerly, we were irreligious, but now, we think we must be religious. On Sundays we go to church, and we daily are expected to read our Bible, and daily we are supposed to pray. And, then, there are certain activities we should not engage in and certain places to which we should not go. We are even being told or *taught* to observe all these instructions. And as a result of following all these do's and dont's most religiously, we eventually come to believe that we are living differently and that we are extra-ordinary.

Nevertheless, having done all that, we sense deep within our hearts that there is something lacking. Though we try to be righteous and do the will of God, we discover we do not have the strength or power to carry it out. This was the experience of the apostle Paul which he described in Romans

7: "I will to do the will of God, but I cannot. I do not want to do the things that are sinful, but I do them anyway." Why is this so and what does it tell us about ourselves? I think the answer is very clear.

This failure of Paul's in trying to live his life in a religious way reveals the fact that it was the wrong life-source by which he was living. He was not living by the life of Christ which was in him. Like Paul had, we too have the life of Christ in us, but just as Paul failed to do, we today do not live by that life. We are still using our natural Adamic life to live— and we end up living religiously. Even in this matter of doing the will of God, we have tried our best to do it, but we find we are unable. Sometimes we are puzzled by this failure, and our conscience bothers us. If a person continues to live that way—that is, by the natural soul-life in him—his conscience may gradually become dull, resulting in his feeling very happy, satisfied, and untroubled.

When I first believed in the Lord Jesus I was fifteen, and I really meant business. I truly thanked God for saving me. And right away I thought I needed to be different. So every morning I got up before the other members of the family, and I would shut myself in my room and have my daily devotions. I would kneel down, sing some hymns, read the Bible, and pray. I faithfully performed these religious duties every day. I was also quite zealous, sharing Christ with my fellow students. Some of us Christian students would even organize gospel teams and go out to the villages to preach the gospel. Outwardly, everybody thought I was a good Christian. I attended the church service, of course, because at that time I was in a Christian school, and on Sundays we would march into the church building and attend the service there because it was required of us. I also kept the Sabbath; for with respect to Sundays I was told that I could not do any labor; so I dared not study because that was considered to be labor. Therefore, whenever an exam fell on a Monday, I feared this the most because I could not study for it on the Sunday immediately before. And hence, on my Sundays I had nothing to do, so I played ball. One could say, therefore, that I was a very religious Christian, but I still lived by my natural life rather than by the inward life of Christ. In other words, I was a reformed believer in Christ but not a transformed one. Outwardly, I appeared to be quite good, but it was all religion.

What is religion? Religion is the manufacture of man, it is something man-made. Man begins to be conscious of his sin, and he tries to overcome it by doing something good in order to cover his conscience. Man finds that he can be very religious outwardly, but when we who are believers in Christ do these same things, are we actually any different from the world? There are people in the world who are very religious, perhaps even more religious than we are. Where, then, is the difference between the religious man of the world and the religious believer in Christ? There is none, for all is being done by self-effort and not by the life of Christ. Therefore, we who have believed in the Lord Jesus need to realize that there is a vast difference between religious life and spiritual life: spiritual life comes from our spirit whereas religious life emanates from our soul. Sad to say, too many Christians today are only living a religious life—and the source of it all is the old Adamic life—it is all through self-effort and not through spiritual life. Spiritual life has to come from our spirit and its expression is the result of spiritual exercise. And such is the right way or path for living which lies before every believer in Christ to choose. By choosing this way the Christian will be able to live differently than he did before and differently from the world.

LIVING THE CHRIST-LIFE AS PAUL LEARNED

What, then, is living differently? What is living an extra-ordinary life? Briefly stated, it is setting forth the excellencies of God. Yet, how can we set forth those excellencies? The only way, and it is God's way for us, is very simple. He does not expect *us* to live differently. Indeed, if living our life is going to be by the old Adamic life, how can we possibly expect to live the heavenly life? For the old life is earthly, natural, fleshly. On the contrary, the Lord does not expect us—in, of, and by ourselves—to live the life He wants us to live; He knows it is impossible; yet we all try. Even the apostle Paul tried, and he tried *very* hard. He failed and failed and failed, until finally he gave up. Cried Paul at that point: "O wretched man that I am, who shall deliver me from the body of this death?" (see Romans 7:24) Have we come to that point in our Christian experience yet? If we have not, it shows that we are trying to live a Christian life by our self-life. Whether it is by the good self or the bad self, it does not matter. It is still self. For did not the apostle Paul acknowledge that in his flesh "no good dwells"? (Romans 7:18) We know this to be true, but it seems as though we do not recognize it as truth for our lives. It is not until we realize and acknowledge this that we will arrive at the point of saying that it is impossible to live a personal Christian life by our old self-life. It was only upon arriving at that point in his failed

Christian experience that the apostle Paul finally declared: "Thank God, it is through Jesus Christ" (see Romans 7:25a). His eyes were at last opened to see that there is but one way that he and all other believers in Christ are able to live as Christians—not by self, only by Christ Jesus.

I would like to challenge everyone, including myself, to face honestly the following questions and respond with candid answers: Are we living a Christian life today by the effort of our self? Are we cheating ourselves? Have we come to the point that we see what God has always known, that it is impossible for the Christian to live an extra-ordinary life with his old self? If so, God has a way through for each one of us.

When the apostle Paul was the unbelieving Saul of Tarsus, he was a young man who was so religious, so moral, so zealous, so concentrated, and was one who—as best he knew how—gave himself unreservedly to God. While other young people of his time were questing after the things of *this* world, he was seeking after the things from above. He became a devout Pharisee. Today we have a very bad impression of those Pharisees of old, but actually they were the strictest and most orthodox sect among the various religious groups of Judaism. There were not many Pharisees at any one time because they gave themselves up totally to the study and implementation of the Scriptures, that is, they tried to keep every letter of God's word. Moreover, they were the interpreters of the Scriptures at the time of Saul; and so, whenever people conduct themselves in this fashion they usually end up becoming hypocritical. However, this young man Saul was a *true* Pharisee in every sense: he did everything he could to follow the directions and the instructions of the Law and all its commandments. In fact, outwardly, he seemed to have been able to observe all such requirements faithfully; inwardly, however, it was a different story. Having become so zealous for the traditions of the fathers, Saul had naturally considered Jesus to have been an impostor of Judaism and His followers should therefore be eliminated; and hence, he became most zealous—even fanatical—in persecuting Jesus' followers. This resulted in his committing acts which no ethical, moral gentleman would ever do. Most likely, therefore, his conscience began to trouble him, but he turned to trying to bribe his conscience in an attempt to suppress it by redoubling his efforts to persecute the Christians. But we know from Jesus' words to Saul on the Damascus road that in reality he was kicking against the goads and was attempting to live by means of his self-life the kind of life which God requires.

I wonder if this is true with many Christians today. If so, then probably they are actually living like Saul the unbeliever had been doing in his former days. They are trying to be Christians by living differently outwardly by means of keeping a few laws and commandments, yet realizing inwardly that they have not succeeded, and thus they end up bribing their consciences to sleep.

Let us each realize that God's verdict upon our living by the old self-life is death. God has no intention of improving our old self-life by making it more ethical or more religious. All such conduct is merely outward in its impact; there is nothing real inwardly about any of it, and hence, all of it will ultimately be cast into the fire. This is what Saul of Tarsus learned in his becoming Paul the Christian. After he received a heavenly vision on the road to Damascus, his life instantly began to change. In his later life Paul would testify in a letter he wrote to the Philippian believers while a prisoner in Rome, what the secret of his Christian life had been. It was quite simple, for he long before this had learned the lesson of Romans 7; wrote Paul: "For me to live is Christ" (1:21a). Outwardly, he was the same person with the same features, but inwardly the source was different. He did not live his life anymore by his old Saul-of-Tarsus life. He instead lived his life by the life of Christ.

REPLACING THE SOUL-LIFE WITH THE CHRIST-LIFE

We who believe in the Lord Jesus have Christ in us. The Bible makes this clear: "Christ [is] in you, the hope of glory" (Colossians 1:27b). That is the mystery of the gospel. We believers all have Christ in us. He dwells in our new spirit. The Holy Spirit is there in us as well to see to it that the Christ-life is being exercised, used, is growing and maturing. God has already made every provision for our daily life. By which life, therefore, are we living today?

How could Saul the Pharisee become Paul the apostle? How could his soul-life be replaced by the Christ-life in his daily living? In Galatians 2:20 he explained the secret: "I [my very self] am crucified with Christ." This is the facet of the gospel for believers. The facet of the gospel for *un*believers is this: "You do not need to die because Christ has died for you." This latter is the side of the gospel for the world. But there is another side of the gospel for the believers which declares: "You do not need to try to live any longer because you were crucified with Christ, and now the resurrected Christ lives for you."

I wonder if we really have a heart for the Lord. Probably we have lived a Christian life in such a manner so long that we have become weary of it all. It has become a huge burden. That, to us, is what being a good Christian is. If we were not good Christians, we would not care to the point of it becoming burdensome. We may think that so long as we try to live religiously, it is enough. But we are cheating ourselves. If, however, we are real with ourselves, we are not satisfied within. We have tried our best, yet we have failed again and again. The struggling and fighting to be good has been fierce. Even when we have gained a small victory, we sometimes shortly thereafter have experienced a big defeat. Is that not our experience? But let us thank God that when our Lord Jesus went to the cross, He not only bore our sins in His body but also took us there in himself. When He died, the old man—the old Adam—in us died with Him. This is God's doing. Let us understand that God does not deal with each and every one of us individually. Rather, He deals with the head of the human race. Which means that when Christ died at Calvary, the Adamic race was terminated. What Christ did on the cross was immense and is something we have to believe.

We believe, of course, that when Christ died on the cross He took our sins away. How do we know this? Even though He was crucified two thousand years ago, we were not yet born and thus had not committed any sins. Nevertheless, upon confessing Christ as our Savior we believe that He has borne our sins in His body. And upon our believing this, our sins are forgiven because what Christ has done on the cross is eternal. Its effect is as effective today as it was two thousand years ago. So if Christ has in fact taken the old Adamic man with Him to the cross, then our old man is now and forever dead. It is because we do not believe this fact that its efficacy for us does not work. It is similar to what our situation was before we were saved: we did not believe that our sins were borne by Christ on the cross; instead, we tried by every means to wipe away our sins by attempting to accumulate merits in order to counter-balance the sins we had committed. It was foolish, yet we all have done that. Just so, we who are now Christian believers find the same situation is too often true of us today: what is needed is for us to believe that we too were crucified on the cross with Christ.

CRUCIFIED WITH CHRIST

Now if it is true that you and I were crucified with Christ on the cross, then it can no longer be we who live: our "I" has been crossed out, and it is therefore Christ who now lives in and through us. Yes, it is quite true that we still live in the flesh—that is, we still live in our bodies. Outwardly, it is still I who lives, but inwardly, it is not I but Christ. And hence, what is required of us is simply to live by faith. Oftentimes we will say that this person or that person lives by faith because he does not have a job and thus he depends on God for his daily existence. Hence, we deem that circumstance to be one of living by faith. That is not true, however, since every one of us lives by faith; that is to say, we all believe that we were crucified with Christ and it is therefore no longer I who live but it is Christ who lives in me; consequently, we believers are those who indeed live by faith.

This faith, strictly speaking, is not your faith or my faith; rather, as Paul has written, it is the faith of the Son of God who has loved us and given himself for us (Galatians 2:20b).

Moreover, the Lord is also faithful: He will see to it that whatever He has done works and will be efficacious in us. Accordingly, for us who have believed in Christ, our living today is to be by faith, faith in the Lord Jesus, so that we can know that we live by Christ and not by our self-life any longer. It is a matter of the faith of the Lord Jesus. If we do not believe this, then we do not have faith.

Consider once again that if an unbeliever does not believe that the Lord Jesus has taken his sins away, then his sins are still with him. Yet so is it true with Christians that if you and I do not believe what Christ has done for us, then *we* are still living—not Christ: it is we who are trying to live a Christ-life, which is an impossibility. "Not I but Christ" is the true gospel, the real glad news.

Let us therefore exercise faith in believing that it is no longer I but Christ who lives in us. When Christ who is our life is released from within us, we will live and please God in our daily life. So the question confronting us is this: By whose life are we living today?

RELEASING THE CHRIST-LIFE

It is vitally important for us to know how to release the Christ-life in us. Do realize that the Christ-life in us is surrounded and imprisoned by our soul-life. How, then, can it be released? The only way is through spiritual exercise—the exercising of our spirit. It is the responsibility of the Holy Spirit, who dwells in our spirit, to make sure that the life of Christ is released in us so as to be strengthened and ultimately replace our soul-life entirely. But for this to happen, the Holy Spirit, while working in us, will need to have our response and cooperation. In other words, whenever the Holy Spirit works upon our conscience, He expects us to respond positively, because even our soul-life's human reasoning may be opposed to His working. Our mind may say, "What is wrong with doing this or doing that? Is not everyone doing it?" But the Holy Spirit is saying, "No." What, then, must we do? We must submit ourselves to the Holy Spirit, and as we do that, our self-life is put to death and the Christ-life is released. It is by the process of spiritual exercise on a daily basis that the release of Christ's life in us will be realized.

WALKING IN THE LIGHT OF THE SPIRIT

Sometimes the Lord gives us some light on our path as we find described in I John: "God is light. If we walk in the light as God is in the light, we have fellowship with one another and the blood of Jesus Christ cleanses us from all sin" (see 1:5b, 7). As we walk on this earth, sometimes we discern a light shining within us regarding a certain matter which has arisen. Such shining of light is the anointing of the Holy Spirit within us. He is wanting to teach us, not only with regard to the big issues of life but also concerning the small things of the day. In our daily lives He will teach us. There may be matters which everybody else thinks are acceptable to do or observe, but in some cases the Holy Spirit may say, "No, that is the world's standard; God's standard is different." What is occurring here? The Holy Spirit is giving us light, and our response is to walk in that light as God is in the light. Then we believers can have fellowship with one another. Sometimes we will experience God touching us by His Spirit when we are in communion with Him. The more we draw near to God, the more we will be enlightened to be like Him.

Are we exercising our spirit? The Holy Spirit never fails in His work if we respond positively. The Bible says He will never leave us nor forsake us (Hebrews 13:5b). He is in us. We may grieve Him or we might not listen to Him or we may neglect Him or resist Him, but He never leaves us. He is very insistent. He wants to see that Christ is being released, and the only way for that to happen is through the cross—our self-life has to die. It is a daily experience (cf. II Corinthians 4:10-12). So let us ask ourselves one simple question: Who is living in me today—I or Christ?

HUDSON TAYLOR'S DISCOVERY

Perhaps you have heard of Hudson Taylor, who was the first missionary to open up inland China to the gospel. He went there and lived by faith—trusting in God to supply all his needs. He formed the China Inland Mission composed of other missionaries who also came out to China. They tried to live as Chinese—wearing Chinese dress and living right among the Chinese themselves in inland China. How they suffered persecution! And even many were martyred. But, because of that, the gospel came strongly to inland China.

After Hudson Taylor had been in China for a few years, leading the China Inland Mission, he became dissatisfied with himself. He came to sense that he was not what he should be as a Christian, for he was worried over the fact that he was not perfect as the Father is perfect. So he sought earnestly after God and studied the Bible very carefully. He often prayed, even fasted, and tried to become like Christ, but he could not. Said brother Taylor to himself: "If only I can be connected with Christ, His power will come into me, and then I shall be able to live a life that will truly glorify God." Accordingly, he began to pray that he would be joined with Christ.

But one day he was reading John 15 which tells of the Lord saying, "I am the vine, and ye are the branches" (v. 5a). Suddenly light flashed within him, to which his response was: "I was trying to join myself to Christ. I did not know that I am already joined to Him, because He is the vine and I am the branch. Therefore, all that is His is mine, and I do not even need to ask for it. I can simply rest in Him." That was a revelation to Hudson Taylor, the result of which was that his life was revolutionized. By the time of the Boxer Uprising of 1900-1901 he was already an old man and very weak. But praise God, the Lord gave him rest.

Do we see the point here? If we are intending to live the Christian life by our self-effort, we are doomed to fail. Indeed, many of us have tried that path and have ended in failure. There must come a day when we need to cry out as did the apostle Paul at his lowest point of failure and utter disappointment: "Oh wretched man that I am, who can deliver me from this body of death?" Light finally came to him, for Paul answered his own question by declaring: "Thanks be to God through Jesus Christ the Lord!" (see Romans 7:25a) From that moment forward God was able to begin turning Paul's eyes away from himself to look off to Jesus, the Author and Finisher of faith, thus bringing to an end his spiritual crisis (see Hebrews 12:2a).

SUGGESTIONS ON HOW TO LIVE THE CHRIST-LIFE

Beginning the Day with God

How are we going to live out the Christ-life? I would like, in the time remaining, to offer two or three simple suggestions. Here is the first one. In the Bible there are many passages which reveal the importance for God's people as to how they start each day of their lives. All our days on earth, of course, begin in the morning, but how do we spend each morning? How we do so will determine the course and character of our day. There is a Chinese proverb which says: "The beginning of the year is spring; the beginning of the day is the morning." Do we commence each morning with God or with ourselves? That choice will make a great difference.

There are many places in the Psalms which address this very matter, but I will only mention two such places. One is in Psalm 5:3: "Jehovah, in the morning shalt thou hear my voice; in the morning will I address myself to thee, and will look up." Another one is Psalm 63:1: "O God, thou art my God; early will I seek thee. My soul thirsteth for thee, my flesh languisheth for thee, in a dry and weary land without water."

I feel it is very important to begin the morning in the right way. If we begin it with God, then it will be His life which will govern our day. If, however, we begin our day without God—that is to say, without drawing near to Him—and thus we go out into the world by ourselves, then it is no wonder that we live by our self-life. How we decide this issue will make a tremendous difference.

It is true that modern life is not conducive to our engaging in spiritual exercise. For instance, today, people sleep in very late. As a matter of fact, it has almost become a universal habit. So if you go to sleep very late, you cannot be expected to rise up early; instead, you will linger in bed as long as you can and then dash out into the world. Yet if your daily life is shaped in that way, it is not surprising that it is *you* who live and not Christ. One of the secrets to living the Christ-life is to be found right here. In this matter of rising early, there is nothing technical surrounding it.

In this connection, I recall the words of Miss Groves, a fellow worker with Miss Margaret Barber—close friend and counselor to brother Watchman Nee. Miss Groves once said that one of our battles as Christians is that which is fought out between our bed and ourselves: whether we wish to continue to linger upon our bed or rise up early. That, she added, is one of our problems.

Communion with God

Everyone is different, but before we do anything, the first action on our part is to draw near to God. The Bible says, "Draw near to God, and he will draw near to you" (see James 4:8). It is very simple. We do not do it as a duty or religious act. We do it for the sake of communion. We want to present ourselves before God. We want to have a time with Him and open our hearts to Him. We want to give ourselves to Him for the day. We want to hear from Him, and this does not really need lots of time. Yes, we can read three chapters a day in the Old Testament and one chapter in the New Testament and cover the whole Bible once a year, but we can do that at some other time. Such spiritual exercise is for reading and knowing what is in the word of God. Communion, on the other hand, is an entirely different matter.

George Mueller, whom I mentioned in the message on Communion much earlier, was born in Prussia (now part of Germany). After he was saved he went to England and studied theology. He tried to be a missionary to the Jews but the Lord met him, and by faith he was led to take care of thousands of orphans for the rest of his life. The secret of life is to be found in what he did at the beginning of each day. Every morning he would spend a little time in going before the Lord and opening God's word. From those books of the Bible which are more conducive to meditation brother Mueller would simply read one verse and meditate on it before God. But while he was meditating he would sometimes feel he had to confess and repent before God— and so he would repent. Sometimes when he read, however, he would feel so lifted up by the mercy of God that he would begin to thank and praise Him. In other words, this brother opened his heart to the Lord and would have a talk with Him and allow the Lord to talk to him. Perhaps this time took only ten or fifteen minutes, and yet, whenever he would come out it was from having been in the presence of the Lord. It can be just that simple.

KEEPING A CLEAR ACCOUNT WITH THE LORD MOMENT BY MOMENT

You do not need to be consciously supernatural. You just need to be spiritually natural. You emerge from the presence of God and with His presence you are ready to go out into the world. There you may touch different things. Yet you need to ask yourself that while doing these things, by whom are they being done? Remarkably, when there is something in your life that is not righteous in the sight of God but is deemed to be all right in the sight of the world, your conscience will tell you that this matter is not acceptable to God. When your conscience tells you this, then you are to obey. If you do not obey right away, you will sense a darkness beginning to descend upon you—as though there is a distance that has been created between you and God. Should you wait until the evening and gather up all these failures and tell God about them? No. You instead need to ask God to forgive you right away. In other words, you must keep a clear account with the Lord throughout the day. Moreover, should the Lord show you anything from the word of God, you ought to obey and do so immediately. On the other hand, if you are not sure about the matter, then you must wait and seek Him; yet such waiting is never to be accompanied by a rebellious spirit or used as an excuse for ignoring or neglecting the matter. Instead, be sure to maintain contact with the Lord.

We do not need to analyze whether it is we who live or the Lord who lives. It is simply a matter of living by faith. As we are engaged in these suggested spiritual exercises we will discover that our lives will truly be changed. It is not as hard and difficult as we may think. It is easy and light, for as the Lord Jesus declared to His disciples: "Yoke with Me and learn of Me, for I am lowly and meek in heart; and you shall find rest in your souls. For My yoke is easy and My burden is light" (see Matthew 11:28-30). That is the way we are to live our personal life. The principle to be followed is simply this: we live our daily life not by self but by Christ. Nevertheless, that principle has to be applied. But when it is applied, we may find that there will be issues over which we struggle. Even so, it can be very simple and childlike. That is why the Lord, in His praise-prayer to the Father, indicated that if a person is worldly-wise and learned, it will be kept from that person; but that if someone is childlike, it will be revealed to that one (Luke 10:21b). To sum up, then, this way of life can be, and is, simple and easy. Therefore, let us allow the Lord to apply this principle to our personal life. And may He have mercy upon us and help us.

Chapter 10

FAMILY LIFE

Ephesians 5:21-6:4—Submitting yourselves to one another in the fear of Christ. Wives, submit yourselves to your own husbands, as to the Lord, for a husband is head of the wife, as also the Christ is head of the assembly. He is Saviour of the body. But even as the assembly is subjected to the Christ, so also wives to their own husbands in everything. Husbands, love your own wives, even as the Christ also loved the assembly, and has delivered himself up for it, in order that he might sanctify it, purifying it by the washing of water by the word, that he might present the assembly to himself glorious, having no spot, or wrinkle, or any of such things; but that it might be holy and blameless. So ought men also to love their own wives as their own bodies: he that loves his own wife loves himself. For no one has ever hated his own flesh, but nourishes and cherishes it, even as also the Christ the assembly: for we are members of his body; we are of his flesh, and of his bones. Because of this a man shall leave his father and mother, and shall be united to his wife, and the two shall be one flesh. This mystery is great, but I speak as to Christ, and as to the assembly. But ye also, every one of you, let each so love his own wife as himself; but as to the wife I speak that she may fear the husband. Children, obey your parents in the Lord, for this is just. Honour thy father and thy mother, which is the first commandment with a promise, that it may be well with thee, and that thou mayest be long-lived on the earth. And ye fathers, do not provoke your children to anger, but bring them up in the discipline and admonition of the Lord.

J. HUDSON TAYLOR'S GREAT-GRANDFATHER

In our considering together today this topic of spiritual exercise and family life, I would like to begin with a story about J. Hudson Taylor's great-grandfather. As a young man he was carefree and not very devout in his Christian faith. Most interestingly, however, on the day he was going to be married, upon his arising that morning he suddenly remembered: "I am going to be married today!" Realizing what a great responsibility this was going to be, he went out to the field to pray. He prayed and prayed and prayed, having lost all sense of time. When he finished praying it was already noon, and suddenly he remembered that this was the very hour at which he was supposed to be married! So he rushed to the church building where the bride, relatives and friends were waiting, all wondering what had happened to the bridegroom. And so, Hudson Taylor's great-grandfather was married.

During the evening, as he and his newly-wedded wife were preparing to go to bed, he told her that they had to pray. He knelt down, at the same time gently pressing his wife down on her knees, and started to pray. His wife was in shock because she did not know what was happening. For they both had loved dancing and other worldly activities; and hence, she immediately thought that perhaps she had just married a secret Methodist! So that was how they had commenced their life together. We know from the Taylor family literature that for several generations this family had served the Lord well. In fact, it is now even the fourth generation of this family that is serving the Lord.

THE WRONG CONCEPT OF FAMILY

Marriage or family life is a big problem today, not only among the worldly people but also among God's people. Many books by Christian authors are being written with much advice offered. Such advice is good as far as it goes, but it does not solve the problem because all of the discussion in those books is at the surface or superficial level. As I meditated before the Lord I came to feel that probably the reason for this is that we Christians have forgotten what God has said about this subject of family. God's people have fairly much considered the family as being that which is earthly and natural and which, therefore, they can and are to manage themselves. To put it another way, too many of us view the family as being solely ours—as being *our* castle; and hence, we try to have family life by means of our natural life. We believe we know what to do, for are we not naturally born to be a father, mother, husband, wife, or child? So we know how to conduct ourselves in this area of life. We thus use our personal wisdom, experience and all else that we have in creating and building up our families.

Yet, has it ever occurred to any of us what God's concept of the family is?—what God's purpose for the family is? For this to be understood we must go back to the beginning. Concerning the creation of man, whose narration we find in Genesis 1:27, we read: "God created Man in his image, in the image of God created he him; male and female created he them." Here we learn that when God created man He created him male and female. In other words, God obviously had the family in view here. We incorrectly assume that we are created solely as individuals. We overlook the Biblical fact, however, that in creating man, God created a *corporate* being: consisting of both male and female, and that they were meant to be joined into one flesh.

From Genesis 2 we learn that the Lord God announced that "it is not good that Man should be alone; I will make him a helpmate, his like" (v. 18). So God made the woman out of man and brought them together. Why did God say that it is not good for man to be alone? We usually take this word as meaning that man has needs which must be satisfied. In other words, we look at God's word purely from our viewpoint. Yet if that be our viewpoint, it is no wonder that we find family situations today in such a serious and terrible state.

So why *did* God say that it is not good for man to be alone? In God's purpose of creation He did not want man to be by himself; rather, He desired to create man who would be a union of both male and female. In short, the Adam God created was only one half; therefore, His creation at this point was not yet complete. Not only was it not complete, it could never in this state fulfill God's purpose in His having created man. God's purpose is so noble that no one person can fulfill it: it requires the family to fulfill it. And *that* is the reason God said what He said.

THE FAMILY IS HOLY

In the sight of God family is a holy entity, which means that from the very beginning of creation the family is set apart unto God, that it is something both spiritual and heavenly—not something worldly or earthly. Too many of us are ignorant of the fact that the family is holy, and hence we treat it as though it is natural. Accordingly, we attempt to solve every family problem with our natural wisdom, experience, or good will, but we find that the solutions are beyond us.

Now in discussing family life, we need to see from the very outset that the family does not originate with man but with God and that He has a definite purpose in having families because He wants to use them to fulfill His work on earth.

Furthermore, when considering family life, we need also to see that there must be the undertaking of spiritual exercise on our part. I wonder if we have ever exercised our spirit concerning our families. Do we truly seek the Lord when we each are seeking for a mate? Do we consider the family we have as being "our" family or do we consider it as the Lord's and that the Lord is for the family? There is an incorrect concept in our thinking which needs to be changed. If we truly see that the family is *from* God and that the family is *for* God, then we shall immediately realize that we cannot fulfill family life by means of our natural self-life. On the contrary, that self-life of ours needs to be dealt with! There is only one way to fulfill family life, and that is by the life of Christ and not by the self-life. Has this thought ever occurred to any of us? Just as the *personal* life of a Christian cannot be lived out by the natural life, even so, the Christian's *family* life cannot be fulfilled unless that person is willing to accomplish it by the life of Christ instead of by one's natural self-life. Living out the family life in the right way is equally as important as doing so in living out the personal life.

THE FAMILY EXISTS TO SERVE THE LORD

As I waited upon the Lord for this message, I came to feel that there is a concept here which needs to be dramatically adjusted. We need to view our family as the Lord's instead of ours. What *we* benefit from the family being the Lord's is a by-product. But what *God* benefits, if I can phrase it that way, is the primary reason for our having a family. Succinctly put, our family is His—not ours. And if we take *that* stand, I believe there will be a tremendous change in our family life.

Joshua, who led the children of Israel into the Promised Land, challenged them in his old age. He said to them: "Who will you live for? If you want to live for the idols of the Egyptians or even those of the Canaanites in the Promised Land, you may; but as for me and my family we will serve the Lord" (see Joshua 24:14-15).

I think these words of Joshua form the basic principle that must govern the believer's family. Why do we have a family? How are we to live as members of the family— whether that be as a husband or wife, mother or father, children or siblings? How do we live out our family life? The first fact we need to realize and acknowledge is that our family exists for one reason and that is to serve the Lord. Our thought usually is that our family serves us and our purpose. How wrong we are! We must acknowledge the fact that our family is to serve *God's* purpose. If this be true, then we cannot live out our family life with our natural self-life. That is the reason I believe there is a need for us to return to the basic principles in the Bible which ought to govern the believer's family. How, then, can we restore our family life as God has purposed for it? It is these principles which we would now like to look into as a help to us in the restoration of family life as set forth in God's word.

GOD'S ORDER FOR THE FAMILY

Now in all the work of God, there is a definite order. God governs this world with an order, not only in government but also in the family. We read in I Corinthians 11 that "Christ is the head of every man, but woman's head is the man, and the Christ's head is God" (v. 3). The basis of divine order has already been demonstrated on earth by Christ Jesus. So far as divine life is concerned, the Son shares the same as that of the Father. Indeed, He declared, "I and the Father are one" (John 10:30). Moreover, He is the fullness of the Godhead: "All the fullness of the Godhead dwells in Christ bodily" (see Colossians 2:9). Father, Son, and Holy Spirit are equal and that is not a reality which the Son had to grasp after or hold onto. It is and has been His from before the foundation of the universe. So far as divine life is concerned, therefore, the Persons of the Godhead are equal. Yet, for the sake of the work of God, the Lord Jesus emptied himself of the attributes of that life and took upon himself the form of a human being and even that of a bondslave (Philippians 2:5-8a). In other words, throughout His time on earth, the principle governing His earthly life was to submit to the divine order by obeying His Father in all things, even to the extent that He was obedient unto death, and that the death of a cross (Philippians 2:8b, c). On earth Christ the Son fully demonstrated to us that divine order. Oh, how He placed himself completely under the authority of His Father! He even said He had no right to say anything out from himself: He could only say what He heard His Father say. He could not do anything or go anywhere unless He first saw His Father doing it. Even His time was not His: He waited for the time that His Father had ordained (see John 5:19ff., 30; 8:28; 12:49-50; 14:10, 24b; 7:2-10). Thus Jesus the Son of God showed us that it is not a matter of life but of order.

There is a kind of misunderstanding over this. Why should the husband be the head of the family? And why should the wife submit to the husband? Are not male and female equal? Is it not true that oftentimes sisters in the church are more spiritual than the brothers? It is almost a universal phenomenon that the wife is more spiritual than the husband. So why should God ordain the husband to be the head of the family and the wife to be, as it were, the body of the family for carrying out the tasks which need to be done? Is this not unequal and unfair? But our human thought here is focused on the issue of equality. Yet, so far as life is concerned, God's grace knows no prejudice. Just because a person is a man does not mean that he has to be more spiritual than a woman. No, oftentimes it is exactly the opposite. Life in the family is the same—it is for the sake of God's purpose and work. It is for the sake of the family that God's purpose may be accomplished. There must be cooperation from both sides.

THE WAY TO AUTHORITY: THROUGH SUBMISSION

Naturally speaking, everyone wants to be the one in charge. Why, we may reason, should I be under anyone?— Why should I submit myself to anyone? We all want to be the master, and that is human nature. In examining the behavior of the disciples of Jesus, we will notice that even though they came from a humble background, they were always arguing among themselves as to who was the greatest. What does that tell us about them? Simply that they desired authority and not submission. The Lord Jesus had to teach them again and again, not only by words but by example. For instance, on one occasion He took a little child, placed him in the midst of His disciples, and taught, saying: "If you are not converted as a little child, you cannot enter the kingdom of God. The greatest in the kingdom of God is one who will humble himself as this little child" (see Matthew 18:2-4). It is in our very nature as fallen humanity not to want to submit; instead, we want to assume the place of authority. This is not only true in family life but also in church life. We do not want God's order because we want to be in authority; but the way to authority is always through submission.

When reading Ephesians 5 we usually begin the family portion from verse 22, and that is the way we find it divided in various versions of the Bible. Before that verse, we read how we need to live before the Lord, be thankful towards Him, sing songs to Him, etc. And following that section we find the portion of verses on the family. And various Bible versions usually add verse 21 to the preceding paragraph because those translators reasoned that it does not seem to fit in anywhere else. And if we compare Ephesians 5 with Colossians 3, we find that this verse 21, which reads:

"submitting yourselves one to another in the fear of Christ," is not in Colossians. Rather, Colossians 3 ends with thanking God and then the next paragraph begins with a section dealing with the wives. Where should we put this verse 21?

I believe that this verse naturally—or should I say, supernaturally—should be placed at the beginning of the Ephesians 5 section on the family. For how can any wife submit to her husband? Or how can any husband be responsible as the head of a family? The only way for these roles to be properly fulfilled is to abide by what verse 21 says: "submitting yourselves one to another in the fear of Christ." In other words, unless Christ comes into the picture, neither the wife can ever submit to her husband nor the husband ever be the right authority. Instead, the husband will abuse his authority by thinking and demanding: "You listen to me!" But that is being a despot. And the wife will say, "Who are you that I must submit to *you*? I know more than you do." Such will be the natural outcome, if Christ is left out. Probably we all have been guilty of doing this. But let us ever bear in mind that the family, in God's sight, is something supernatural, and the only way to live it out is by supernatural means; that is, it has to come from above—it has to be by the life of Christ in us.

Christ showed us by His earthly walk that He arrived at the place of authority through submission. Consequently, because of this, God has highly exalted Him and given Him a Name which is above every name—that to that Name every knee shall bow and every tongue confess that Jesus is Lord (Philippians 2:10-11). Now in our further considering this matter of authority and submission, it would seem to be harder for a person to be in authority over a given situation in the family than to submit because when a person submits, the responsibility is not his. But when one exercises authority, it is that person's responsibility. Yet, in reality it is not easier to be either the one in authority or the one in submission. Furthermore, according to our fallen human nature, we cannot do either one. For either to be achieved in our family life we need the life of Christ. Therefore, family life must start with husband and wife submitting to one another in the fear of Christ.

Naturally speaking, we—whether husbands or wives—cannot submit. But if both have the fear of Christ, recognizing and acknowledging that God has made Him Head over all things and that He is Head of both man and woman, then submission will be the supernaturally, natural reaction of both.

SUBMITTING TO EACH OTHER IN THE FEAR OF CHRIST

Now the fear of Christ being spoken of here is not that which we usually contemplate. The fear we usually think of is that of a slave towards his master, of whom he is much afraid. Of what is he afraid? He is afraid of *punishment*.

But the fear of Christ of which Ephesians 5:21 speaks is not the fear of a slave but that of a son. It is the fear which Christ had towards His Father and is not negative in character at all. No punishment is in view there. It is instead having a fear lest He should displease the Father whom He loves. So far as the fear of punishment is concerned, the Bible makes clear that "perfect love casts out fear [of punishment]." There is no such fear in perfect love (see I John 4:16b-18). But there *is* the fear of Christ which, as God's children, we must all have: we should be fearful that we might displease our Father God: we should have the attitude of wanting to be very careful lest we displease Him because we very much want to please Him. If the spirit within us has this kind of fear—the fear that was in Christ—then we shall find that submission is always the attitude to have and to act upon: that is, the husband will want to submit himself to his wife and the wife will want to submit herself to her husband. Neither one is thinking of taking authority to himself or herself, because they both recognize and acknowledge that actually Christ is the authority. They both desire to please their Lord God.

Such is the spirit which we all must have, and this is not only to be true with the family but is also to be true with the church. As Watchman Nee once observed: "When you go to the church, you do not seek for those over whom you can have authority, but you look for those to whom you can submit." That is the right attitude to have because it was the attitude of Christ when He was on earth. He submitted himself willingly, gladly and joyfully to His Father (cf. John 8:28b-29).

Therefore, having the love of Christ in us and having the life of Christ being manifested in our lives, we learn that an attitude of submission is one of the characteristics of our spirit. We shall not be trying to lord it over anyone; instead, we shall be willing to submit ourselves. And with this kind of spirit present in us, divine order can and will be established. Then the husband will tremble in the fear of Christ and acknowledge: "Lord, if it is your will that I be the head of the family, I dare not assume this role in and of myself. I must seek after You. I have to know what is Your will in every family situation which may arise." That is the right way to exercise authority in being the head of the family. And the same spirit of submission must be true in the wife. Let us continually think of Christ who ever and always submitted himself to God the Father; and because we have the same spirit, we, too, as husbands and wives, are willing to submit to each other in order that we may work together as one. Otherwise, how can two people live together as one? How can any work be done if each becomes the head? If that be the situation in the family, where is the body?—for all which the head desires to see done can only be done through the body. The body must be there to express and manifest the glory of the head—who in reality is *not* the husband but is Christ.

If both husband and wife are willing to manifest the kind of spirit betokened in verse 21—"submitting yourselves to one another in the fear of Christ"—then the divine order will naturally appear in the family. The husband is to be the head of the family, but for this to be a reality he must himself be submitting to Christ *the* Head. Otherwise, he has no right nor ability to be the head of the family. Husbands should be humble. They should be trembling before the Lord lest they misrepresent Christ. Yet the same demeanor must be true in the wife: wives are not being submissive to their husbands as men but to their husbands who as heads are representing Christ as *the* Head. If we can view this in that light, then the family life will be beautiful. There will be harmony, and both spouses will cooperate in accomplishing the work of the family. Such cooperation between these two will be a beautiful reflection of what is expressed in Ecclesiastes: "Two are better than one and a threefold cord cannot be easily broken" (see 4:12). Both husband and wife cooperate together in order to serve God. And that will be the glory of the family.

CHILDREN: OBEY PARENTS

Now we know, of course, that the family is not just limited to husband and wife. There are also parents and children, and the Scriptures additionally give us advice concerning children. One such Scripture is as follows: "Children, obey your parents in the Lord, for this is just [that is, this is the right thing to do]. Honour thy father and thy mother, which is the first commandment with a promise" (Ephesians 6:1-2). Obedience, not submission, is spoken of here, for it says, "Children, obey your parents."

There is a difference between obedience and submission. Submission is an attitude whereas obedience is an act. In our relationship with God we submit and obey Him absolutely because He is God. However, nowhere do we find commanded in the Bible that we should submit and obey completely a human being. We need to have the spirit of *submission* to human beings in all things, but God does not demand of us to *obey* them in everything. When the obeying of God and the obeying of man are in conflict, we have to obey God. We can clearly see this played out in the experience two of Jesus' disciples—Peter and John—had had on one occasion. When they were brought before the Sanhedrin council, which at that time was the highest human authority in Judaism, they were forbidden to preach anymore in the name of the Lord Jesus. What were they to do? They countered this pronouncement of man by saying: "Whether to obey God or obey man—which is right? But we must preach what we have seen and heard" (see Acts 4:19-20).

Here in Ephesians the Scripture says, "Children, obey your parents." The word children here speaks in particular of minors. When you are not grown up yet but are still a minor in the family, you are under your parents. In that case, you should obey them in all matters because you cannot decide for yourself.

Take for instance the Lord Jesus. When He was twelve years old and while with His parents in Jerusalem, He went into the temple. At that point in His earthly life He had become a son of the Law. In other words, at that age He had the right in the temple or synagogue to ask and answer questions. And when His earthly parents were returning home from Jerusalem, He had stayed behind in the temple. Returning to Jerusalem and after searching for Jesus for three days, His parents finally found Him still in the temple and said to Him, "Why have you done this to us?" He replied, "Must I not be occupied with my Father's business?" (see Luke 2:49) Did Jesus then continue to stay in the temple, refusing to go home with His parents back to Nazareth? On the contrary, the Bible record tells us that He obeyed His parents by returning home with them—and, the Scripture meaningfully adds, "He was obedient to them" (v.51). And the reason is the boy Jesus was still a dependent minor who not only had to submit in attitude but also to obey in action.

CHILDREN: HONOR PARENTS

The passage in Ephesians 6 next says, "Honor your father and mother" (see v. 2a). Probably this command refers to those children who have grown up. You are independent now. Therefore, you do not think you need your parents anymore. Nevertheless, you have a responsibility to honor your father and mother, to respect them and to provide for them, if necessary, because this is the first commandment with promise—you will have a long life (vv. 2b-3).

As earthly children we are rebellious—that is our natural inclination. We want to be on our own and be our own master. We rebel against anything or anyone that might contradict that. As minors who are therefore dependents, you must learn to obey your parents, but when you are grown up, they are still your parents and you are obligated to honor them. You may not obey them or do what they want you to do anymore, but your attitude needs to be one of submissiveness. Do not think: "Well, you are old fools." No, you have to respect and honor them.

FATHERS: BRING UP CHILDREN IN FEAR OF CHRIST

Whenever I read the passages about the parents in both Ephesians and Colossians, there is something that continues to puzzle me. For they only speak of the fathers and not of the mothers, as though to say that the mothers know and do no wrong in relation to their children and therefore have no need to be instructed. This is strange, and I do not know the true answer to it. So far as I understand it, it may be because the husband is the head of the family and hence is responsible not only for the physical needs of the family but also for its spiritual needs. So that may be why the passage states that the fathers must bring up their children in the admonition and discipline of the Lord and that they should not hurt their children to the point of their losing their willingness to do good (Ephesians 6:4, Colossians 3:21).

Is it not true that husbands are usually negligent of their responsibilities in this regard? Men are so busy with worldly affairs that they have no time to bring up their children in the admonition and discipline of the Lord. Also, when men discipline their children, usually they overdo it—perhaps because their anger has been deeply stirred up. This may therefore explain why the passage calls for the fathers to not provoke, exasperate or hurt their children to the extent of them becoming discouraged and losing their willingness to be good. Clearly the responsibility belongs to the fathers. They need to admonish their children.

This word admonish (the verbal form of the noun, admonition) in the Scriptures has a twofold meaning: one is "to encourage," the other is "to warn." On the one hand, fathers must encourage their children in the Lord and also warn them concerning certain risks or dangers they may encounter in their young lives. On the other hand, we do not like the word discipline; rather, we prefer the word child-training. In either case, it has the same meaning. Fathers must train their children in the fear of the Lord. They should not be so much occupied with the worldly tasks of supplying their families with abundance that they neglect their responsibility of bringing their children up in the fear of Christ.

Nevertheless, that does not mean that mothers are always perfect in bringing up their children. It is very true that recorded history tells us that usually the mothers spend more time with the children than do the fathers in attempting to bring them up in the right way. That was the case with

Monica the mother of Augustine. That was also the case with Sussanna Wesley in bringing up her many sons. Every day she tried to spend time with them—perhaps not all of them together in the same day. Rather, she would meet with her boys one by one and try to help them spiritually. No wonder that John Wesley, Charles Wesley, and all her other children turned out the way they did because she was faithfully fulfilling her duty as a mother. If the family can have the fear of Christ as its foundation, then that family will be built up, and God will be glorified.

THE FAMILY ALTAR

Finally, I would here offer up one last suggestion. In the old days among Christians, the family altar was a must. That is to say, Christian families would usually gather together as one every day and read the Bible and pray together. Now this is a practice which is almost unknown among God's people today because modern life is so hectic and demanding that they tend to neglect it. As a result, how much families suffer for it!

In my family there were seven brothers and sisters. I can still remember that when I was a child my father would gather us together before supper every day except when he was away. He would read from the Bible, and then we would all kneel down and he would lead us in prayer. I often wondered back then why Father never asked us children to pray. I later realized that it was because he knew us very well. He would not ask us to pray until he was sure we were truly the Lord's. That impression has been with me throughout my life ever since.

In this connection, I remember one particularly relevant story. There was a certain professor who deeply loved the Lord. He had family altar every evening; but one of his boys became very rebellious and would not attend the family altar. One day when he went home, however, he heard his father leading the family in prayer and praying specifically for him. This son became quite furious. Regarding his father he thought: "Why do you pray for me and not for the others?" So he left home. But God disciplined him and eventually brought him back home.

How important the family altar is! I would suggest that in spite of your modern busy life parents should find a time for this spiritual exercise. It does not require much time— perhaps only ten or fifteen minutes. Gather your family together because—as the well-known saying goes—the family that prays together stays united together. If everyone is simply doing what he or she wants to do, the family scatters and lacks a real cohesive family life. That is the reason I believe spiritual exercise is so important. All of us need to exercise our spirits to be a good husband, a good wife, a good father, a good mother, or even a good child. It is not natural for any of us to be like that; rather, it is supernatural. Family life is for the increase of the glory of God. May the Lord help us all!

Chapter 11

CHURCH LIFE

Ephesians 4:1-16—I, the prisoner in the Lord, exhort you therefore to walk worthy of the calling wherewith ye have been called, with all lowliness and meekness, with long-suffering, bearing with one another in love; using diligence to keep the unity of the Spirit in the uniting bond of peace. There is one body and one Spirit, as ye have been also called in one hope of your calling; one Lord, one faith, one baptism; one God and Father of all, who is over all, and through all, and in us all. But to each one of us has been given grace according to the measure of the gift of the Christ. Wherefore he says, Having ascended up on high, he has led captivity captive, and has given gifts to men. But that he ascended, what is it but that he also descended into the lower parts of the earth? He that descended is the same who has also ascended up above all the heavens, that He might fill all things; and He has given some apostles, and some prophets, and some evangelists, and some shepherds and teachers, for the perfecting of the saints; with a view to the work of the ministry, with a view to the edifying of the body of Christ; until we all arrive at the unity of the faith and of the knowledge of the Son of God, at the full-grown man, at the measure of the stature of the fulness of the Christ; in order that we may be no longer babes, tossed and carried about by every wind of that teaching which is in the sleight of men, in unprincipled cunning with a view to systematized error; but, holding the truth in love, we may grow up to him in all things, who is the head, the Christ: from whom the whole body, fitted together, and connected by every joint of supply, according to the working in its measure of each one part, works for itself the increase of the body to its self-building up in love.

Colossians 3:5-17—Put to death therefore your members which are upon the earth, fornication, uncleanness, vile passions, evil lust, and unbridled desire, which is idolatry. On account of which things the wrath of God comes upon the sons of disobedience. In which ye also once walked when ye lived in these things. But now, put off, ye also, all these things, wrath, anger, malice, blasphemy, vile language out of your mouth. Do not lie to one another, having put off the old man with his deeds, and having put on the new, renewed into full knowledge according to the image of him that has created him; wherein there is not Greek and Jew, circumcision and uncircumcision, barbarian, Scythian, bondman, freeman; but Christ is everything, and in all. Put on therefore, as the elect of God, holy and beloved, bowels of compassion, kindness, lowliness, meekness, long-suffering; forbearing one another, and forgiving one another, if any should have a complaint against any; even as the Christ has forgiven you, so also do ye. And to all these add love, which is the bond of perfectness. And let the peace of Christ preside in your hearts, to which also ye have been called in one body, and be thankful.

Let the word of the Christ dwell in you richly, in all wisdom teaching and admonishing one another, in psalms, hymns, spiritual songs, singing with grace in your hearts to God. And everything, whatever ye may do in word or in deed, do all things in the name of the Lord Jesus, giving thanks to God the Father by him.

BORN INTO THE FAMILY OF GOD

As we continue considering together this subject of spiritual exercise in relation to our present life on earth, we would like to look next at church life. The people of the world may have a religious life—and some of them can be quite religious—but they cannot experience church life or body life. Only those who are born again into the family of God can enjoy church or body life. After we have been saved we soon discover that salvation not only has its personal and individual side, it also includes our having been born into the family of God. So we must not forget that our being born again of God is not just for ourselves. Indeed, we ought to thank God for that! Yes, we cannot ignore the fact that our individual spirit is renewed by our having been born anew of God's Holy Spirit; yet, simultaneously with that experience we also are born into God's family. That is why we are told in Ephesians: "ye are ... of the household of God" (2:19). From the moment we believed in the Lord Jesus we became a member of a tremendously huge family by the new birth. It is truly a tremendous privilege in our belonging to the heavenly family: God is our Father, Christ is our Elder Brother, and we are brothers and sisters by virtue of all of us being brethren in the Lord.

The moment we were saved we began our experience of church life. Intuitively, we know within our hearts that we are not alone and that we are not to be independent of one another. Indeed, we soon realize that we have been born into a very large family and that it is a heavenly and spiritual one. Oftentimes we sense that the bond among brothers and sisters in the Lord is actually stronger than that within our natural family. A closeness is there because we Christian brethren share the same life, the same God and Father, and the same Lord Jesus. A bond is within us which cannot be broken. Is it not true that right after we were saved and we met another Christian, we sensed a special bonding with each other? It is something which has supernaturally been birthed within us.

The Lord Jesus declared: "I will build my church upon this rock and the gates of hades shall not prevail against it" (see Matthew 16:18b). The Greek word translated here as church is *ecclesia*. Strictly speaking, this English word church is not a correct translation of *ecclesia*. If we translate this Greek word according to its true meaning it would be "assembly" or "the called-out-and-gathered-together-ones"; that is to say, the church consists of those who have been called out of this world and are assembled or gathered together. The so-called church life is therefore basically assembly life. We need to assemble or gather together for the purpose of exhorting and encouraging one another in the Lord. Now *that* is what *ecclesia* is all about.

In Matthew 18:20 we read what the Lord Jesus declared on this matter: "Where two or three are gathered together in my name, there am I in the midst of them." That is exactly what the *ecclesia* of God signifies—two, three, or more people gathered together. But it is not merely several or more people gathered together, since there can be two or three persons who are gathered together on merely a social basis. No, this of which we are here speaking is a being gathered together in the name of the Lord Jesus. Whenever two or three place themselves under the headship of Christ, acknowledging Him as the Head, then the Lord will be in the midst of them. This, in the true Christian sense, is what assembling together means.

THE GATHERING OF THE EARLY CHURCH

We learn from the early chapters in the book of Acts that as soon as the one hundred and twenty Christian brethren assembled in "the upper room" at Jerusalem were baptized in the Holy Spirit into one body, three thousand new brethren were added to them. And Acts 2:42 tells us that "they persevered [or, continued] in the teaching and fellowship of the apostles, in breaking of bread and prayers." In those early days of the church those who had believed in the Lord Jesus assembled every day. It so happened that many, if not most, of them had come to Jerusalem from other parts of the world to attend the Jewish Passover, but when they were saved there, they did not return home but remained in Jerusalem. So they had plenty of time on their hands. Every day they would gather together in the name of the Lord at the Porch or Colonnade of Solomon, since that was a place spacious enough to accommodate them (Acts 5:12b). They broke bread—that is, they observed the Lord's Supper or Table— from house to house every day, thanking and remembering the Lord. That is the way they lived in those early days of the church. Obviously, they could not continue in that manner forever because persecution eventually arose and thus they were dispersed elsewhere in Israel and to other lands.

Nevertheless, wherever they ended up being they took the gospel with them and continued to meet together.

So we see that in the early church assembling together unto the Lord became their life. To put it another way, it would appear as though church life or the gathering together in the name of the Lord replaced their former social life. That had now become their real life together. In the case of Saul of Tarsus who became Paul the Lord's disciple, as soon as he was saved, he gathered together with the other disciples in the city of Damascus. He went in and out among them and testified concerning the Lord (Acts 9:19-22). Then, he went to Jerusalem where he sought to have fellowship with the brothers and sisters there; but they were afraid of him because of his past history of having persecuted many of the Christians before he himself believed in Christ. Finally, brother Barnabas, the "son of consolation and encouragement," befriended Paul and brought him to the apostles (Acts 4:36, 9:26-27).

It was the habit of these early believers to gather together to encourage one another in the Lord. It became the central part of their very existence. Generally speaking, an earthly family stays together. Yet there is something more about life in the family of God than the life as members of one's natural family. Though a natural family's members share the same blood, each of them is still an individual. And though it is true that they do come together, there is a bonding together in God's family which is even closer than that; and this is because the church—the family of God—is also the body of Christ.

ONE HEAD—ONE BODY

Not only are we members of God's family, we also are members of one body, and Christ is the Head. There is but one Head and one body. There cannot be one Head with many bodies or one body with many heads. There is only one Head and one body (Ephesians 4:4a, 15b; Colossians 3:15b). As members of this one body we are bonded closer together than even the members of the same earthly family. Just as the members in our physical body are very close and cannot be separated, even so, as members of the one body in Christ we are united together and cannot be divided. There is such a closeness that no member can be separated. Such is the spiritual reality of church life.

Church life, *outwardly*, is the assembling together of the believers in Christ. On the other hand, church life, *inwardly*, is the fellowship among the members of the body of Christ. Take, for example, our physical body. All its members are in continual relationship with one another, and every member of our body is also in close connection with the head. If the head were to be cut off, the body would become dead. All of my body's members are connected to my body's head by means of my body's blood and nervous systems. Similarly, all the members of my body are so related to one another that they flow one to another and help one another to complete a given task. If, for instance, I see an object in front of me and I wish to take hold of it, my feet and hands have to help. Every member of my physical body is coordinated together as one under my body's head. Hence, from this, we who are members of the body of Christ can see how close we members truly are one to another.

We may sometimes think that church life is simply a matter of being assembled together—that is to say, when we are assembled together, we have church life; and by the same token, if we do not assemble together, then we do not have church life. In one sense, that is true, but there is something deeper involved in all this than that. Assembling together is definitely a must for God's people, for I have seen what happens to those who in their personal individual life love the Lord very much but who—when for whatever reason, they became isolated—gradually, suffered the loss of their faith. The believer in Christ cannot stand in his Christian walk by himself—just he and the Lord. There must be the assembling together of the saints. We need not only the Lord, we need one another as well.

WE NEED ONE ANOTHER

I well remember hearing that when brother Watchman Nee went to England he visited George Cutting. He was the one who wrote the well-known little booklet, "Safety, Certainty, and Enjoyment." When I was young, that small publication had a distribution that was second only to the Bible among all published Christian literature. It has been used by God to save many people. Now at the time of brother Nee's visit, George Cutting was quite old, his mind sometimes became confused, and he would doze off much of the time. On the day of his visit brother Nee sat by brother Cutting's bedside waiting for him to wake up. And when he finally did awaken, he said to brother Nee: "The Lord cannot do without me and I cannot do without Him." Then he would fall asleep once again.

How true it is that I cannot do without Christ and He cannot do without me. Have you ever thought of that? Obviously none of us can do without Christ, but let us contemplate for a moment the other half of that statement: that Christ cannot do without you and me. He is the Head, and each of us is a member of His body. If that member were to be cut off, there would be something terribly missing. Our relationship with the Lord is such that we cannot do without Christ; but thank God, He cannot do without us.

Now when brother Nee returned to China from England, he took this statement of brother Cutting's somewhat further by saying that beyond the vertical implications of it he wanted to apply it to our church life on the horizontal level as well. By which he meant: you cannot do without me and I cannot do without you. Not only is there our relationship with the Lord, there is likewise our relationship with one another. No brother or sister can do without other brothers and sisters. We all need one another. And because of that, how important it is for us to have an assembly life!

FORSAKE NOT ASSEMBLING TOGETHER

In Hebrews 10:25 we are exhorted as follows: "Not forsaking the assembling of ourselves together, as the custom is with some; but encouraging one another, and by so much the more as ye see the day drawing near." It is unfortunate but very true that among God's people there are some who have developed the habit of not assembling together. They even despise the practice and object: "I can be as spiritual by myself as when I am assembling together. If I am by myself I can be free from problems, for if I meet with brothers and sisters, I will have problems." Consequently, for such people it becomes a habit not to assemble with others and their conscience eventually does not bother them about this particular disobedience anymore. When you first fail to assemble with other brethren your conscience will tell you that that is not the right thing to do. But if you continue not assembling, it will develop into a habit, and your conscience will ultimately fall silent. How spiritually dangerous this will be to one's Christian life. Let none of us therefore forsake the assembling of ourselves with the saints as has become the custom of some.

THE DAY OF CHRIST'S RETURN IS DRAWING NEAR

Another reason for assembling with other Christian brethren is because—as this same verse in Hebrews tells us— the day is drawing near when the Lord shall return; and because we do not know when that day will be, we all need to be prepared, encouraged, and protected. In this regard, I recall a story about Evan Roberts, who was the person used greatly by God in starting and furthering the Welsh Revival of 1904-1905. As a young man he was a miner, and he loved the Lord so much that he would never miss any church meeting. And the reason he gave for his faithful attendance was this: "If I miss a meeting and the Lord should pour out His Spirit at that meeting, what a loss it would be for me." Throughout his occupation as a miner, he attended every meeting of the church. And one day, while he was praying with other brothers and sisters, he offered up a simple but meaningful prayer which launched the revival. As he was kneeling before the Lord he prayed: "Bend the church and save the world."

Knowing brother Roberts' heart very well, the Lord used him mightily in that revival; for let it be noted that there were great positive effects from the revival.

For instance, the miners back then used donkeys to carry the loads from the mine, and prior to the outbreak of the revival the men would curse those donkeys terribly. But because so many miners were saved in the revival, they did not curse those animals anymore. Interestingly enough, when they now spoke to the donkeys, the latter were confused because they no longer understood the miners' gentler words! Other positive effects of the revival should be noted as well: one example was the fact that the judges would sit around with white gloves on because they had no cases to judge; and a second example was that even the liquor stores had to close down. It was a great revival, and in various ways it impacted for good much of the world. In fact, the revival's effect was still being felt long afterwards. For in 1970 I was invited to New Zealand to minister God's word by a group of believers which had been the result of the Welsh Revival. But let us be reminded that all this began with a young brother who had determined in his heart to never miss a church meeting.

Let us consider the story of another brother who was determined to be with the saints as often as possible. I knew a Christian brother in China who happened to be a banker. He not only was a banker, he also—before he became a Christian—was one of China's foremost fortune tellers. He earned more money by telling fortunes than by being the president of his bank! But one day the Lord saved him. After he was saved, he tried to attend all the various meetings of the church throughout every week. He placed a Bible on his bank office desk, and whenever people came to his office, he would use the opportunity to share the gospel with them. As a prominent banker in China he would be invited out and entertained every evening. Upon his being saved, however, he made it clear that whenever the church had a meeting he would not attend any entertainment. So people began to ask him: "Other Christians go to church only on Sundays. Why is it that during the week you go to church so often?" He would reply as follows: "Yes, according to Christians, Sunday is worship day, but what is Monday? We still must worship. It is Worship Day One, then comes Worship Day Two, Worship Day Three, Worship Day Four, Worship Day Five, and Worship Day Six. Therefore, every day we Christians ought to gather for worship together, if at all possible." Does that sound reasonable to you? To me, that is truly living the church life.

Let us not neglect or forsake the assembling of ourselves with the saints. It is an absolute necessity. We not only need the encouragement, we also need the warning and discipline as the day of Christ's return draws nearer and nearer. Yet this is only the outward side of church life. There is the inward side as well, which is fellowship. And this we must next inquire into.

FELLOWSHIP VS. FRIENDSHIP

What is fellowship? The very word signifies a sharing together—sharing what we all have. The Son fellowships with the Father, and the Father fellowships with the Son. They share everything with each other. All which the Father has is given to the Son. All which the Son has is offered up to the Father. And by the grace of God this divine fellowship has been extended to us: we believers have all been called into the fellowship of God's Son Jesus Christ (I Corinthians 1:9; cf. also with I John 1:3). What a fellowship that is! We are to share, yet not only with God the Father and His Son the Lord Jesus, we are to share also with one another what God has given us. This fellowship is not limited to our being assembled together in one place but is so wide and broad that throughout our Christian life we are in fellowship with one another no matter where we may be.

It seems to me that the Scriptures emphasize fellowship among God's people rather than friendship. In the world friendship is of great importance because we humans are social beings. Friendship with others is an interaction which is a natural inclination of mankind. Nevertheless, in my search into the Scriptures I have discovered that they do not emphasize friendship; they instead emphasize fellowship. What is the difference between these two?

Well, how do you strike up a friendship in the world? Who do you consider as your friends? Often people become friends because they discover they have the same temperament. Or they have the same likes and dislikes, the same interests. Or it may be that they have the same or similar social or cultural background, and that creates a kind of closeness between them and thus a friendship develops. People find comfort and strength in such friendships, and that is understandably a very natural development. Friendship, as it is conceived of today, is actually based upon ourselves and our natural life, and our temperament and all the other things just now mentioned are part of that. We are brought up in our natural environment, and all these various traits or characteristics seem to determine our friendships.

However, fellowship is a relationship whose foundation is on a higher plane. It is not based upon the manifested similarities of our natural soul-lives; rather, fellowship is based upon the same life we all have and share in Christ Jesus, which is a relationship that is heavenly and spiritual. That is where the difference lies between these two kinds of interaction.

It seems as though as soon as we believe in the Lord Jesus God begins, as it were, to raise our relational interaction with others to a higher level—from friendship to fellowship. Let me use a very practical example from life that is familiar to most, if not all, believers. Before you were saved you naturally had some close friends. I certainly did. After you were saved, however, you most likely went through the experience of the Lord leading you to develop another kind of relationship; that is to say, He began nudging you towards those who are of the same faith as yours. You began to grow closer to those of like faith with you. You were able to share with others and they with you without restraint. You and they could comfort, strengthen, and open up to one another.

Moreover, you probably noticed that after you believed in the Lord Jesus, He gradually began changing your friends. It definitely happened to me. But we should understand that that does not necessarily mean we should terminate our former friends: the kind of friendship we had before with those who were unbelievers will still be there; but we may have found that if that friendship did not increase, it soon died away. And that is what happened in my case. Those close friends of mine continued to be friends, but we ceased to build up the friendship, and it gradually disappeared. I believe such experience is sovereignly arranged by the Lord.

What He is doing is gradually delivering us from befriending the world and moving us into the spiritual fellowship which is in Christ Jesus.

We all need fellowship. We all need one another. We need to pray for one another. We need to bear the burdens of one another. We need to stand together with one another. We even need to warn one another in the Lord. That is what true Christian fellowship gives us and does for us. The Bible tells us that through fellowship we have the joy of the Lord (I John 1:3-4). If we do not have that joy, then it reveals that there is something missing in our fellowship. Church life should replace our social life but not to the extent of completely terminating the social life. However, according to Biblical principle we come to realize that it is the will of God that we should move onto higher ground. We *have* to live on a higher plane. In other words, we must live by the life of Christ—not by our natural life. If we continue to live by the latter life, sooner or later we shall realize we are no match for the world. Moreover, it will become clear that to befriend the world is to be at enmity with God (James 4:4).

Yes, we need to strengthen our assembly life, but we also need to cultivate the fellowship which we all have in Christ Jesus. When a person is truly saved, immediately he or she becomes conscious of their heavenly Father. Therefore, the Bible teaches us that the Holy Spirit witnesses to us in such a way that we cry out to God, "Abba, Father" (Romans 8:14-16). Yet we not only are conscious that we have a heavenly Father, at the same time we also are conscious that we have brothers and sisters: for when you and I meet another believer, we instantly sense a bond between that one and ourselves. And this body consciousness needs to be cultivated continually. How, though, can our body consciousness be cultivated? The answer is to be found in the book of Romans.

CONSECRATION AND BODY CONSCIOUSNESS

Romans 12:1 says: "I beseech you therefore, brethren, by the compassions [mercies] of God, to present your bodies a living sacrifice, holy, acceptable to God, which is your intelligent service [that is, it is your reasonable worship]." Here we are exhorted to present or consecrate our bodies as a living sacrifice. The word bodies here is cast in plural number because each one of us believers has his or her own body, and this body of ours actually represents the entire being of each one of us, because further on in Romans 12 Paul speaks of numerous aspects of our daily living. Indeed, we live by this individual body of ours which embraces our entire being. Therefore, how important it is to offer up to God our bodies as a living sacrifice! And when we do, something happens in our minds as the Holy Spirit begins to renew them (12:2). We not only begin to *see* things differently, we also commence *evaluating* things differently.

What accounts for this difference? Verse 5 tells us: "We, being many, are one body in Christ." In other words, body consciousness will be nurtured, increased and cultivated by the consecration of one's whole being. The more you consecrate yourself to the Lord, the more your mind will be open to discern the importance of the body of Christ and to behold the wonder of being a member in that body. You will become more thankful and more responsible in being a member. Consecration is therefore not only to be a daily act, it is also to be an increasing, continual experience in your walk before God. And the more you consecrate yourself to the Lord, the more you shall become conscious of the Head, and the body shall become more and more real to you.

Assembling together with brothers and sisters is actually a necessary habit in the Christian's life. After you are saved you begin to realize that there are many *old* habits you have to drop. We are told in Colossians 3 to take off the old man and put on the new man (vv. 9-10a): so, there are new habits which need to be formed, and one of these new habits is that of your assembling together with other brethren in Christ. The more you assemble together with others the more you shall feel the need to assemble. On the other hand, the more you neglect being gathered together with the saints the more it will become the habit of *not* gathering together.

SPIRITUAL EXERCISE NEEDED IN FORMING THE HABIT OF ASSEMBLING

Gathering together is a habit which needs to be formed, and to form this habit you will need to exercise your spirit continually. Frequently you may feel tired and wish to stay home; so you may say to yourself: "Why should I go to the church meeting? Is it not enough that I go on Sunday? Why, then, should I attend the weekly prayer gathering?" Yet by staying away you will not know what you shall be missing. Hence, you may in fact be tired, but if by the grace of God you can overcome such tiredness and gather yourself with the saints, you shall find your spirit being strengthened and you will grow in the Lord. It requires the exercising of your spirit so that you may be able to really enter into all the fullness of the Lord's church and of His body life. Do not ever allow to be formed in your life the habit of forsaking the assembling of yourself with the saints. Do not ever miss out on the experience of body consciousness. Even when you are doing something by yourself in physical isolation, bear in mind that you are not alone. Not only is the Lord there, the body of Christ also is there. Whatever you do or wherever you may go, it shall affect the body and affect the Head. This is a practical recognition which we all need to cultivate increasingly as we go forward in the Lord.

PRINCIPLES OF CHURCH OR BODY LIFE

Headship

There are a few principles of church life which need to be observed diligently by all. The first one to be observed is that of the headship of Christ. If we read Colossians 2:19 in a positive way by removing the negative word not, then this first church-life principle we are to follow is: "Holding fast the head, from whom all the body, ministered to and united together by the joints and bands, increases with the increase of God."

How can we live the body or church life? Each of us must hold fast to the Head of the body, who is Christ the Lord. By that it means that everyone needs to remove himself as his head and let Christ be his head. Yet for this to occur it truly needs spiritual exercise. Naturally speaking, we all want to be head. Even the disciples of the Lord Jesus often argued among themselves as to who was the greatest. Furthermore, towards the end of Jesus' life John and James had their mother attempt to obtain from the Lord the position for them of being seated at His right and left side in His coming

238

kingdom (Matthew 20:20 ff.). That is the natural inclination of all of us, is it not? Thank God, though, we who possess the name of Christ are not to live by our natural life but by a supernatural life—even the life of Christ which is in all of us who have believed. By engaging in spiritual exercise and through the consecration of our entire being we develop a willingness in our renewed minds to hand over *our* headship and let Christ be our head. Only when we hold fast to the Head—that is to say, when we as the members of the body of Christ maintain connection with Him as Head—then quite naturally we will be joined together and can work together because it is the Head who directs. And in his Ephesian letter Paul expressed a similar sentiment when he wrote: [God] gave him [Christ] to be head over all things to the assembly, which is his body, the fulness of him who fills all in all" (1:22-23).

Keep the Unity of the Spirit

Another principle in living out the body life is for the saints of God to diligently keep the unity of the Spirit in the uniting bond of peace (Ephesians 4:3). We who have believed in Jesus are called to be the body of Christ. We need to diligently maintain, that is, make every effort to keep, the unity of the Spirit, and this is a part of the seven "ones" mentioned in the very next verses of this passage in Ephesians 4: "There is one body and one Spirit, as ye have been also called in one hope of your calling; one Lord, one faith, one baptism; one God and Father of all, who is over all, and through all, and in us all" (vv. 4-6).

We find here the three "ones" of the Spirit—first and second, the one body and the one Spirit: that is, it is the one

Spirit in whom we have been baptized into one body; and third, there is the one hope of our calling as the body of Christ: when the *body* of Christ is matured, it will become the *bride* of Christ, and that is the work of the Holy Spirit who is preparing us members to be a grown and matured body so that when Christ comes again He can take us as His bride.

Then we find here the three "ones" in God the Son— "one Lord, one faith, one baptism." We have but one Lord— who is Jesus Christ. There is also but one faith—we believe Jesus is the Christ, the Son of the Living God, and that is the fundamental faith for all of us who have believed. And there is likewise but one baptism—we are not baptized to Paul nor to Peter nor to anyone else but baptized into Christ (cf. I Corinthians 1:12-13).

And, finally, we find here the "one God and Father of all, who is over all, and through all, and in us all." We all have but one Father.

There are these seven "ones" in the triune God of Father, Son, and Holy Spirit. The unity of the Spirit is our oneness in God, and that is shared by every believer. That is something most precious which we need to keep diligently. We find too often in church history and in our lives today the sad fact of God's people being divided because of, and on the basis of, different teachings and different experiences. We need to rise above these differences in understanding and make every effort to maintain the unity of the Spirit and to continue to fellowship with one another. And as we continue to fellowship, what will be the result? Verse 13 of Ephesians 4 describes it for us: "Until we all arrive at the unity of the faith and of the knowledge of the Son of God, at the full-grown man, at the measure of the stature of the fulness of the Christ."

There is no possibility of arriving at the unity of the faith and of the knowledge of the Son of God if we do not diligently keep the unity of the Spirit, and do so in the uniting bond of peace. However, if we continue fellowshiping with one another, gradually we will all come to the same faith. In other words, our individual understanding of the word of God will, all together, gradually become one. As we continue to share with one another, our experience of the Son of God will likewise become one. Such spiritual exercise will be the way for all of God's people together to arrive at the unity of the faith and of the knowledge of the Son of God.

The Universal Priesthood of Believers

A further principle of body life to be upheld and observed is the recognition and reality of the universal priesthood of believers. From I Peter 2:5 and 9 we learn that we Christians are a holy priesthood—that is to say, every believer in Christ is a priest. We may not have the name or title but we are to bear the reality. Being priests simply means we live for God and serve Him. Moreover, according to Ephesians 4, to every one of God's people there has been given by God both grace and gifts (vv. 7ff.). Grace has been equally dispensed to all God's children but gifts have not. We all receive differing gifts, and we all share in the grace of God with one another. What *grace* God has given you and me is not meant merely to make you and me spiritual individuals but has been granted also for the benefit of the whole body of Christ. What *gift* God may have given you and me is likewise for the whole body. We are all priests and we are to exercise our priesthood, taking up our responsibilities in the church. We serve in whatever capacity or according to whatever ability God has given us. Yet not only are we to serve, we also are to receive from the other members of the body of Christ. In other words, it is to be a mutual sharing with one another of the grace and gifts of God. If all of us do that, the body will grow (v. 15), and thus we as its members will not remain as babes, easily swayed by every wind of teaching (v. 14).

Love: the Perfect Bond of Unity

Finally, the most important principle to follow in cultivating body life is that of love. The Scriptures bear witness to this principle: "to all these add love, which is the bond of perfectness" (Colossians 3:14). Without manifesting love, we cannot live church life or love body life. 1 Corinthians 13, which is the Bible's love chapter, shows us that the first ingredient in the love of the body is a willingness to suffer long. The number one quality necessary in the body of Christ is for its members to suffer long—a willingness in them, for the sake of the body, to suffer greatly and to be kind towards one another (v. 4a). Love is the perfect bond of unity. In our fallen natural constitution we do not have that love: our love is limited, conditional, and natural: sooner or later our love will fail us. By contrast, God's love is everlasting, for it withstands and rises above all resistance and enables the believers to genuinely love one another, forgive one another, forget one another's faults, and to press on together.

Such church or body life as here presented today in our consideration together, and which ought to be an important part of our daily walk with the Lord, can only be attained through spiritual exercise. If we do not exercise our spirit, we will not be able to enter into the fullness of body life. May the Lord show us that there is a life experience for each one of us which is far better than we ever expected. Let us ask the Lord for His help in enabling us to enter into the reality of that life experience.

Chapter 12

SOCIAL LIFE

Ephesians 4:17-32—This I say therefore, and testify in the Lord, that ye should no longer walk as the rest of the nations [the unbelieving Gentiles] walk in the vanity of their mind, being darkened in understanding, estranged from the life of God by reason of the ignorance which is in them, by reason of the hardness of their hearts, who having cast off all feeling, have given themselves up to lasciviousness, to work all uncleanness with greedy unsatisfied lust. But ye have not thus learnt the Christ, if ye have heard him and been instructed in him according as the truth is in Jesus; namely your having put off according to the former conversation [conduct or behavior] the old man which corrupts itself according to the deceitful lusts; and being renewed in the spirit of your mind; and your having put on the new man, which according to God is created in truthful righteousness and holiness. Wherefore, having put off falsehood, speak truth every one with his neighbour, because we are members one of another. Be angry, and do not sin; let not the sun set upon your wrath, neither give room for the devil. Let the stealer steal no more, but rather let him toil, working what is honest with his hands, that he may have to distribute to him that has need. Let no corrupt word go out of your mouth, but if there be any good one for needful edification, that it may give grace to those that hear it. And do not grieve the Holy Spirit of

God, with which ye have been sealed for the day of redemption. Let all bitterness, and heat of passion, and wrath, and clamour, and injurious language, be removed from you, with all malice; and be to one another kind, compassionate, forgiving one another, so as God also in Christ has forgiven you.

Colossians 4:5-6—Walk in wisdom towards those without, redeeming opportunities. Let your word be always with grace, seasoned with salt, so as to know how ye ought to answer each one.

SOCIAL BEINGS

We know from the Scriptures that spiritual exercise is profitable for everything, having the promise of life in this age—that is, the present time—and in the time to come. Our focus in today's message, as it has been in the previous three messages, is on the promise of life for the time in which we presently live—day by day—and how through spiritual exercise we can receive eternal life. And our three previous discussions together have centered on three of four key areas of the believer's current life on the earth; namely, the Christian's personal life, family life, and church life. In today's message, however, we would like to focus our attention together on spiritual exercise in relation to the fourth key area of interest: the Christian's social life.

Let us take note of the fact that upon our being born into this world, we automatically become part of the world. We are not alone. For instance, we are part of our family, which includes both parents and siblings. And within our family there is a social life which develops through our interaction with each other. Then, as we grow older we go to school and thus we acquire schoolmates and friends with whom we interact. And when we graduate from either school or college, or both, and enter the general society, there are those colleagues, neighbors, and friends of ours with whom we likewise interact and relate. In other words, these interactive or relational activities of ours reflect the fact that we are social beings. We are constantly *with* people, *relating* with people, and *living* with people. And hence, it can be said that we human beings experience social life.

As was indicated earlier, when we believe in the Lord Jesus, something quite remarkable happens—we are born into the family of God. Consequently, there is added to our personal life, social life and family life another and important facet of interest, which is church life: we become members of the body of Christ. And if we live by the life of Christ within us, we shall see that His life fosters such an intimacy, closeness and oneness among the members of God's family that it will appear as though church life begins replacing our social life.

OUR LIFE BEFORE CHRIST CAME INTO US

Let me take a few moments to explain and lay some background. How did we live in this world before Christ came into our lives? Though every human being is different, there is one thing which is common to all of humanity: the life which all we humans receive from our parents is from our common fallen ancestor Adam. It is a fallen, sinful life; it is a life of the flesh and is therefore self-centered. That is the nature of the life we all receive from our parents. And hence, it is by that life that we live on earth. Whether it is in our personal life, family life or social life, we live by that natural life. However, according to the word of God, the social life we as unbelievers had formerly engaged in on earth is not the kind of life God wants us to engage in any longer.

We are told in verses 1 to 3 of Ephesians chapter 2: "And you, being dead in your offences and sins—in which ye once walked according to the age of this world." How did we formerly walk in the world? We did so according to the age or fashion of this world.

Worse than that, the apostle Paul went on to observe that we had walked in this world "according to the ruler of the authority of the air, the spirit who now works in the sons of disobedience." Outwardly, we walked in times past according to the fashion of the world, but actually we were walking according to the dictates of God's enemy, Satan, who is the one controlling the world. So even though in outward appearance we walked according to the current of the world, in reality we were walking according to Satan's command.

Those first three verses in Ephesians 2 reveal even more about ourselves and how we had walked on this earth formerly—"Among whom we also all once had our conversation [that is, our behavior or conduct] in the lusts of our flesh, doing what the flesh and the thoughts willed to do, and were children, by nature, of wrath, even as the rest." That was what we once were and did. That was how we had previously conducted ourselves in this world in our social life.

Again, in chapter 4 of Ephesians we read this: "Walk[ing] in the vanity of their mind" (v. 17b). Formerly, whatever we thought about, we engaged in it. We became "darkened in understanding" (v. 18a) and therefore we walked in darkness.

Then we read further in this verse 18: "Estranged from the life of God by reason of the ignorance which is in them, by reason of the hardness of their hearts"—in other words, we did not have the life of God in us. And finally, in verse 19, we have the sorry conclusion to it all: "who having cast off all feeling, have given themselves up to lasciviousness, to work all uncleanness with greedy unsatisfied lust." That was the way we behaved in the world before we received Christ's life.

OUR LIFE AFTER CHRIST COMES IN

As soon as we believed in the Lord Jesus, however, something drastic happened. In the same introductory passage for today from Ephesians 4 we are also told this: "But ye have not thus learnt the Christ" (v. 20). When we have Christ Jesus in us, a radical change occurs. This is because the life now within us is a different kind: it is no longer the life of Adam but that of Christ: it is no longer earthly but heavenly: it is no longer fleshly but spiritual. Since we now have the life of Christ in us, how are we going to live in this world? Can we continue to live in this world as we did before? Are we to continue to live by our self-life—by the way we think, by the way we want, by our being self-centered? No! Upon our receiving the life of Christ within, our walk in this world should henceforth be drastically different.

Let us recall that when the children of Israel were slaves in Egypt, the Lord delivered them by the Pascal (Passover) lamb. God had commanded them to sprinkle the blood of the Passover lamb on the doorposts and lintels of their homes, to gather within their homes, and to eat the flesh of the lamb. Then they had to put their sandals on, gird themselves, and take hold of their staffs in preparation for fleeing Egypt. Accordingly, on that same night the children of Israel marched out of Egypt, and the Lord took them through the Red Sea so that they could not return. Formerly, the Israelites had belonged to Pharaoh and had served him as his slaves. Now, however, they had come out of Egypt and had been baptized, as it were, unto Moses (see Exodus chs. 12, 14).

In like manner, that is exactly what happened to us believers of a later day. When we believed in the Lord Jesus, it was not a matter of merely having our sins forgiven and having eternal death passed away from us. No, like those Jewish believers of old, we are not to remain any longer in Egypt—which in the Scriptures represents the world—but must march out of Egypt without delay, not waiting to do so one day, one month or one year later but doing so immediately and forever. Being saved from eternal death, we can no longer, spiritually speaking, remain in the world.

Then, too, in Colossians 1 we are told that "[God] has delivered us from the authority of darkness, and translated us into the kingdom of the Son of his love" (v. 13). Simultaneously in our being saved from sin and death we are also delivered from the world. God has translated us out of this world of darkness and has put us in the kingdom of His beloved Son. That is where we now belong.

That is why, when we believe in the Lord Jesus, we need to be baptized. Otherwise, some newly-saved believers may think along the following line: "Well, I am saved. I have the life of Christ in me now and have eternal life. Why, then, should I be baptized? The water will not cleanse me from my sins." This is the wrong attitude to take, for we have been commanded to be baptized (Acts 2:37-38, Matthew 28:19) because it is our responsive testimony to what God has done: He has transferred us from this worldly kingdom into that of Christ (Colossians 1:13). In baptism, therefore, we respond with faith by publicly testifying: "Yes, we are being baptized into Christ" (Romans 6:3a). We go down into and under the water to portray the fact that like our being buried in the waters of baptism the old man has been put to death and is buried out of sight (Romans 6:4a, 6a); and we also rise up out of the baptismal waters, demonstrating the fact of our having been resurrected unto newness of life in Christ Jesus (Romans 6:4b). Thus baptism portrays the fact of our having been brought into an entirely new and different realm: we have been transferred out of ourselves and the world into the life and kingdom of God's beloved Son. In short, upon our being saved, there is a total change of our position in terms of our relationship with the world.

FOUR ASPECTS OF THE WORLD

We call the lengthy prayer recorded in John 17 the high-priestly prayer of the Lord Jesus. He is found here praying for His own—those persons who are His. And in that prayer He mentioned four different aspects of the world.

The World System That Satan Organized

The first aspect of the world is found in verse 6: "I have manifested thy name to the men [Jesus' disciples] whom thou gavest me out of the world." In other words, in applying this passage to ourselves, we see that God has delivered us out of the world and given us to Christ. What does the phrase "out of the world" mean? Does it mean we are no longer here on earth? No, the Greek word translated as world here is *cosmos*. It signifies a system which Satan has organized. He has organized all the different facets or aspects of this world into one giant system. And with that system—which is the world as we know it today—God's enemy tries to oppose God and His purpose. But thank God that He has already delivered us out of this *cosmos* of darkness. Therefore, we are no longer a participant of this world system.

The World and All Who Dwell Therein

In verse 11 the Lord Jesus is recorded as praying: "I am no longer in the world [a reference to the fact He is soon leaving it], and these [His disciples] are in the world." Even though He has delivered us out of the world system, we who believe in the Lord Jesus are still in the world. What does the Greek word translated as world here mean? It simply signifies the earth and all whom God has created. This very thought is found in Psalm 24:1: "The earth is Jehovah's, and the fulness thereof; the world, and they that dwell therein." In Hebrew poetry the writers often employ repetition to reflect emphasis. Hence, the phrases "the earth ... and the fulness thereof" and "the world, and they that dwell therein" convey the same thought and meaning. So we learn from Jesus' prayer that the world has another facet or aspect about it— the earth and all those who dwell on the earth. Our relationship with the world in this aspect is that God's people today are still living on earth or in the world. We believers have not been raptured yet.

The Things of the World

According to Jesus' prayer, a third aspect of the world can be discerned in verse 14: "I have given them thy word, and the world has hated them, because they are not of the world, as I am not of the world." Having been delivered out of the *cosmos*—the world system—we are nonetheless still living in the world, and yet we are not of the world. Though we continue living on this earth and despite the fact Satan continues being the god or prince of this world system of his, nevertheless, we are not of the world even though in one sense we are still surrounded by the things of this world. In other words, we do not belong to this world. Regarding this aspect of the world, the Greek word for world employed here is defined by the things in it, as we learn from I John 2: "Love not the world, nor the things of the world. If any one love the world, the love of the Father is not in him; because all that is in the world, the lust of the flesh, and the lust of the eyes, and the pride of life, is not of the Father, but is of the world" (vv. 15-17). We who now have the life of Christ in us are not of the world. Yes, we are still in the world but we do not belong to it, for to befriend the world is to be at enmity towards God (James 4:4).

A Witness and Testimony to the World

Jesus' prayer makes reference to one final aspect concerning the world: "As thou hast sent me into the world, I also have sent them [His disciples] into the world" (v. 18). Yes, we have been delivered out of Satan's world system; yes, we are still living in the world; yes, we are not of the world; and, yes, we now also learn that we have been sent into the world just as God had sent Christ into the world. In other words, when we today go into the world, there is a purpose behind it. It is not because we want to be a friend of the world, for to do so would be contrary to God's will since any befriending of the world by us would mean we become His enemies; rather, it is because we want to testify to its people concerning the Lord Jesus.

When we believe in the Lord Jesus, our social life begins to undergo a dramatic change. Formerly, the world was our friend and it was our desire to befriend it. But after we are saved, a radical change begins to take place in our life as Christians. We continue to live in this world until the Lord should remove us from the world, and yet we do not belong to it. We will have nothing to do with it. Nevertheless, that does not mean we are to be anti-social—not at all! For though church life does take the place of our social life, it does not totally do so, since just as the Father sent His Son Jesus into the world to bear testimony to it, we too have been sent into the world for the same purpose: we must go out into the world and be a witness and give testimony concerning the Lord Jesus in order to rescue those who are still dead in sins and transgressions. This is what our position towards the world is now to be. Because God has given us such a position, what should be our response?

God has already transferred us out of this world. Can we therefore continue to live out our life in it in the same way as do the worldly people? Can we continue to desire after such a life? If we do, what will happen? In his epistle the apostle James tells us that if we befriend the world, then we become the enemy of God (4:4). In II Corinthians we are told that there is no communication or fellowship or sameness between those who are in the light and those who are in darkness, between those who have life and those who do not have life, nor between those who are in Christ and those who are not of Christ. There is no fellowship whatsoever between the two (see 6:14). This is a very basic understanding of what it means to live the Christian life. Therefore, if we really wish to follow the Lord, then bearing a witness and testimony to the world concerning Christ is the way we must proceed in our Christian walk in the world.

OVERCOMING THE WORLD BY THE WORD OF GOD

How can we overcome the world? The world and the things of this world are very tempting. In I John 2 the apostle John writes: "I have written to you, young men, because ye are strong, and the word of God abides [dwells] in you, and ye have overcome the wicked one" (v. 14).

The way to overcome the wicked one and this world is by the word of God. It tells us what the world really is, that it is a deception. The only way we can see through the enemy's deception is by the word of God. If we have God's word dwelling in our hearts, then we have the wisdom, the discernment, and even the power to overcome the world and the wicked one who controls it.

Let us consider the Lord Jesus when He was on the earth and see how He lived in the world and overcame it. Having come into this world, He shared in the same humanity with us, yet without sin; for He continually lived by the divine life within Him whose governing principle in all of life for Him was ever and always: "My Father's will." Jesus therefore did not live by His natural life; rather, He walked the way of self-denial, took up His cross daily, and followed God the Father. Such is the path we too must tread.

Now when the Lord Jesus was about thirty years old, He was baptized by John the Baptizer in the river Jordan. Then the Holy Spirit led him into the wilderness where He was tempted in three very substantive ways by the enemy. These three temptations recorded in the Gospels actually include or sum up all the temptations which can come to man. Satan used the things of this world—"the lust of the flesh, the lust of the eyes, and the pride of life"—with which to tempt Jesus. But with every temptation He overcame by the word of God. He did not try to argue with Satan nor reason with him. He simply quoted the relevant passages from the Scriptures which were already stored up in His heart. By the word of God He overcame.

The only way to overcome the world and the enemy is to store up God's word in our hearts. Sad to say, in our day many believers know positionally that the Lord has delivered them out of the world, but experientially they are like the Israelites of old. God had delivered them out of Egypt—out of the world—but later in the wilderness they were tested and were found wanting. For in their hearts they still longed for Egypt and desired after all the savory spices and foods which were to be enjoyed there (Numbers 11:4b-5). Because of their continual hankering after the world of Egypt, that entire Israelite generation died in the wilderness and was unable to inherit its inheritance in the Promised Land because of unbelief (Hebrews 3:15-19). Similarly, God's people today are in danger of the same outcome. God has delivered us out of the world, too, but if we still hanker after the world and the things of the world, we—like the children of Israel—may not be able to inherit our inheritance in Christ who is our Promised Land. God has promised us a kingdom and an unfailing, undefiled, and incorruptible inheritance reserved in heaven for those who believe (I Peter 1:3-4). Nevertheless, only those like Joshua and Caleb—who had a different spirit—are able to enter their Promised Land (Numbers 32:10-12, 14:21-24).

Upon our believing in the Lord Jesus there needs to be a drastic change in our social life. Some of God's people may react to such a challenge by declaring: "Are we to be that unsocial? Even those believers discussed by Paul in his first Corinthian letter enjoyed an earthly social life." Let us understand that in those olden days their social life was carried on in the temple of the idols. The best food would be there, and the best socializing experiences would take place in the temple. They wanted to engage in the unbelieving world's social life so much that they rationalized the problem away by saying: "We have the only true God, and these idols of the unbelievers are not gods. Therefore, we can go to their temple and eat the temple food because it really signifies nothing." But those believers among them who were weak in their conscience stumbled at the actions of those who reasoned this way. So the apostle Paul responded to the problem by writing: "If I eat meat, and even though it is lawful but causes my brother to stumble, I will not eat food which has been offered up to the temple gods. For that would not be love" (see I Corinthians 8). This desire of those rationalizing Corinthian believers is a very natural sentiment that can be found in the thinking of too many of God's people today, who continue to long after, or cling to, their current social life. We need to understand that God does not at all want to deprive us of a social life, since He as our Creator is very much aware that we are social beings. But He does want to replace it with body or church life, which is a far different experience and on a much higher plane because it is to be found in the realm of the Spirit of God. So far as the world is concerned, our only relationship with it is for us believers in Christ to be sent out into it for but one reason—which is, to be a witness for Christ and give redemptive testimony to the people still ensnared in Satan's world system.

BIBLICAL FRIENDSHIP

Now we said last time that for the Christian, friendship is replaced by fellowship because friendship is established and carried on on the basis of man's natural life whereas Christian fellowship is a relationship based on the spiritual life—the Christ-life—which is within those of us who have believed in the Lord. Having said that, however, we nonetheless find in the Scriptures that there is an exception to that general understanding. For there is a kind of friendship which we do indeed find in the Bible. Yet it is a different kind of friendship altogether, as the following examples from the Scriptures will make clear.

We read, first of all, that God called Abraham His friend (II Chronicles 20:7, Isaiah 41:8, James 2:23). Abraham was the friend of God with whom He freely conversed. God likewise treated Moses as a friend and talked to him as a friend (Exodus 33:11a). Then, too, when the Lord Jesus was on earth, He called His disciples His friends on several occasions. For instance, we read in Luke 12:4 that He said to them: "I say to you, my friends, Fear not those who kill the body and after this have no more that they can do." Again, we learn from John 15 that He called His disciples friends of His once more: "I call you no longer bondmen, for the bondman does not know what his master is doing; but I have called you friends, for all things which I have heard of My Father I have made known to you" (v. 15). Jesus often shared His heart with them. Strangely, He even called Judas His friend; for in Matthew 26 we are told that when Judas came with the armed group to seize and arrest the Lord, Jesus approached him and kissed him, saying, "My friend, for what purpose art thou come?" (v. 50a) On the other hand, when in his old age John the apostle wrote his short third epistle, he at one point said, "The friends here greet you, and greet each of our friends there by name" (see v. 14c).

We see, then, that there is indeed a friendship to be found in the Scriptures, but let us be very clear that it is not a friendship with the world—it is a much higher and far different type of friendship. In a non-derogatory sense, it is a kindly and gracious condescension shown by a higher person towards a lower one—as was exemplified when God condescended himself by taking Abraham and Moses to himself as His friends. In the same way, the Lord Jesus took His disciples to himself, calling them His friends and sharing His heart with them. In like manner, Jesus became a friend of sinners and tax collectors (Luke 7:34) and even called His enemies His friends (see again Matthew 26:50). Such behavior reveals to us the virtues of kindness, grace and love. And that kind of friendship is sanctioned in the Bible.

MANAGING AND APPORTIONING OUR TIME

Finally, let us not forget that as we live on this earth, we have a personal life which must be fulfilled. This is very important for us to mention once again and to expand somewhat further upon it. We cannot neglect our personal life and try to hide ourselves among the crowd. Yes, we do have obligations of family life, church life, and social life to fulfill. Yet these other aspects of life are quite demanding; indeed, it is as though they demand our whole time. Nevertheless, we only have twenty-four hours in a day. And of these twenty-four hours some are needed for rest and sleep. How, then, on the one hand are we going to live a balanced personal life as a Christian and on the other hand manage to deal effectively with all these other demands placed upon us?

Back when I was living in China, we believers had emphasized church life so much that we had meetings every night, and because of this we neglected our family life. That was a real problem for us Christians there in China, but when I came to this country I witnessed a reverse situation. Here in America many Christians were sacrificing their church life for the sake of family life. Family life is very demanding, especially here in this country: not only is school itself demanding, the many activities *after* school are likewise quite demanding. American parents feel very obliged to cater to their children, and thus the latter become more important than Christ; which means that family life is more important than church life. It is exactly opposite to what I experienced in China.

Now I will acknowledge that it is very difficult to apportion the right amount of time to handling the right and proper responsibilities in all these areas of our lives on earth. That is the reason the words in Colossians 4 are so relevant to this matter: we must "walk in wisdom." We need wisdom to properly walk before the world and redeem all the opportunities afforded us. We need wisdom in how best to redeem our time so that it may not be wasted but be used according to the word of God. In the book of James it is made clear that if we need wisdom, we are to pray with faith, believing, and God will give us the necessary wisdom to carry out our various obligations and responsibilities demanded of us (see 1:5-6a).

Consequently, every one of us must go to the Lord in prayer. No one else can decide for us. If we are going to live out our lives properly in all of these four areas of our present life on earth, then we must continually do so by that one Life only. We must ever and always live by the life of Christ—whether it be in our personal life, family life, church life, or social life—and not by our natural life. That is a must, for sure.

Yet, if that be true, how do we correctly apportion the time in a manner acceptable to God? For that to happen it requires wisdom which we do not have. In too many instances we end up being lopsided in dividing up our time. God alone has the wisdom, and we know that He is the source of all wisdom. Therefore, we need to pray and ask Him to show us how to use our personal time wisely in order to fulfill our responsibilities in all these areas of life. If we pray and believe, God will show each of us, for there is no fixed rule or standard equally applicable to everyone. I cannot tell you to set aside five hours for this or two hours for that or one hour for the other. No! No one can decide for you. As you grow in the Lord, what is required, time-wise, for this or for that obligation changes according to the need of the time and according to the leading of the Holy Spirit. It is not something legalistic or fixed but is something that is constantly changing. As you truly seek out God on this matter, He will show you how to apportion your time.

THE EXPERIENCE OF JESUS

In this connection, let us consider the experience of Jesus. We will recall that when He was twelve years old, he went to the temple in Jerusalem and became a son of the Law. He had begun sensing in His spirit that it was His responsibility to begin minding the things of His heavenly Father. When His parents—with whom Jesus had come to Jerusalem—departed back to Galilee, He remained behind in the temple. After anxiously searching three days for Him, the parents finally, and with great relief, found Him, for by that time they had become quite worried as to His whereabouts. And in response to their inquiry as to why He had remained behind, the Lord Jesus said to them: "Why were you worried? I am now a son of the Law, and therefore it is now the time that I must attend to my Father's business." Yet did He insist on lingering further in the temple and refuse to go home with His parents? On the contrary, Jesus sensed that it was now the time to leave. So He obeyed His earthly parents and went home with them (Luke 2:41-51).

In other words, Jesus knew exactly how to apportion the entire period of years afforded Him on the earth by His heavenly Father. As a minor, and even though in His heart He would rather have stayed in the temple, He sensed in His spirit that it was the right thing to do to return with His parents and resume obeying them. He then remained at home until He was some thirty years of age. Probably the reason for this was that His earthly "father" Joseph must have passed away early on, since he was much older than His mother Mary. As the so-called firstborn son in the family, Jesus had to assume responsibilities for His family's welfare. Most likely, therefore, as a trained carpenter He now supported the family. In Scripture He is called *the* carpenter— meaning that He had become a model carpenter. Were these years a waste of time? Not in the least, because while He was acting responsibly for His family, He was also serving God, for in either case it was to be the same servant-life consecrated to God His Father. Then, by the time Jesus had turned about thirty in age, His earthly brothers and sisters had all grown up; hence, His responsibility for the family was now over. Accordingly, He stepped out and devoted himself completely to ministry. Even so, when He was on the cross, He was still concerned in taking care of His mother. He committed her into the care of His disciple John (John 19:26-27).

Furthermore, we can discern from the Gospel accounts of His life that throughout Jesus' life on the earth, He knew how to use His time. Whenever His heavenly Father wanted Him to, Jesus would show compassion for the people. And because He was constantly preaching to them and serving them, He had almost no time to eat. And although He would urge His disciples to take time for some rest, He himself would rise up very early in the morning to go to the wilderness and pray. Jesus knew exactly how to divide up His time wisely in order that He might accomplish what His heavenly Father wanted Him to do. From all of this we come to realize that just as it was for Jesus, life for His followers is not static either, but is living.

LIVING OUT THE LIFE OF CHRIST BY SPIRITUAL EXERCISE

I do believe that if we lay our hearts before God, we shall know our position in the world—which is, to live by the life of Christ in us. And whenever necessary, we shall come to our Father and ask for wisdom, and He will faithfully show us what and how to do in all four of these key areas of our life on the earth. This is a matter of spiritual life—not of law but of grace. And if we conform ourselves to living this kind of life, we will have peace in our hearts.

Nevertheless, I would again remind ourselves that spiritual exercise is an absolute necessity. We will not be able to have the necessary wisdom unless we exercise our spirits and pray. We will not be able to experience any of these areas of life in the way God wants us to experience them unless we live by the life of Christ which is in us. Did not Paul emphatically declare, "For me to live is Christ"? That is, and can only be, the result of spiritual exercise. May the Lord help each one of us!

PART FOUR:
HOW SPIRITUAL EXERCISE AFFECTS
OUR FUTURE LIFE

Chapter 13

THE SECOND COMING OF THE LORD

I Timothy 4:7b-10—Exercise thyself unto piety [godliness]; for bodily exercise is profitable for a little, but piety [godliness] is profitable for everything, having promise of life, of the present one, and of that to come. The word is faithful and worthy of all acceptation; for, for this we labour and suffer reproach, because we hope in a living God, who is preserver of all men, specially of those that believe.

John 14:1-3—Let not your heart be troubled; ye believe on God, believe also on me. In my Father's house there are many abodes; were it not so, I had told you: for I go to prepare you a place; and if I go and shall prepare you a place, I am coming again and shall receive you to myself, that where I am ye also may be.

Philippians 2:12-13—So that, my beloved, even as ye have always obeyed, not as in my presence only, but now much rather in my absence, work out your own salvation with fear and trembling, for it is God who works in you both the willing and the working according to his good pleasure.

Luke 21:34-36—But take heed to yourselves lest possibly your hearts be laden with surfeiting and drinking and cares of life, and that day come upon you suddenly unawares; for as a snare shall it come upon all them that dwell upon the face of the whole earth.

Watch therefore, praying at every season, that ye may be accounted worthy to escape all these things which are about to come to pass, and to stand before the Son of man.

We have mentioned before that if we exercise our spirit, it will bring the promise of God's life to us in this present age. In other words, spiritual exercise will provide us with God's life as we live day by day during the present time. Do we enjoy the life of Christ which is within us? Are we living by the eternal life of Christ in us? Or are we still living by our fleshly natural life? That makes all the difference. With regard to our personal life, can we say with the apostle Paul: "For me to live is Christ"? Or must we acknowledge: "For me to live is myself"? We can readily see how different the consequences of these two kinds of life lived out currently on the earth will be.

It is the same issue with respect to our family life. Are we fulfilling our family life by ourselves? Or are we enjoying our family life by the life of Christ? And the same is true concerning our church life and social life. So from this we realize that spiritual exercise is profitable for everything, and it is to be profitable for us *now*. And my hope is that every brother and sister will be able to benefit from and enjoy such spiritual exercise.

HAVING ETERNITY ALWAYS IN VIEW

Spiritual exercise is not only profitable for today; it is profitable for the age to come. Our God is eternal, being the same yesterday, today, and forever (Hebrews 13:8). Indeed, everything He does is for eternity—not just for a short while here on earth. That is why we who are the Lord's do not live for the present time only; we live for eternity.

I always remember the saying of that great English Anglican open-air preacher, George Whitefield (1714-1770), who is considered to have been the greatest evangelist of the eighteenth century. He it was who helped spread the Great Awakening revival in Britain and especially in the British North American colonies. Said Whitefield: "I always preach with eternity in view." That meant for him that it was not only for his day; it was for eternity. I believe that like him every one of us should always have eternity in view because what we can see today is temporal whereas what we cannot see is eternal (II Corinthians 4:18). How, then, can we enjoy life in the age to come? For we know that the Lord Jesus is coming back to the earth soon. He *will* return, and we are, or ought to be, here waiting for His return.

THE LORD'S FIRST COMING

We are all aware of what happened to the Jewish people when the Lord Jesus came to the earth the first time. They, of course, had known of all the Old Testament prophecies: they knew that their Messiah was coming, and thus the whole nation of Israel was waiting for Him. They were under the rule of the Roman government at that time, and because of that, they were hoping and expecting that when the Messiah did come, the Roman yoke would be cast off and that their nation would become the greatest in the world. But, strangely, when their Messiah—in the Person of Jesus—did come, they were disappointed and even frightened by His presence, and ultimately they rejected Him.

But we must thank God that there were a few Jews at that time who were truly waiting for the Messiah to come and would recognize and acknowledge Him as such. We are told of the old couple Zachariah and Elizabeth, also Joseph and Mary, and Simeon and Anna (see Luke 1:5-6, 26-55, 67-79; 2:25-38).

God was to work mightily in the lives of Zachariah and Elizabeth. Meanwhile, however, He had not given them a son; and according to the Old Testament Scriptures, if a person loved the Lord he would be blessed with many sons and daughters and thus be surrounded by his children. It was also understood in the Old Testament time that if a person did not have a child, that one was considered to be under a curse. Despite all of that, however, this elderly couple still loved God even without having been blessed with a child. They probably prayed much about it, yet there was no answer except that of silence from God. But through this experience God brought them, as it were, to a higher understanding of His purpose. Most likely, they had even ceased to pray for a child of their own and simply prayed that God—in fulfillment of the relevant prophecy—would send His messenger and forerunner to prepare the way for the promised Messiah. And in the end God fulfilled that particular prophecy by giving this elderly couple a son who turned out to be that forerunner, even John the Baptizer.

On the other hand, Joseph and Mary were an engaged couple who had not yet entered into marriage. However, Mary conceived through the Holy Spirit—an event unheard of in human history. Under Jewish law, of course, she would have been considered an adulteress, and Joseph would have had the responsibility of casting the first stone at her to kill her. But Mary was obedient to the Lord and chose to give up her very life, if necessary, in order that the Messiah might come. The same heart attitude was true of Joseph. He was willing to take Mary despite a possible scandalous future so that God's purpose might be realized.

Then, too, there were Simeon and Anna. How they had longed to see the Messiah in their lifetime! They prayed and fasted through many years, and before their deaths they were rewarded by being granted the opportunity by God of seeing His salvation in the Person of that Child of Mary's.

THE LORD'S SECOND COMING

These few had been waiting for the Messiah to come, and because of their faithful expectant waiting, it would seem as though the Messiah came in direct answer to *their* prayers. So as we consider the second coming of the Lord, and surely He is coming soon, it would appear as though every believer in Christ is waiting for Him to return. But are we all truly waiting for Him? Or do many of us harbor the hidden notion that if He delays, then we shall have more time to get ready? Are many of us afraid of His return? Or are we truly looking forward to it—having been prepared, made ready, and by our conduct of life hastening His coming? This latter circumstance constitutes a great, great difference.

The soon coming of the Lord Jesus is a fact. Though its realization still lies in the future, we who believe in Him know it to be a fact because He himself promised us. And near the very end of the book of Revelation we find the resurrected and ascended Lord's emphatic declaration: "Surely I come quickly" (22:20a). But the question to be asked of each of us is: When He does come, will we be able to enjoy that event and the kingdom life the Lord will be bringing with Him? Let us recall again the words of I Timothy that if we exercise ourselves unto godliness we will have the promise of life in the age to come. Therefore, we want to specifically consider today how spiritual exercise can prepare us for the coming back of the Lord to the earth and the establishment of His kingdom.

WHY IS CHRIST COMING AGAIN?

The first point to be addressed in our discussion together on this subject is this: Did not Christ finish the work He came to do during His first coming?—why, then, should He need to come again? Did Jesus not declare from the cross: "It is finished"?—meaning that His mission was accomplished, that what He came to do has already been finished and fulfilled (John 19:30). If, therefore, it is finished, why should it be necessary for Him to come again? We are told that Jesus was resurrected and has ascended back to heaven where He is now seated at the right hand of the throne of God waiting for His enemies to be made His footstool (Hebrews 10:12-13, 12:26; Psalm 110:1; I Corinthians 15:25). Now we realize that a person engaged in some task does not sit down until he has finished the work at hand. So that the fact of Jesus being now seated in heaven demonstrates that He had indeed finished the work of redemption during His first coming. And there is nothing to be added to it. If that be the case, then, once again, it needs to be asked: Why should He come again?

Moreover, is the Lord Jesus resting in heaven, even perhaps dozing off and having nothing to do because everything has been done? Not so; for we know from the word of God that the Lord Jesus, after He ascended back into heaven, was anointed by the Father and made High Priest for us. Furthermore, the Bible also states that Jesus ever lives to make intercession for us, and that He is able to save to the uttermost those who approach Him by faith. Thus we know that the Lord Jesus is very, very busy in heaven in His having undertaken another and different kind of ministry on our behalf. He is there in heaven praying and interceding for us (Hebrews 5:5-6, 9-10; 6:19-20; 7:24-25). And as He intercedes for us, the Holy Spirit, whom He sent to dwell in us, commences to do His transforming work in us.

CHRIST OUR HIGH PRIEST AND THE INDWELLING HOLY SPIRIT

When the Lord Jesus first came to the earth, He was the Apostle (that is, the sent One of God) who had come to accomplish a mission—the work of salvation. But then He ascended back to heaven, and there He is our High Priest. He is praying for us that all He had done and finished on Calvary's cross would become experience and reality for each one of us.

Now what He accomplished at Calvary is an objective truth. It will never change but is forever. Yet how can this objective truth of what the Lord Jesus accomplished on the cross become our daily, personal, and even corporate, experience? Well, that is precisely the work He is engaged in doing today. As our High Priest He is praying for us, and as He prays for us, the indwelling Holy Spirit in us begins to work to make that *objective truth* become our *subjective experience*. And it is as the Holy Spirit works in us to make what Christ accomplished on the cross two thousand years ago a reality in our life, that that is the time when our spirit must cooperate with the Holy Spirit—that that is the time for us to engage in spiritual exercise, because if we fail to do so even as the Holy Spirit is working in us, then we will neglect it: we will not listen to His still small voice within us nor will we walk in the light with which He has enlightened us. Though by our so doing we will grieve Him, nevertheless, thank God that the Spirit will never leave us nor forsake us (Hebrews 13:5b) but will continue to work in us despite our being rebellious in not listening, in not being obedient, and thus not cooperating with Him. If all that be true of us, then what Christ completely finished at Calvary two thousand years ago will not become our personal experience.

There was nothing incomplete or defective in what Christ objectively accomplished on the cross—it is an eternal fact and shall never change; but whether it becomes our subjective experience or not is our responsibility. The Holy Spirit who dwells in our spirit is ever so faithful: He is there to show us Christ: He is there to bring Christ into our life: He is there to remove any hindrance: He is there to deal with our old nature: and He will never fail in working to bring all this about in our lives. But the question is: Will we continually respond to the Holy Spirit's touch upon our conscience, our intuition, our worship and communion? Now if *that* becomes our ongoing experience, then we shall be prepared for the coming again of the Lord and the setting up of His kingdom on earth.

"THE SPIRIT OF PROPHECY IS THE TESTIMONY OF JESUS"

I realize that the coming of the Lord is a very popular subject these days. People like to hear about the events which are to happen before the coming of the Lord. We are all very curious regarding the future, and we try to satisfy our curiosity by trying to learn as much as we can with respect to what the coming events must be that are to precede the coming again of the Lord. However, in the book of Revelation we are told that "the spirit of prophecy is the testimony of Jesus" (19:10). If we look at prophecy merely for the purpose of searching out future events, we are simply looking at the *letter* of prophecy; yet God's purpose in giving us prophecy is not for satisfying our curiosity but for helping us to be spiritually prepared for the return of Christ. That is why we have been given to understand that the *spirit* of prophecy is the testimony of Jesus. And because I know that all of us believe that Christ is indeed coming back, I will therefore not approach this subject of the coming of the Lord from the prophetic point of view; rather, I prefer to approach this topic of the coming of the Lord from the very practical standpoint of our being prepared for it.

THE LORD IS PREPARING A PLACE FOR US

How can we practically prepare ourselves for the return coming of the Lord as we wait for it to come to pass? We will recall from John's Gospel chapter 13 that Jesus had gathered with His twelve disciples for the observance of their last Passover feast together. During that occasion the Lord had shared with them that He would be leaving them, that He would be betrayed, persecuted, and would die. Because of this news, the disciples were very sorrowful. They had followed the Lord for some three years, and He had taken care of them. He had been their guardian, protector, provider—He had become everything for them. But Jesus was now going to leave them, so they assumed that they would be left as orphans. No wonder they were quite sorrowful. I believe had we been there, we too would have been sorrowful, and for the same reason. The Lord Jesus therefore tried to comfort His saddened followers. He said to them: "Let not your heart be troubled; ye believe on God, believe also on me. In my Father's house there are many abodes; were it not so, I [would have] told you: for I go to prepare you a place" (John 14:1-2).

From these words of comfort we learn that the reason the Lord Jesus would be going back to heaven was to prepare a place in His Father's house for us, and after making such preparation, added Jesus, "I will return to earth to gather you up so that you can be with Me" (v. 3). That clearly tells us why the Lord Jesus is coming back a second time. Hence, I do not intend speaking here about the Lord's coming back as being due to the world's chaotic situation or because of the restoration of the Jewish nation. No, the reason the Lord must return is because of us. He went to prepare a place for us in His Father's house, and then He will come back and receive us to himself.

Now the conventional, ordinary, common interpretation of what the Father's house refers to is heaven. Many of God's people express this interpretation this way: "One day we will go to heaven. That is what the Father's house means; so to us heaven is a place. There is the street of gold for us to walk upon, etc., and thus it will be such a wonderful place to live." Yet if we know the character and tenor of John's writings, we shall realize that he is not interested in anything physical. He is instead always interested in the spiritual reality of such things.

"MY FATHER'S HOUSE"

So what is the meaning of "My Father's house"? We read in Isaiah that the Lord declared: "Heaven is My throne, and the earth is My footstool. Where is the house that you are building for Me, the place for Me to rest?" (see 66:1) From this we learn that in one sense heaven and earth are God's office.

But God also said here: "Where is My home? Where is My house you are building for Me? Where is the place where I can rest?" Ever since God began His creation work He had had in mind a house for himself. God does everything according to His will, and when He created heaven and earth and man, He had in mind a house. He wanted to dwell with man who himself would become His house. And elsewhere in the Old Testament we learn that after God had delivered the children of Israel out of Egypt and brought them to Mount Sinai He began to reveal His mind to them as to why He had brought them out: "I want you to be My people. I want to dwell among you. So you must make a sacred tent for Me so I can live with you" (Exodus 19:3-6, 25:8-9). Thus there came into being the tabernacle. During the Israelites' travels God dwelt in the tabernacle because they were not holy enough in themselves for Him to dwell in, and hence, He had to have the tabernacle established as His *temporary* dwelling place.

But His thought and purpose had always been to dwell eventually with man, for that was to be His house.

We will recall that when the Lord Jesus began His earthly ministry, He went up to Jerusalem and there observed to His dismay all the commerce which was then occurring in the temple—the buying and selling and profit-making for both the priests and the merchants. And in cleansing that now-defiled house He had lamented: "You have made My Father's house a house of merchandise" (see John 2:16). Now we know that this physical temple was but a type or shadow of what was to come; the reality of the house of God would be the church: indeed, in I Timothy Paul wrote that "the church is His house" (see 3:15).

In view of all this, therefore, and in considering further what the Lord Jesus had said to His disciples on the night of His last Passover feast with them—"My Father's house"—we realize that He was not referring to heaven or to some *physical* entity but to a *spiritual* reality, which is the church. Said Jesus further to His disciples that same night: "In My Father's house there are many abodes." Now in some Bible versions the phrase "many abodes" is translated as "many mansions." We all are attracted to mansions and large houses, but Jesus clearly stated, "in My Father's house"—a reference to *one* house, not houses. In God's thought and purpose there is to be only one house; nevertheless, that one house is to have many apartments or suites, thus signifying from Jesus' statement that each one of us is to have a suite. How wonderful! Yet let us always bear in mind that there is but one house.

Let me try to illustrate it this way. I came from an old Chinese family that lived in a very large house. My grandfather had been a builder, and he had built for him and his extended family a very large house with many suites in it. Every son in the family had his suite. And for his married daughters he had constructed an auxiliary accommodation for each one of them that was placed by the side of the house. Briefly stated, therefore, we all lived under one roof. It was a truly wonderful experience. Grandfather took care of everything, and my grandmother managed the entire house. All of us enjoyed living in such an arrangement because we had no responsibility! Now that is something of the idea being expressed here by the Lord Jesus: in My Father's house there are many apartments—you will have a place and you and you and you will also have a place. In other words, we each will have a place of our own in the one house of God. And thus the Lord has returned to heaven to prepare a place for each of us.

Now what does all this mean? It means that in God's mind He has a place for all of us in His house. It is an expansive wonderful mansion, as it were, because He desires each of us to be conformed to the image of His Son. What a marvelous suite that will be for each of us. And because of this which from the very beginning has been in the Father's heart and mind, the Son, our Lord Jesus, needed to return to heaven and prepare it all for us. Otherwise, should He *not* be preparing for us by interceding unceasingly in heaven on our behalf as the Holy Spirit works in us, we could not and would not ever be transformed and conformed to the image of the Father's beloved Son. But praise God, this is what the Lord is now doing. And after He has prepared a place for each one of us, He will then come back and receive us to himself. Anything short of this purpose of God in each of our lives, anything short of our being conformed to the image of Christ, means that our place is not yet prepared.

WHY THE LORD DELAYS HIS COMING

Can this be the reason the Lord Jesus is delayed and delayed and delayed in returning? It is not because He does not want to come back to take us as His bride but because the body of Christ—the church—has not grown to maturity. He cannot marry a child. It is not Christ who is responsible for the delay. It is we who delay His coming. So this is a most serious practical issue. Our Lord is preparing a place for each of us, and He himself cannot fail in fulfilling His responsibility as our High Priest. The Holy Spirit is working in us and He, too, cannot fail in carrying out His responsibility. So why is there the delay? Who delays the return of the Lord? Is it not we who are the ones responsible? I believe this is actually the case, and thus we bear a very serious and great responsibility. Instead of delaying the Lord's return we should be *hastening* His return by our faithful obedience.

We all have a new spirit, with the Holy Spirit indwelling us there. God has made every provision—not only for saving us but even for us to become like Him—because the Bible declares that by God's "divine power He has given us all things which relate to life and godliness" (II peter 1:3). He has given us a new spirit and sent the Holy Spirit to indwell us as our Guide, Teacher, Comforter, and Empowerer. Hence God has made every provision to enable us to grow up into full maturity in Christ and be conformed to the image of His beloved Son.

"WORK OUT YOUR SALVATION"

But where exactly lies our responsibility? Is it not that we should be responding positively to the work of the Holy Spirit in us? When He shows us where we are wrong, that in us there is some unrighteousness, that this or that or the other is not holy or glorious in our lives—and given the fact that He will not fail in His responsibility to show all this to us—how do we react? Do we grieve Him? Do we offend Him? Do we rebel against Him? Or do we submit to Him, take up our cross, and follow Him? Truly, therefore, the responsibility unmistakably lies with each one of us. And this thus explains why spiritual exercise is so vital. We have to engage in such exercise daily. If we neglect it, we jeopardize our future status in the coming age.

In Philippians 2 we are told to "work out [our] salvation with fear and trembling." Now we may respond to this statement by saying that since salvation has already come to us, we having been saved by grace because God has done everything for us, then why is it that we must work out our salvation with fear and trembling? Is it because we are not believing and are lacking in faith? No, that is not the reason we are instructed to work out our salvation. What this instruction means is that as the Holy Spirit works in us according to God's purpose and desire, we need to respond positively by working out that salvation with fear and trembling. Even though we are involved in the work, it is not by our work but is still by grace: all of God's salvation, from beginning to end, is by grace and not by works. By God's grace the Holy Spirit begins to speak to us, to touch us, and to show us wherein we may have departed in some way from God's standard of righteousness or holiness. And as the Holy

Spirit continually works in us along this line we are to work out, with fear and trembling, what He works into us of God's salvation. Therefore, it is not the case of our doing the work but that of the Holy Spirit doing the work. We simply cooperate by responding positively; and when we say "Yes" to whatever the Holy Spirit is doing in us, He will accomplish the work. Can we now see how essential this is? If we cooperate in this way of spiritual exercise, we can enjoy life when the Lord returns to take us to himself.

THE PARABLE OF THE TEN VIRGINS

In order to impart some spiritual lesson to His disciples the Lord Jesus often spoke in parables, some of which are relevant to our current discussion. Two come to mind here. Let us notice in the parable of the ten virgins that all ten are indeed virgins (Matthew 25:1-13). The Bible only calls those people virgins whose sins have been cleansed by the blood of Jesus. Otherwise, they would be referred to as adulterers or adulteresses. These ten virgins are divided into two groups— five foolish and five wise. They all have torches as they go out to meet the bridegroom, who symbolizes the Lord Jesus himself. Before proceeding any further here, let us be clear in our understanding that no one will go out to meet the Lord unless they are believers—the people of the world will not do that; hence, all ten are Christians. Then, too, all ten virgins have oil in their torches since every torch at this point in the story is shining forth light. But because the Lord, as it were, delays His coming, all ten virgins fall asleep. At midnight, however, they hear a voice proclaiming: "The bridegroom cometh!" They all are awakened by this and commence to trim their torches, but the five foolish virgins had not provided extra oil in their vessels. Only the wise ones had extra oil because they had wisely prepared in advance for the days ahead; whereas the foolish virgins had merely been living for the present day—their motto having been, "Let us eat, drink, and be happy, for tomorrow we die." The oil in each torch itself was given, but the oil in each vessel had to be purchased at a cost. Now it is while the foolish virgins go out to buy extra oil that the bridegroom arrives. Only the five wise ones can enter into the marriage feast, for once *they* enter, the door is closed behind them.

From this parable we are given to understand, spiritually speaking, that in our present life we torches—for we Christians are called lights in the world (Matthew 5:14a; Philippians 2:15b)—not only need to have in us the already-provided oil, which gift of God is the Holy Spirit, but we also need to have extra oil, and it has to be bought; which means that it costs something. Spiritually speaking, therefore, are we willing to pay the price that we may be filled with the Holy Spirit? If that be the case, then we can enter in to the marriage feast of the Lamb of God (Revelation 19:9). If not, then the door will be closed to us latecomers. We can thus discern from this parable that there is a huge difference in outcome for us believers in the future age resulting from how we live during this present age.

THE PARABLE OF THE TALENTS

From the parable of the talents we can detect a similar teaching (Matthew 25:14-30). The owner in the story gave talents to each one of his servants according to each's ability—one received five talents, one two talents, and one a single talent. The master then left, and after a long time he came back to receive an accounting from his servants. The one given five talents was faithful, for he had earned another five. The two-talent servant earned another two, and so he, too, proved to have been faithful. But the one who had received one talent had hidden that talent in the ground, and in his accounting had even accused his master of being very hard on him, and further, indicated his fear of his master.

What is the spiritual lesson we can derive from this parable? God has given to all of us gifts according to *our* ability, for if such gifts were *beyond* our ability we could not accomplish what our Master intended in giving us such gifts. Even so, within whatever He has given us according to our ability we should faithfully labor to increase it for the Lord. That is a reference to service. We serve with whatever He has entrusted to us, and if we are faithful, then at the moment of reckoning, we will be rewarded; but if we are not, we—like the one-talent servant—will be cast out into darkness.

So when we consider this parable in relation to the coming of the Lord, let us be clear that when He returns to the earth, not every believer will be taken up and receive a reward. Not so; for some will indeed be taken immediately because they had been faithful, but others will be taken later. Nevertheless, what will immediately be common to all believers is that all will experience the judgment seat of Christ (II Corinthians 5:10). That event will decide whether we will enter into the joy of the Lord during the kingdom age or whether we will be cast into outer darkness during that age to experience profound regret, but also to repent and to receive whatever discipline necessary in order that we might be matured and made ready for the coming ages of ages (eternity).

WAITING-WATCHING-PRAYING

In the Bible passage of Luke 21 which heads this message we are exhorted to not be occupied with eating, drinking, and the cares of life. If we make these activities and concerns our way of life, then the day of the Lord's return will come upon us suddenly unawares. If we are not engaged in the spiritual exercises of waiting, watching and praying, and are thus made ready for the kingdom, His coming will be sudden and unexpected. For as a snare it will come upon all who dwell upon the face of the whole earth. To the world the second coming of the Lord is something of which they are unaware, but to us who are sons of light we should be aware of it. We should be preparing for His coming by watching and praying at every season in order that we might be accounted worthy to escape all things which are about to come to pass on the earth and be able to stand before the Son of man.

So when we contemplate the coming of the Lord, let us approach this matter in a most practical way. Are we watching? Are we praying? Are we preparing ourselves for His coming? If so, then it will be the most joyous of times. But if we are not prepared, the judgment seat of Christ awaits us to determine whether we will or will not enjoy life in the kingdom days to come.

"EVER READY, NEVER READY"

What should be our attitude as we await the Lord's return? It is summed up in a slogan or motto of mine which I constantly say to myself as a way of being reminded of its truth: "Ever ready, never ready." By which I mean that if we ever think we are ready for His return, we most likely are not. If we ever reach the point of thinking we are ready for His return, then we should adopt the reverse attitude that we are never ready. It is important to have *that* kind of spirit as we wait for the coming of the Lord. Let us continually ask ourselves: At the coming of the Lord will we see Him joyfully or be in sorrow and regret? That will depend on whether or not we exercise our spirit during this present age of grace. It is that vital an issue.

I do not know how I can best impress upon ourselves the importance of spiritual exercise. Yet the truth is that the Lord is coming—and soon—sooner than most people think, because all the prophecies which concern those events which were to *precede* the coming of the Lord have now been fulfilled. Yes, there are some other prophecies yet to be fulfilled, but those are to be fulfilled both at the coming of the Lord and after His coming—not before. In view of that, and if we look at all this from a prophetic point of view, can we not therefore say that the Lord can come at any time? It can even be today—indeed, why not? Yet the central question for each of us to answer is, Will we be in a right spiritual condition to enjoy life when He does come? The only way for this to happen is if meanwhile we exercise our spirit daily and cooperate with the Holy Spirit who is so faithful. He is even now working in each one of us in a constant attempt to bring us out of ourselves and out of the world and bring us into Christ. May the Lord encourage us all.

Chapter 14

THE KINGDOM OF THE HEAVENS

Matthew 4:17—From that time began Jesus to preach and to say, Repent, for the kingdom of the heavens has drawn nigh.

Matthew 11:12—But from the days of John the Baptist until now, the kingdom of the heavens is taken by violence [force], and the violent seize on it.

Matthew 24:14—And these glad tidings of the kingdom shall be preached in the whole habitable earth, for a witness to all the nations, and then shall come the end.

We have been considering this very basic issue of spiritual exercise which, to repeat again, is profitable for everything. It has the promise of life, and the life promised is not our physical life; it is our spiritual life or the life of Christ in us. If we exercise our spirit we will have the promise of this life eternal in us, and this is not only for now, it is also for the age to come.

THE AGES OF TIME AND ETERNITY

From the Bible we learn that our God is eternal, but He uses time to work out His eternal plan. According to the Scriptures there is the age of grace which we are now in, and then there will be the age to come which is the age of the kingdom of the heavens—a thousand-year period on earth.

And after that kingdom age to come there will be the ages of ages—which is eternity.

We find this demarcation of these ages in part in the words uttered by the Lord concerning the unforgivable sin. Said Jesus: "Every sin can be forgiven but one. That sin cannot be forgiven in this age or in the age to come, and that is the sin against the Holy Spirit" (see Matthew 12:32). From this remark of the Lord's we see that there is not only this present age in which we live but after this age is concluded there will also be, in God's timing, the coming age—the thousand years of the kingdom of the heavens upon the earth. Only after that age will there be the unending "ages of ages" which we know of as eternity (Revelation 1:6, 22:5).

THE KINGDOM AGE AND
THE FALSE NOTION OF PURGATORY

Many Christians are only conversant with the idea of this present age and the eternal ages of ages. These Christians seem completely unaware of the age to come; and because of that, they harbor the notion in their minds that because they have believed in the Lord Jesus and are saved, eternity is guaranteed for them—meaning, that after they are finished with this present life, they will go to heaven and enjoy eternity with the Lord. Apparently they overlook the fact that in between these two ages there is the age to come—the kingdom age.

The glad tidings of the kingdom of the heavens is an integral and very important part of the gospel of Jesus Christ. It is not *another* gospel, for there is only one gospel, even as the apostle Paul constantly maintained (e. g., Galatians 1:6-

9). Let us therefore realize that the gospel of the kingdom of the heavens is the gospel of Jesus Christ. Indeed, He himself *is* the gospel, but because He is so rich and full, His gospel includes far more than we can possibly imagine.

We too often think of the gospel only in terms of the gospel of grace; that is to say, our conception of the gospel is only what Luke has emphasized—that the Lord Jesus Christ came in order that we might believe and have our sins forgiven. Now most certainly this is true; we do thank God most heartily for what He has done for us in that regard. Nevertheless, according to the entire word of God this is just the beginning of the gospel of Jesus, because His gospel is not according to our needs but according to the nature and thus the glory of God.

Now *we* may be satisfied by merely being saved but God is not satisfied. He gave His multifaceted gospel to us so that we may attain to His eternal purpose concerning us. Therefore, the gospel not only includes the grace of God but also the kingdom of the heavens.

Unfortunately, Christians' awareness of the kingdom age has either been nonexistent or else misinformed throughout the centuries. Before proceeding further, however, permit me to lay an historical foundation for better understanding what I mean here.

During the Reformation, which arose in the sixteenth century, the Reformers had come to realize the falsity of the unbiblical doctrine of the Roman Catholic Church known as Purgatory and the abuse to which it had been put by that church. In essence the teaching of this doctrine signified that the Catholic Church did not know that people are saved by grace through faith and not by works. That church's teaching of Purgatory meant that everyone needed to be saved by one's own merits; yet who can gain enough merits in this life which would enable a person to go straight to heaven after he dies? Moreover, there were only a few saints, it was claimed, who had been able to accumulate enough merits in their lives to go straight to heaven after their death, and these few even had additional merits to spare for allotting to others who lacked. Therefore, further went this teaching, people could pray to these saints, who would share their extra merits with them, which would thus enable such folk to be extricated from Purgatory more quickly.

At this same time in Church history, the Catholic Church needed huge funds for building its immense cathedral in Rome known as St. Peter's, so they began to sell what were called indulgences. The church sent out representatives to every country, who went about proclaiming that if a person paid a certain amount of money, that one could receive an indulgence for, say, a hundred days or two hundred days or whatever—all according to the amount of money an individual might give. By giving the money, it signified that one's sins were forgiven. People back then naively believed this; it even reached the point that whenever people wanted to commit a sin, they would pay the indulgence first so that if and when they were caught sinning, they could show the document of indulgence and be forgiven immediately. The people had even been told that at the very moment when their money to be paid for these indulgences would fall into the collection box their souls would rise up out of Purgatory and go into heaven. Thus everything pertaining to the obtaining of salvation was by merits, even with respect to the way by which to gain heaven.

But the Reformers, as they carefully read the Scriptures, received revelation from God by His Spirit that they were not saved by their meritorious works but by grace. Salvation, they realized, could only come to a person by faith in the Lord Jesus who is the sinless One and who was made sin for us that we might become the righteousness of God in Christ (II Corinthians 5:21). And because of their emphasis on justification by faith and not by works, these Reformers overthrew, as it were, this whole system of merits and indulgences and all other aspects surrounding the doctrine of Purgatory. Because of that false system, however, it created a big problem for Christianity of a later day.

TWO SCHOOLS OF THOUGHT IN CHRISTIANITY CONCERNING SALVATION

There are two schools of thought today in Christianity concerning salvation. One school believes that once a person is saved, he is forever saved. In other words, if you believe in the Lord Jesus and you are saved, then you are saved forever. The other school believes that though you may have accepted Jesus by faith and are saved, if you do not properly behave thereafter you will lose your salvation. Here, then, in part, is the problem which the false Catholic system of merits and indulgences had created for the Christian church of a later day. We must thank God for raising up the Reformers who by revelation through the Holy Scriptures saw afresh that before anyone is saved, whatever good deeds or works of righteousness which a person may have accumulated are as "filthy rags" in the sight of God (Isaiah 64:6a). Such so-called earned merit cannot in the least save anyone. We can only look by faith to the Savior, the Lord Jesus Christ, for salvation; His blood shed on Calvary's cross will cleanse us of all sins and, by our believing, God will grant us life eternal. Hence, our being eternally saved is gained by grace through faith in the Lord Jesus Christ plus nothing else. That is the teaching of the first of these two schools of thought.

On the other hand, what of the conduct and behavior of Christians *after* they are saved? For the second school had raised the question—Can it be acceptable in the sight of God that since people are now saved they can nonetheless be careless, live loosely, even bring shame upon the Lord Jesus, or act unrighteously? After all, goes the reasoning of this second school of thought, since people are assured of going to heaven, why should they be concerned or worry about how they live?—can they not have the best of both worlds?—they thinking to themselves, Let us eat, drink and be merry in this present world and later happily enter the other world of heaven. So, confronted by what appeared to be an unsolved problem, there arose this second school of theological thought which posited the teaching that if a believer in Christ does not behave himself in a holy and righteous manner after being saved, he would lose his salvation. And hence, we have in Christianity today these two opposing opinions.

For instance, the Baptists believe that once saved believers are forever saved, whereas the Methodists believe that if believers do not behave themselves in holiness and righteousness, they can lose their salvation; and this problem of differing opinions has never been resolved to the satisfaction of either theological camp for these hundreds of years because both have somehow overlooked the age to come—the kingdom age—as that which provides the solution to this knotty problem. Now it is quite true that if we have in fact believed in the Lord Jesus for our salvation, we are forever saved eternally, because once we have been taken into the hand of God, nothing and no one can remove us out of His hand (John 10:29 ASV). By this fact our salvation has been eternally determined, we having been saved by none other than God himself. But it is equally true that upon our receiving the grace of God, that grace in us ought to transform us into gracious people of God in order that we may be as gracious as is our God. In other words, His life in us ought to manifest His character, and if we indeed have His life in us but do not manifest His character by the way we live, then we are guilty of abusing the grace which God has graciously bestowed upon us. In short, we, as it were, have fallen from grace, and even though we are eternally saved, during the kingdom age to come we will suffer great pain and loss. Consequently, this matter of the kingdom is very, *very* significant for us believers.

WHY REPENT?

When the Lord Jesus came to earth the first time, He was born not only as a savior but also as a king. And when He first began to minister (see Matthew 4:17a), this is what He as the Savior-King proclaimed: "Repent, for the kingdom of the heavens has drawn nigh" (4:17b).

Now we know that the children of Israel were God's chosen people. They had the temple, the Law, the priesthood, and all other elements of their religious culture (cf. Romans 9:4-5). They observed and depended upon their Jewish religious culture, yet they did not live a godly life.

Therefore, God sent John the Baptizer, the forerunner of the Lord Jesus, to proclaim the very same message: "Repent, for the kingdom of the heavens has drawn nigh" (Matthew 3:2).

Why must people repent? Unfortunately, too many of us view repentance only in terms of its relation to our sins. Quite true, if we have committed anything unrighteous or unholy we do need to repent of it. Here, though, is a further reason for us to repent: "the kingdom of the heavens has drawn nigh." Let me explain this by saying that we can infer from this statement that the King of kings is coming, and when He comes, He will establish His kingdom upon this earth. But the question arises, Are you and I qualified to be in that kingdom? If we recognize and acknowledge that we are *not*, then we need to repent because our religious life will not save us; it will not make any of us a son of the kingdom to come. We need a new life—even the King's life. The King is coming to build up His kingdom upon the earth, and if we repent He will bring us into His kingdom.

When the Lord Jesus came the first time, He came to minister, and this, as we have seen, is the message He gave from the very outset of His ministry: "Repent, for the kingdom of the heavens has drawn nigh." Why was *that* His message? For had not the King already come? Yes, the Lord Jesus as King did come, but where was His kingdom at the time of His first coming to the earth? For the most important possession for a king to have is people, since without people a king *has no kingdom*. We find, therefore, that when Jesus the King came to the earth, He had no people and thus no kingdom yet. The earth's people did not belong to Him but to God's enemy. So that is why Jesus' message was necessarily one of repentance when He came: "Repent, reverse course in your lives, and become My people." And if that should happen, then it could rightly be said that His kingdom is indeed come. So the work of the Lord Jesus on the earth during this age of grace is calling people to repent and believe in Him. In other words, His work is to make preparation for His kingdom.

After the Lord Jesus preached, "Repent, for the kingdom of heavens has drawn nigh," there were some people who repented and believed in Him. Further, we learn from Mark 1:14-15, Luke 4:43-44, and Matthew 4:23 that He continued to proclaim this soon-coming kingdom truth, especially in Galilee; and He also began to call for disciples (Matthew 4:18-22, Mark 1:16-20, Luke 5:1-11). He said in so many words to those who would listen: "Come, and follow Me. You are not only to come and receive salvation from Me but you are also to follow Me. Walk after Me. Do what I do. Be what I am. Be My disciples. Be My citizens. Prepare to be kings in the kingdom of the heavens."

SEIZING HOLD OF THE KINGDOM BY FORCE

In Matthew 11 there is to be found this remarkable statement uttered by the Lord Jesus: "From the time of John the Baptist until now the kingdom of the heavens is to be taken by violence, and the violent seize upon it" (see v. 12). Now we do not take kindly to the word violent because of its negative connotation. We deem violence to be something bad, unpleasant, and to be avoided; yet the word itself is neutral in content, for it depends on whom the violence is being meted out. If you do violence to other people, that is wrong, but if—in spiritual terms—you do violence to yourself, that is considered commendable by the Lord. Now if we do not like the word violence or violent, there is another word which can legitimately be substituted: the word force or forceful. A Christian is to take the kingdom by force, and the forceful one is to seize upon it. In other words, such action does not arise spontaneously; rather, by an act of the believer's will the kingdom is taken forcibly and the forceful one seizes hold of the kingdom.

Are we not saved? Thank God, we are. Are we not in the kingdom of Christ? Yes, positionally, we are. Revelation tells us: "To him [Christ] who loves us, and has washed us from our sins in his blood, and made us a kingdom, priests to his God and Father: to him be the glory and the might to the ages of ages. Amen" (1:5b-6). The Lord Jesus loves us so much that He has not only washed us from our sins in His blood but has also done something more—He has made of us a kingdom.

Moreover, Revelation 5 reveals the fact that in heaven the twenty-four elders and the four living creatures worship the Lamb and "sing a new song, saying, Thou art worthy to take the book, and to open its seals; because thou hast been slain, and hast redeemed to God, by thy blood, out of every tribe, and tongue, and people, and nation, and made them to our God kings and priests; and they shall reign over the earth" (vv. 9-10).

And Colossians 1:13 tells us that the Lord Jesus has delivered us out of the authority, domain and power of darkness and transferred us into the kingdom of the Son of God's love. Before we believed in the Lord Jesus we belonged to the kingdom of darkness. The authority of darkness was upon us, and thus we were under the control of the enemy of God, who is Satan. So the whole world lies under the Satanic authority and power of darkness. Therefore, when we were born into this world, we automatically came under the power of darkness and thus under Satan's control. Accordingly, that was where we were positionally. Praise God that the Lord Jesus came to this earth and delivered us out of the authority of darkness and transferred us into His kingdom—into what the Scriptures describe as the kingdom of the Son of God's love. So our position as believers is now situated in the kingdom of the heavens and no longer in the kingdom of the world. That is a true statement, but if our relationship to the kingdom of the heavens is only positional in nature, that is not enough to satisfy God's purpose for us since that is but something objective: we have not entered into the subjective experience of the kingdom.

For example, if you only know as factual that the Lord Jesus died on the cross two thousand years ago, but you do not believe in Him, you will not be able to benefit from what He did at Calvary. The objective truth of salvation is there but unless you believe the truth it will not be yours experientially. Whatever your experience may be does not change the objective truth. What the Lord Jesus did on the cross is able to save the whole world; therefore, none should have to go to hell. Yet why is it that only those who believe in Jesus actually go to heaven? It is because they have experienced the reality spiritually of what He has done for them. The objective truth of salvation has to become every person's subjective experience if that person is to benefit from what Christ accomplished on the cross.

Likewise is it with this matter of the kingdom of God. We believe that God has transferred us, positionally, out of the authority and kingdom of darkness into the kingdom of the

Son of His love. He has done it all. We are there positionally in the kingdom of the heavens but experientially we have to forcefully seize upon the kingdom and take hold of it by force. If we do not do so, we will not be able to benefit from what God has done in having brought us into the kingdom. And hence, that is why it is so important for us to do as Jesus proclaimed: "The kingdom of the heavens is to be taken by violence, and the violent seize upon it." We must do violence to ourselves—that is, we must not cater to the needs and desires of our flesh all the time. We must enter by our forceful will, as it were, into the kingdom of the heavens.

WHAT DISCIPLES ARE

It was mentioned earlier that when Jesus continued to proclaim the kingdom truth ("Repent, for the kingdom of the heavens has drawn nigh"), He began to call for disciples to come and follow Him. Why did the Lord do this? Why, too, is it that though we are believers, that is not enough? After we have believed in the Lord Jesus, why does He call those who believe in Him to come and follow Him and be His disciples?

First of all, what do we mean by this term disciples as used in the Scriptures? As employed in the Bible, the word disciples is not to be construed as being like modern-day students who, as it were, hire teachers in order that they might learn as much knowledge as possible. No, a disciple is quite different from that. A disciple in the Biblical sense was like being a candidate in the apprentice system of old. If back then you had wanted to learn a specific trade or skill, you had to be apprenticed to a master by leaving home and everything else to go forth and live with him and become a part of his very household. Moreover, during the first year he usually would not teach you any skill of the trade. If you were learning carpentry, for example, the master would not allow you to touch any of the relevant tools or instruments. Instead, you would become like a servant in his house—performing such tasks as cleaning the house, washing the floor, helping with the babies and/or children, and even waiting upon your master while he ate—just as though being like a slave. Only after perhaps a year would the master begin to allow you to touch the instruments or tools of the trade and begin teaching you how to use them. It would require a few years before you could graduate, but afterwards, you had not only learned the trade skills of your master, you had also learned the very lifestyle of your master. You ended up walking like him and talking like him; in fact, you ended up being like him in almost every way. Now that was what the olden days of apprenticeship had been like.

    Christian discipleship is actually quite similar. And when the Lord Jesus began calling for disciples to come and follow Him, that was what happened. He saw at the Lake of Galilee one day Peter and his brother Andrew, who were fishermen. At this moment they were fishing, and the Lord Jesus said: "Come and follow Me." They left their boat, their net, and even their home and followed the Lord. The Lord walked on farther along the lake and saw two more brothers—the sons of Zebedee, James and John. They were mending the nets which they had previously used because there were holes in them. And the Lord Jesus said to these men, too: "Come and follow Me." They left their nets, their boat, and their father, and went forth and followed the Lord. We also will recall the tax gatherer, Levi, who later became known as Matthew. He was sitting in the customs office one day, and the Lord came up to him and said, "Come and follow Me." He left that office and, like the others, followed the Lord Jesus (Matthew (9:9; cf. Mark 2:13-14).

From all this we can discern the fact that the Lord wants and expects us to *simultaneously* believe in Him and follow Him. Strictly speaking, there is no time interval between believing in Jesus and becoming His disciples. They are two aspects of the same spiritual event in our lives. If we believe in the Lord Jesus we should automatically become disciples of His.

Viewed another way, can you continue to live by yourself and for yourself once you have believed in the Lord Jesus?—can you still live your old life? The answer is obviously, No, for you have been saved out of sin, death, the world, and Satan's authority of darkness. You now need to follow the Lord in light, righteousness, and love. He is to live in you as the very life of your spirit, and then, by continual spiritual exercise as His disciple in training, your life will ultimately be completely transformed and conformed to the image of God's Son. This is what the nature and content of true Christian discipleship really is.

CONSECRATION

It is most important for us to understand that believing in the Lord Jesus alone is not the beginning of Christian life. We may believe in the Lord Jesus and be saved, but our Christian life has not yet begun. It does not begin until we consecrate ourselves to the Lord—that is, not until we present our bodies as living sacrifices, because this is God's will, this is what is acceptable to Him, this is what in His sight is our true spiritual worship and reasonable service (Romans 12:1-2). For actually, to present our bodies as living sacrifices means we rise up and follow Him as His disciples. We cannot do it physically as did the two sons of Zebedee or Peter and Andrew or Matthew; nevertheless, spiritually speaking, that is what we do. In short, consecration is absolutely essential in becoming a disciple of the Lord Jesus. We put everything of ourselves into His hands and say, "Lord, it is all Yours. You have the right to my life and all which pertains to it because You have saved me. Therefore, Lord, do whatever You want to do with me. Turn me about and transform me to be like You in order that Your character may become my character, and I will be a true follower—a true disciple—of Yours." This is what true consecration to the Lord is. And as a result, He will take us in His hands and begin the work of discipling us as His followers. He will begin to shape and mold us according to His will.

Now that is the only way by which we can enter and reign as kings in the kingdom of the heavens. If our relationship to the kingdom is only positionally, it means we will not gain entrance into the kingdom of the heavens to come.

PARABLES OF THE KINGDOM

In Matthew 13 we read how the Lord Jesus taught different parables regarding the kingdom. The first parable is concerned with the sowing the seed of the gospel and the truth of the kingdom, whereas the second parable is not concerned with these matters but with the sowing of the sons of the kingdom. Once a person believes in the Lord Jesus he becomes His disciple and a son of the kingdom. Then He sows these sons of the kingdom throughout the world to be His testimony to the world. More than that, however, we need to grasp hold of the fact that in the kingdom of the heavens everyone is not only a citizen, not only a son, but is also a king. Has that fact impressed itself upon our thinking yet? Who is to be in the kingdom of the heavens to come? There can only be kings. That is what everyone in the kingdom of heaven is.

Then Matthew 24 records the Lord telling us what will precede the coming of the kingdom of the heavens upon the earth: the gospel of the kingdom of the heavens is to be proclaimed to all the world as a testimony, and only then will the kingdom come (v.14). We find, therefore, that the essence of the gospel according to Matthew is unmistakably the kingdom of the heavens, with the Lord Jesus himself stating that only when the preaching or proclamation of the kingdom gospel to all the world has been completed will the end come, ushering in the kingdom.

We also find this same theme concerning the gospel of the kingdom and its proclamation in the book of Hebrews chapter 2. There we are told that this so-great salvation was first launched forth through the preaching or proclamation of the Lord Jesus and was later confirmed by those who heard this message. The apostles, in turn, continued to confirm it as exemplified in Peter's preaching in Jerusalem on the day of Pentecost when he declared: "The One whom you rejected and crucified God has made both Lord and Christ" (see Acts 2:36b). That, in essence, is the gospel of the kingdom. And it is also as exemplified later in the ministry of the apostle Paul;

for when he was under house arrest in his apartment at Rome, he continuously proclaimed to his visitors the gospel message concerning the kingdom of God and taught all things concerning the Lord Jesus (Acts 28:30-31). In other words, the gospel of the kingdom was the gospel preached by the Lord's apostles because this was, and still is, the will of God.

THE TRAINING OF KINGS

Thus we can see that discipleship is centrally related to the coming kingdom and is actually the preparatory training up of a person to be a king in that coming kingdom. Do we think it is easy to be a king? Here in the United States we have a democratic republic, so we do not have kings in our country. But if we look at America's former mother country, Britain, we see that it has had a long political history as a monarchy, and the training of its king- (or queen-) to-be is a very strict one. The training of that country's future monarch is far more extensive and disciplined than that of any citizen growing up in the monarchy of Great Britain. Even though the heir to the throne is a son or daughter, he/she must experience all aspects of such preparatory training. If the heir is a son, he usually will enter one of his country's armed services and begin as a common serviceman. He must learn submission and obedience rather than himself be the one in authority. Otherwise, no authority could be given to him in the future because he would abuse that authority. He must go through very strict and diverse kinds of training to be the king.

Now the Lord Jesus is today training us, His disciples, to be kings. Think of that! Do you want to have an easy time? Do you want simply to get by? If you do, you are not qualified to be a king, and because of that you are not able to reign with Christ during the thousand years of His coming kingdom. For the sake of a few enjoyable years on earth, for the sake of a little of this world, for the sake of gratifying your flesh, you are unaware how much you will miss by not being allowed into Christ's kingdom. How long do you have to live on the earth? How long can you enjoy this world? How much time do you really have—40, 60, perhaps 80 or perhaps even 100 years? How can that short period be compared with the kingdom's thousand years? Suppose you could gain this whole world but in the process lose your soul—what, then, is the profit? (Matthew 16:26)

One day, when the Lord returns, those who have allowed themselves to be trained as kings will reign with Him for a thousand years—yet not in the sense of reigning as would a king in this world: sitting on a throne giving orders and everybody serving him. *That* is the kingdom concept of this world. No, they shall be kings of the kingdom of the heavens, which shall be of a totally different character.

THE HEAVENS INVADED THE EARTH THROUGH JESUS

What is like the kingdom of the heavens? We will recall that day on which the Lord Jesus was brought before Pilate, the Roman governor, who asked Him: "Are You a king?" The Lord Jesus replied: "I am. Indeed, I was born King, but My kingdom is not of this world. If it were, My people would rise up and rescue Me, but My kingdom is not of this world" (see John 18:33-37). Jesus' kingdom is the kingdom of the heavens, and He is its King. In fact, the heavens have come in the Person of the King above all kings. At the birth of the Lord Jesus, therefore, the heavens actually invaded this earth. And while He was on earth He once observed that He was still in heaven (John 3:13). Thus, Jesus had brought with Him all the atmosphere of the heavens. He was not governed by the law of *this* world; rather, He was governed by a higher law—even His Father's will. So that even while He was on earth He was yet in heaven. Truly, *His* kingdom is not of this world.

One day His disciples were arguing among themselves: "Who will sit at the Lord's right and at His left in His glory? Who among us will have the authority?" And the Lord interjected with these words: "My kingdom is different. If you want to be the first, be the last—be the servant of all. If you want to be the head, be the tail. As for Me, I have come to serve and not to be served, and to give My life a ransom for all" (see Mark 10:35-45). That is the nature and character of *His* kingdom. And because His kingdom is so radically different from the kingdoms of this world, no wonder the world persecuted Him, no wonder the world cast Him out, no wonder the world crucified Him, because His kingdom is altogether different. And today, we have the privilege of being called into that kingdom. And if we are to be in *that* kingdom, can we in our lifestyle remain any longer the same as those who are in and of the world? Let us not be surprised if by the way we live we will be misunderstood. Let us not be surprised if the world will not understand us. Let us also not be surprised if the world persecutes us because we do not belong to it. We belong instead to the kingdom of the heavens, and that is why we must seize upon it by violence. We, as it were, must do violence to ourselves, and not cater to the desires, and even to the legitimate needs, of our flesh all the time. Instead, if we are truly His disciples, we must be willing to deny ourselves, take up our cross, and follow the Lord.

THE NATURE OF THE KINGDOM OF THE HEAVENS

A Kingdom of Truth

What, more specifically, are the nature and characteristics of this kingdom of the heavens? Retuning once again to John 18, we read that, still within the context of speaking to Pilate concerning His kingdom, Jesus went on to say this: "I have come to bear witness to the truth" (see v. 37). In other words, the kingdom of the heavens is a kingdom of truth. Today, we live in a world of lies and gross hypocrisy, but the Lord Jesus came to bring in a kingdom of truth and transparency. Everything about His kingdom is true, real, and eternal—not false, unreal, and transient.

A Kingdom of Righteousness, Peace, and Joy

What further is the nature and character of the kingdom of the heavens? Romans 14:17 declares that "the kingdom of God is not eating and drinking, but righteousness, and peace, and joy in the Holy Spirit." To put it most succinctly and clearly: the kingdom of the heavens takes its nature or character from its King, from Christ himself. In other words, Christ is himself the kingdom. And that is the reason God wants us—by means of discipleship—to be transformed and conformed to the image of His beloved Son (Romans 12:2b, 8:29a), because that is the only way for any of us to gain the kingdom. And this gospel message of the kingdom of the

308

heavens must be preached to all the inhabited world before the end shall come and His kingdom be ushered in.

THE TRAINING OF JESUS' DISCIPLES

Here I would like to use a few incidents from the New Testament Gospels to show how the Lord trained His disciples; for instance, the disciple Peter. From Matthew 16 we learn that the Father revealed the Son to Peter. When asked by Jesus who He is, Peter replied: "You are the Christ, the Son of the living God." And the Lord Jesus responded with: "Simon Barjona, you are blessed because this is not something shown you by the flesh. It is My heavenly Father who has revealed the Christ to you" (see v. 17).

In our believing in the Lord Jesus as the Christ the Son of the living God, let it be clear that this truth did not come to us through human reasoning or teaching. It came to us by revelation from above. Such revelation lifts us up, as it were, to the third heaven and changes us, as it did Peter. For it was no longer Simon—simply dust—but now Peter—a living stone.

Immediately afterwards the Lord Jesus began to share with Peter and His other disciples how He must go to Jerusalem and be rejected, persecuted and crucified, but on the third day He would rise from the dead. And Peter, having just then received such an immense and marvelous revelation but out of his natural love for the Lord, took literal hold of Jesus and shook Him somewhat and declared emphatically: "No! Never! Lord, You do not need to experience the cross." At this moment Peter did not realize he was being used by God's enemy. For the Lord, having total discernment, turned around and addressed His disciple directly: "Satan, get thee behind Me, because you are not mindful of the things of God but of man" (see vv. 21-23). Think of that! Here, Peter was being disciplined most sternly by the Lord, even being addressed by the Lord as Satan. What personal degradation for this disciple! On the one hand, through this severe discipline Peter learned his lesson. On the other hand, though he did learn *this* lesson, it did not mean he had learned all he needed to learn in completion of his discipleship under his Master, Jesus.

On another occasion the temple tax-collectors came to Jesus' disciples and asked, "Does your Master pay the temple tax?" Without any hesitation, Peter presumptuously replied: "Yes." After so saying, Peter went into the house where Jesus was staying and attempted to encourage the Lord to pay the tax. But before he could do so the Lord asked him this: "Peter, when the king collects taxes, will he collect from the people or from his son?" Peter replied, "Of course, he will collect from the people, not from his son." So the Lord, now alluding to himself, responded: "The son therefore does not need to pay the tax." As the Son of God, Jesus had no need to pay the temple tax. Nevertheless, He additionally said the following to Peter: "For your sake I will pay the tax anyway, and free you of embarrassment with those temple officials. I will provide you the money, but you must go fishing for it. When you hook the first fish, open its mouth, and there you will find the coin for both you and Me with which to pay the tax" (see Matthew 17:24-27).

How gracious the Lord was towards His presumptuous disciple, but how troublesome it must have been for Peter when he went fishing for the money. He was a fisherman who used nets and not a fish hook to try to catch fish. He would not have the patience in using that method to catch any fish. So there he was, seated by the lakeshore and patiently holding in his hands a fishing line attempting to hook a fish. I do not know what he must have been thinking as he waited and waited for that first fish; nevertheless, the Lord by that means was teaching him a necessary lesson. Finally, the fish did come up, and sure enough, there was the coin with which to pay the temple tax. This was rather a simple and relatively easy lesson Peter learned; but that was still not enough discipleship training for Jesus' difficult disciple.

On yet another occasion Peter came to the Lord and inquired: "My brother sinned against me seven times and I forgave him. Isn't that enough?" That was *more* than enough in Peter's mind, he most likely having thought to himself, "How gracious I am being towards my brother!" But the Lord countered with: "I do not say seven times; I say seventy times seven" (see Matthew 18:21-22).

I really do pity Peter: if only he would keep his mouth shut like most of Jesus' other disciples—but he could not help himself! Yet we must thank God, because what an apostle the Lord raised up out of that fisherman! Among all the disciples of Jesus Peter ended up being the most disciplined. Not only had the Lord now and then cut him off; God the Father had also cut him off—on the Mount of Transfiguration. And even the Holy Spirit would cut him off at the house of Cornelius the Roman centurion (Matthew 17:4-6; Acts 10:44). Nevertheless, Peter became a king.

Let us also consider briefly the two sons of Zebedee. Similar discipline was meted out upon these two disciples as well. How the Lord dealt with them! These two, James and

John, thought the kingdom was to be attained merely by asking, and even asking through their mother! But the Lord said to them: "Not so. Are you able to drink the cup which I must drink, are you willing to be baptized with the baptism I am baptized with?" These two disciples did not know what either the cup or the baptism was, but they desperately desired to sit on the right and left sides of the Lord on His kingdom throne, and so they naively replied: "Yes, we are able and willing." Their Master said to them: "Yes, you both will, but the right to sit on My right and left is not for Me to give. It is for My Father to grant" (see Matthew 20:20-23).

OUR NEED TO BE TRAINED DISCIPLES

These early disciples were severely disciplined and trained because the Lord Jesus was about the task of training and preparing kings. Do you want to be a king in the kingdom of the heavens? Do you want to reign with Christ for a thousand years? Such a privilege is not to be construed according to the human notion of being crowned, sitting on a throne, and issuing orders, but in the true sense of the kingdom of the heavens: you rule for God, and you rule as Christ will himself rule. You rule by serving, and you rule by enforcing the will of God (Matthew 20:24-28). Today's service as a servant of God on earth is actually only probationary. Your and my real service will begin in the coming kingdom age.

Meanwhile, the Lord is about the business of training and preparing us for future kingdom service as kings. No one really grows into maturity without discipline. If there is no discipline there will be no growth. We naturally do not like discipline, but the love of Christ constrains us, in that if One has died for us all, then we all have died to ourselves as well, in order that we might live for Him. Accordingly, during this present age we no longer live for ourselves but for Christ who died for us (II Corinthians 5:14-15).

So we need to increasingly acquaint ourselves with the kingdom of the heavens. When it shall come upon this earth Christ the King will need a people who have been well prepared through disciplined training and who can thus reign with Him to the glory of God. But are we ready? Will we be enjoying His life in us during that time? Or must we find ourselves in outer darkness during that period, gnashing our teeth in total regret for having forfeited the opportunity and privilege of reigning with Christ? If we do not exercise our spirit today, we will miss the kingdom when He appears. That does not mean, however, that we will miss out on heaven's eternity. Nevertheless, if we have desired to have the whole world but in the process we lose our soul, what profit and benefit will that be? (see again Matthew 16:26)

So may the Lord encourage us. This has not been a message meant to weigh us down but to lift us up in order that we may understand the true meaning of discipleship and why it is that the Lord allows us to experience all such training. It is for our eternal good. In the words of the hymn we sang today at the beginning of our time together: "Many crowd the Savior's kingdom, Few receive His cross." There is a direct relationship between the cross and the kingdom. So let us rejoice. Whenever we are disciplined, let us thank God for it. Indeed, in the words of Madame Guyon, "Let us kiss the hand of the One who disciplines us" so that we may be transformed and conformed to the image of God's beloved Son and be able to enter His coming kingdom.

Chapter 15

THE OVERCOMERS

Revelation 2:7—He that has an ear, let him hear what the Spirit says to the assemblies. To him that overcomes, I will give to him to eat of the tree of life which is in the paradise of God.

Revelation 3:21—He that overcomes, to him will I give to sit with me in my throne; as I also have overcome, and have sat down with my Father in his throne.

Revelation 12:11—And they have overcome him [the accuser] by reason of the blood of the Lamb, and by reason of the word of their testimony, and have not loved their life [soul-life] even unto death.

THE IMPORTANCE OF OVERCOMING

We are still considering together this subject of spiritual exercise, which—as is true with the many other aspects of the Christian's life we have previously discussed—has much to do with overcoming; and by overcoming in this present age the believer in Christ shall receive and experience His eternal life in the kingdom age to come. I realize that to many of us the word overcomer is quite familiar, but the point I wish to emphasize here is not whether we are familiar with theological terms but whether we are living in the reality and actuality of what overcoming means. Overcoming is the strategy of God for the recovery of the testimony of Jesus in the church. Hence, it is not something minor but is of tremendous importance, especially for us believers who are living in these last days. So I hope this topic of overcoming is not a matter we think we can treat casually or neglect. To the contrary, it is an issue of life or death for us. Moreover, the fact that God calls for us to be overcomers is of immense significance not only for us personally but also for the fulfillment of God's purpose and work. For if we fail to be overcomers, such failure will affect not only us but also the Lord's timing in ushering in His kingdom on the earth. That is why I am deeply burdened concerning this particular spiritual exercise of overcoming.

THE TESTIMONY OF GOD'S NAME IN ISRAEL

God had entrusted His very name and testimony to the nation of Israel. She was supposed to have borne His testimony in this ungodly world, in that the Israelite nation had been destined to testify to the world that there is a living God, but, sadly, she failed to do so. Nevertheless, the Lord would raise up a remnant of the faithful out of the Babylonian captivity which the Jewish nation had to experience as disciplinary punishment for her failure.

We will recall that the Jews were carried off into captivity by the Babylonians, and after seventy years God raised up a remnant from these captives. However, most of these Jews in captivity had become quite contented because they had been granted a certain amount of freedom by their captors: they could build houses for themselves, could and did establish their own businesses, and in the process they became quite prosperous financially. Where, though, was the name and testimony of God on earth? For it is significant to note that during this entire period of captivity of God's people the Biblical account of those days never once refers to God as the God of the heavens and of the earth but only makes reference to Him as the God of the heavens. In other words, He no longer had any testimony concerning himself upon the earth.

But though man may fail, God never fails. For by His Spirit He was able to raise up a remnant of faithful ones from among these captive Israelites. Those people of the remnant were stirred in heart by the Spirit of God: they were not content to live just for themselves but now wanted to live for God and for His testimony. Therefore, a remnant from among the captive children of Israel answered the call of God and returned to Jerusalem—a ruined place. And as we know from the Biblical record, there was eventually built a temple so that the name of Jehovah might be recognized once again on earth as it is in the heavens. Now that is an historical illustration of the remnant principle which is to be found throughout the Old Testament.

THE CHURCH BEARS THE TESTIMONY OF JESUS

We today are in the New Testament period and the Lord Jesus has given His testimony to the church. What, therefore, is the church for? The church is on earth for bearing the testimony of Jesus to the world. Those who have believed in Him and are saved are to declare the excellencies of the One who has saved them (I Peter 2:9b). The name of the Lord Jesus is inextricably intertwined with His church, and that is the reason she exists on the earth. The church is not to speak of herself, she is to declare the name of the Lord Jesus.

When the church had its beginning on earth on the day of Pentecost, the Holy Spirit came upon the one hundred and twenty believers who were gathered together in that Jerusalem "upper room" and were praying there with one accord (Acts 1:13-14). Those gathered believers were baptized that day into one body in the Spirit. They were no longer one hundred and twenty individuals but one hundred and twenty members of the body of Christ (Acts 2:1-4). That was the beginning of the church, and on that very same day three thousand others were added to the body of Christ. And the Bible further tells us in the book of Acts that the Lord added to the church daily, and that those who believed in the Lord persevered and continued in the teaching and fellowship of the apostles, in the breaking of bread, and in prayers (2:41-47). Such was the testimony which they bore in the world. They showed the world by their manner of life who Jesus is.

The disparaging name of "Christian" was given to these believers because the world, as it observed these people who gathered together in the name of the Lord Jesus, saw them praising the Lord, praying to the Lord, ever and always talking about Jesus, and living for Him. The world noticed that these people had a way of life totally different from any other on the earth: for it was neither the Jewish nor the Roman nor the Greek way: rather, these Jews who had believed in the Lord and those believers from among the gentile nations lived out and expressed a manner of life totally different from the lifestyle all other people pursued on the earth: indeed, it was a heavenly manner of life. Consequently, when people watched and observed them, they did not know what to say about them or what to call them. Who were they? And so, people mockingly said, "They are the Christ-ones, the Christians; they are Christ-men and -women" (Acts 11:26c). What a testimony!

Within thirty years the gospel of Jesus Christ had been preached not only in Judea and Samaria but even to the end of the known world of that time, which was the Roman Empire. It had become a conquering church, a victorious church, a church that had faithfully borne the testimony of Jesus to a watching world. It was a church that did not live for herself or make herself known but was a church that made Jesus Christ known to the whole world.

The State of the Testimony at the First Century's End

We learn from the book of Revelation that after another thirty-some years which was at the end of the first century, John, who was an apostle for the testimony of Jesus and for the word of God (1:9b), had been exiled to the island of Patmos in the eastern Mediterranean Sea (1:9a). While there he was continually faithful (again, 1:9a); and on a certain Lord's day he was in the Spirit (1:10a) and saw a vision of the risen Lord ministering to seven of His local churches in Asia Minor (today's Turkey) whose spiritual condition in five of them had become such that the Lord had to call them to repent (1:10b ff.). Of the other two, the church in Philadelphia had the praise of the risen Lord whereas the church in Smyrna had no such praise but He did not find any fault in her, either. These two were encouraged by the Lord to continue to be faithful to the end. However, the church as a whole had lost the testimony of Jesus (Revelation 1:10b-3:22). Now whenever the church loses the testimony of Jesus she has lost the very meaning for her existence.

THE OVERCOMERS

Even to the heretofore highly commendable church in Ephesus the risen Lord had to issue a warning to repent: "If you do not repent I will remove your candlestick" (see Revelation 2:5b). In other words, physically she might remain, but spiritually her testimony before God and the world had gone—she now had no meaning to her existence and no praiseworthy recognition from the Lord. And so, when the church has failed in her mission and testimony, what must God do? For though man may fail, the Lord never fails but reacts with a work of recovery. Similar to the Old Testament principle of the remnant, the Lord will bring in the principle of the overcomers. When the Lord Jesus assessed the deplorable situation in the church of John's day, He was moved to call out again and again: "He that has an ear, let him hear what the Spirit says to the churches. He that overcomes ..." In other words, here is a reaction from the risen Lord: He calls overcomers out of the church (see e.g., Revelation 2:7).

Who are the overcomers? What do they overcome? And why must there be overcomers? We are living at the very end of the age of grace. The end is coming. And while we are living during this critical time we all need to assess our true condition before God. Are we as His people faithfully bearing the testimony of Jesus to the world? Or have we fallen away from that testimony? The summons to overcome constitutes the very last call from God to His church. If we miss this final one we miss our calling and the very reason for our existence. The Lord knows very well what is the difficult, even terrible, environmental situation of the world in which we believers are living today. He fully understands; nevertheless, we are called to overcome in order that we may bear the testimony of Jesus to the world in these last days.

WHAT WE NEED TO OVERCOME

The Power of Sin

What do we need to overcome? What makes us an overcomer? As we look at our outward personal condition, we most likely would conclude that the redeemed of the Lord need to overcome the power of sin. We know that the Lord Jesus has borne our sins in His body on the cross and has forgiven our sins. He has redeemed us; therefore, we are expected to live a holy and righteous life, a life that will glorify God. So, first of all, we must overcome the power of sin in our lives. We must not allow sin to overcome us: what we should not do, we should be able not to do; and what we should do before God, we should have the power to do. However, when we look back at our experience since initially being saved, what has been the outcome for us in this matter of sin? Has it been resolved in our Christian life? Or does that sinning power still trouble and overcome us at times?

This personal experience of defeat after being saved the apostle Paul described for us in his letter to the Romans chapter 7. He tells his readers that he well knew what was the right thing to do—what for him was the will of God—and that he very much wanted to do God's will; but he found to his dismay that what he should do he could not, that what he should not do, that he did anyway. He even wrote that his experience demonstrates the fact that "it is not I who is doing it but the sin in me" (see v. 17). This self-revelation compelled this apostle to woefully cry out: "O wretched man that I am! who shall deliver me from this body of death?" (v. 24)

Do we, too, have such experience? Do we still labor under such a defeatist condition? It seems to many of us as though most of the time in our life we are defeated. Yes, perhaps once in a long while we have some victory, but that, we know, is not what the Lord has ordained for us. How, then, can we overcome the power of sin? We need to realize and acknowledge afresh that when Christ died on the cross He not only bore our sins in His body, He also bore us—our very selves—in himself to the cross. Briefly stated, our old man was crucified with Christ (Romans 6:3-11). Have we experienced our personal co-crucifixion, co-burial, and co-resurrection with the Lord Jesus? We can only find victory in Christ—not in ourselves. No matter how hard we struggle against sin, we will be defeated; but let us thank the Lord that *He* has overcome. Paul eventually discovered the secret to victory, for in that same Romans 7 chapter we find the apostle's answer to his woeful cry for help: "Thank God through Jesus Christ" (see v. 25a). It is only through Jesus Christ that we can experience the continual overcoming of the power of sin.

The World

What else must we overcome? We also need to overcome the world. We live in this world but we are not of it. Is that our daily attitude and inclination or do we find that the world still attracts us? If it is the latter, we realize it not only *attracts* us but even has its *ascendancy over us*. We see that we cannot help ourselves from loving the world.

We know we should not love the world (I John 2:15-16) nor be friends with it because to be a friend of the world is to be an enemy of God (James 4:4); but we must acknowledge that we in and of ourselves cannot cease loving the world. We cannot, but who can? The solution is for us to subjectively experience the fact that in Christ Jesus the world has been crucified to us and we have been crucified to the world (Galatians 6:14).

The Flesh

What more must we overcome? We must likewise overcome our flesh. Though we are saved, we discover that our flesh is still here, meaning that we are still carnal; indeed, the works of the flesh still continue in our lives. I can illustrate this problem we have by relating to you again an incident I and others observed when I was in Albuquerque, New Mexico on one occasion. A few of us Christian brethren were sitting in a room talking one day. In the midst of the room there was a table with a dish full of candy on it. Suddenly, a boy came in and began walking in circles around the room, with the circles of his walk becoming smaller and smaller in circumference until he reached the table itself. He quickly took a piece of candy, put it in his mouth, and went out of the room. After awhile he came back into the room again and did the same thing. He continued to come back several times more until on the final time every eye was now focused upon him, causing him to become quite self-conscious. So upon his taking his final candy piece he sheepishly remarked: "I know I should not do it, but I just love the candy."

Like this boy, is this what we too often are doing today? How can we overcome our flesh—the lust of the eyes, the diverse lusts of the flesh, and the pride of life? (I John 2:15) We in ourselves cannot, yet if we look to the Lord Jesus we will come to recognize this vital Biblical truth about ourselves at last: "I have been crucified with Christ. And no longer do I live, it is Christ who lives in me, and the life I now live in the flesh, I live by the faith of the Son of God who loved me and gave himself for me" (see Galatians 2:20).

The Self-Life

There is yet another obstacle in our lives we must overcome. We must overcome this self-life of ours. That is the life which controls our soul and expresses itself through our thinking or opinion, our emotion or feeling, and through our will or decision-making. Too often what comes out of us is not Christ but self: that is, what *I* feel, what *I* love, what *I* think, and what *I* wish to have or do. Instead of all that, it should be the love of *Christ*, the feeling of *Christ*, the thought and mind of *Christ*, and the will of *Christ*. So, how can we be delivered from ourselves and overcome our self-life? For sure, we cannot, but He can.

SATAN IS THE ENEMY

Now, of course, we know that behind all these obstacles to an overcoming life which have been mentioned here there is Satan, God's enemy. He is the one who brought sin into this world (Genesis 3:1-15; cf. John 8:44). He is the one who is the usurper of this world (cf. John 12:31b). He is the one who is in control of our flesh (Ephesians 2:2-3). He is the one who is at the back of everything negative. How can we overcome Satan? Let us acknowledge at the outset that we ourselves cannot. For he is an archangel and is therefore of higher rank than man (Job 1:6; cf. Psalm 8:4-5). His intelligence is beyond ours and his experience is longer than ours. If we try in ourselves to fight against Satan, we for certain will be overcome. Unfortunately, many people try to do that and instead are overcome by him.

BEARING THE TESTIMONY OF JESUS

As we have said, these obstacles and challenges for God's people to overcome which we have mentioned are negative in character, but we know from the Scriptures that there is a most positive reason to overcome. And that is, that we may have and maintain the testimony of the Lord Jesus to the world—to declare His name and the excellencies of the One who has brought salvation to the earth.

If we read human history aright, we find failure upon failure so far as God's purpose and His testimony are concerned. That is the reason Satan is still considered to be the god or prince of this world (John 12:31b). He is still in charge, as it were (cf. I Peter 5:8; Ephesians 6:12). Yet, it would be such a small thing—in fact, nothing at all—for God to destroy Satan. Indeed, do we not often think, Oh, if only God would destroy him, all problems in the world and in ourselves would be solved—and, oh, how good that would be!

Why is it, though, that God did not do that? The answer is, that were God to destroy Satan it would not give Him any glory, just as in the case that were a strong man to beat a little child no glory in the slightest would occrue to that man. In either case, there would be no contest. And so, in the wisdom of God He chose to have some being lower than the angels as His agent by whom to destroy the work of the fallen archangel Satan. And who is lower than the angels? God's word informs us that man was created lower than them (Psalm 8:4-5); nevertheless, God in His wisdom has purposed to use man to destroy all the works of His enemy and thus bring glory to himself. Hence, that is why, in part, we are on this earth. We are not here just for ourselves. We are here to defeat God's enemy (cf. Genesis 3:15; Romans 16:20). We are here to glorify God by faithfully bearing His testimony to the world. But sad to say, commencing all the way back from the time of our ancient forefather Adam, we have witnessed failure after failure after failure in the record of human history.

Yet in that same human history of failure we find an exception, and that is the Lord Jesus. As God He is higher than the angels, yet He lowered himself and became a man. That, too, as we shall see, was God's wisdom.

JESUS IS THE OVERCOMER

After so much failure among mankind, finally, God sent His Son into this world who would demonstrate success. "The Word became flesh and, full of grace and truth, tabernacled among men" (see John 1:14). In the sight of God there are but two men—Adam, the first man, failed; Christ, the second

Man, succeeded. He came to earth as a man, and this was the Man whose entire life on earth answered to what God had had in mind for mankind all along. When Jesus was twelve years old, for example, He was made a son of the Law; and immediately He declared: "Must I not be mindful of My Father's business?" (Luke 2:49)

Throughout His life Jesus lived as a perfect man. He did not live for himself; He lived for the will of God. Satan tried to tempt Him in diverse ways by saying: "If You are the Son of God, You can do this, or, You can do that." Most certainly, as the Son of God He *could* do all of Satan's proposed tempting acts—for instance, He *could* turn stones into bread, if He so willed. But Jesus did not so will; instead, He always stood on the ground of His being the Son of man and not the Son of God. In response, for example, to Satan's first temptation He said, "Man shall not live by bread alone but by every word that comes from the mouth of God." In each and every one of Satan's temptations Jesus refused to exercise His right as the Son of God; rather, in each instance, He maintained His place on earth as the Son of man (Matthew 4:1-11). As a man Jesus was tempted in all things but as a man He did not fall: He was tempted by sin, by the world, by the flesh, by self; as a matter of fact, He was tempted by everything but did not sin (Hebrews 4:15); rather, the Son of man denied himself, took up the cross, and followed God His Father in all things. He gave himself totally to God and was obedient to God's will even to the extremity of death, and that the death on a cross (Philippians 2:8). In all circumstances and situations He as a man overcame the enemy completely.

We may recall that by the time of the events recorded in John chapter 12 it had become for Jesus, humanly speaking, the most glorious period of His life on earth. The whole nation of Israel, it seemed, had gone after Him. Even some gentiles from Greece sought to speak with Him. This, then, was Jesus' moment of glory. But did He bask in that glory? Not at all. Though Jesus did say, "The time of My glory has come," He was speaking of a different glory—the glory which He would bring to His Father—when He prayed, "Father, I have glorified Thee," referring here to His forthcoming death on the cross. From this we can discern that Jesus' entire life was solely governed by the desire to bring glory to His Father and to bear the testimony of God to the world. His life was never centered upon himself. The Son of man could therefore say at this moment: "This is the time that the god of this world will be cast out" (see John 12:31b). In other words, the Son of man had overcome.

Who actually is the overcomer in the world today? Is it not Christ Jesus? He, in fact, is *the* Overcomer. We cannot overcome, but He has overcome (John 16:33b). And it was on the basis of His having overcome that He could confidently declare: "I will build My church upon this rock, and the gates of Hades shall not prevail against it" (see Matthew 16:18b). The church is built on the overcoming victory of Christ. Therefore, because He has overcome, we too shall overcome. But how? The way we enter into and experience this overcoming life is by the way of faith.

THE WAY OF FAITH

What is faith? Faith is not something we develop in ourselves. Oftentimes we try to hypnotize ourselves into the experience of faith by saying over and over to ourselves—I believe, I believe, I believe. If we continue to repeat "I believe, I believe," it may appear as though we do believe. But such a technique does not work. That is not faith. Faith is neither looking into one's self nor looking at one's environment; the focus of faith cannot be found in those places. Faith is looking away from all these and looking off to Jesus, who is the Author and Finisher of faith (Hebrews 12:2a).

I John declares that "all that has been begotten of God gets the victory over the world; and this is the victory which has gotten the victory over the world, our faith. Who is he that gets the victory over the world, but he that believes that Jesus is the Son of God?" (5:4-5) We see from this Scripture that our victory is based upon and flows out from our faith in the Lord Jesus Christ. It is not based upon our struggling but upon our believing—believing in Him. We take Him at His word and rely upon His finished work accomplished at Calvary—and that is faith.

EXERCISING OUR SPIRIT
TO OVERCOME THE ENEMY

In this connection, I cannot refrain from relating a story which I love so much. Once a little girl believed in the Lord Jesus, and she was most happy in the Lord. A man came to test her and asked: "Little girl, do you believe in the Lord Jesus?" She replied, "I do." "Are you happy in the Lord?" She answered, "I am."

Then the man said, "Suppose Satan came and knocked at your heart's door, wanting to come in. What can you do? You are just a little girl. Your strength is so small, but Satan is a mighty warrior. He can easily push in the door and enter, and you will be finished."

The little girl thought for awhile and then answered: "If Satan comes knocking at my door, I will turn to Jesus and say, 'Lord, will You please open the door?' And the Lord Jesus will go to the door and open it. When Satan sees the Lord, he will say, 'Oh, excuse me, I have knocked at the wrong door.' And he shall flee."

Is that not the secret of victory? We cannot in ourselves overcome the enemy. Yet, how we apply our whole strength against the enemy's attempt to enter our lives and naively say to him: "You cannot come in. I do not want you here." But he just pushes himself in and you are finished and done for. But where is the Lord in all this? Are you in fellowship with the Lord as that little girl obviously was or do you neglect—perhaps even forget—the Lord in your life? If not, are you exercising your spirit? Do you turn to Jesus in the hour of temptation and say, "Lord, You please confront the enemy at the door"? That is engaging in spiritual exercise.

God has made every provision for us to overcome if we will but avail ourselves of it all. The Holy Spirit who dwells in us will remind us of what is not of the Lord and warn us to keep away from it. He will show us where the point of the conflict of wills is. But as He does that we need to respond, and the response required is spiritual exercise. If we do not exercise our spirit, then the voice of the Holy Spirit will just pass into one ear and out the other.

We need to exercise our conscience by responding positively to whatever the Spirit of God speaks to it about. Let us not rebel against our conscience but let us submit to its voice. Yet how can that power come to us enabling us to do this? It is by looking to Jesus who is in us. The Holy Spirit is there in our spirit to bring the victorious power of the Lord Jesus into our life at the moment of conflict or temptation, and if we commence to struggle, the Lord will encourage us by saying: "Don't struggle, but believe in Me. Trust Me and give yourself to Me. Let go of yourself, and let Me take over." For that to happen, however, it will require spiritual exercise on our part.

Unfortunately, our problem is that too often we are exercising our mind instead of our spirit by constantly thinking and trying to figure out what to do and how to do in resolving a given instance of temptation or conflict or challenge. Do we ever consider exercising our spirit at a time like that? Can we not learn to draw near to the Lord and tell Him of the situation? We need to simply tell Him we are not able, but He is able. If in every situation we trust Him and look to Him in such manner, we will discover that He is more than sufficient to meet every challenge victoriously. We can enjoy being more than conquerors over all circumstances around us (Romans 8:37).

Such, then, is the secret of victory. By continually exercising our spirit in the way described, we not only will overcome the unacceptable forces around us and within us, we also will be accomplishing the purpose of God in His having and maintaining—through us—the testimony of Jesus to the world.

THE CONSEQUENCES OF OVERCOMING

What will be the consequences for us of our overcoming? With respect to this present age, overcoming provides us with such a victorious life on earth that we can richly enjoy the Lord and His life and bear the testimony of Jesus to the world. Moreover, with respect to the coming kingdom age, if today we overcome and keep the testimony of Jesus, there will be a further consequence—we will enjoy the promise of eternal life in all its various aspects as described for us in Revelation chapters 2 and 3. For, strictly speaking, all the promises having to do with eternal life which are there recorded as having been promised by the risen Lord to those who overcome are all to be experienced in the kingdom age to come.

For instance, the risen Lord Jesus promised this to every overcomer: "To him that overcomes, I will give to him to eat of the tree of life which is in the paradise of God" (2:7b). Though those who overcome today enjoy life in this present age, the promise made here is to eat of the Tree of Life in the paradise of God. That refers to the coming kingdom age. During the kingdom age the overcomers will enjoy eternal life—the life of Christ—which experience can be likened to that of the five wise virgins who entered in to the marriage feast of the Lamb to enjoy life with the Lord Jesus (Matthew 25:1-4, 6-7, 10b-c; cf. Revelation 19:9).

The risen Lord also promised that the overcomer shall in no wise be injured of the second death (2:11b). Now this has presented a problem for many Christians because of the reference made here to "the second death," which is another way in the Bible of referring to "the lake of fire" (Revelation 20:14). The "first death" in Scripture is a reference to our physical death, but "the second death" is specifically a description of eternal death in the lake of fire (Revelation 21:8). So can it be that a Christian who fails to overcome will lose his salvation and end up in hell? No, the Lord has indicated that those who do not overcome will only be *injured* by the second death. What does this signify for those who are not overcomers?

I think the best illustration of this is to be found in the book of Daniel. The three friends of Daniel had refused to worship the golden image King Nebuchadnezzar had erected, and consequently they were to be thrown into a fiery furnace. Nebuchadnezzar had become so indignant over their refusal that he ordered the fire to be increased sevenfold. It was so hot that only the strongest soldiers he could find were able to approach the furnace close enough to cast these three helpless men into it. In fact, the fire was so intense that it literally came up out of the furnace and burnt the soldiers to death, even though they were not actually thrown into the fire (Daniel 3:1-27).

That provides for us an indication of what it is to be injured by the second death. In other words, for the believer who is not an overcomer it will not be the experience of the second death itself but that of being harmed or injured in some way by the second death. But for those who do overcome in their present life the Lord's promise is that they will not even be injured by the second death. Let us recall Jesus' parable in which the master of a wicked servant in his household declared that he would be cut into two and be assigned to the place reserved for the hypocrites and where there would be weeping and the gnashing of teeth in regret. That, too, speaks of being *injured* by the second death but eternally saved (see Matthew 24:51). For the overcomer, however, there is the risen Lord's promise of life, in that he will not even be injured by the second death.

The next promise of life for the overcomer mentioned by the Lord was this: "To him that overcomes, to him will I give of the hidden manna; and I will give to him a white stone, and on the stone a new name written, which no one knows but he that receives it" (2:17b-c). "Hidden manna" refers to life. We may recall that when God sent down manna from heaven to the children of Israel in the wilderness, some of it was put into a pot and kept in the tabernacle. It thus became, as it were, *hidden* manna (Exodus 16:32-34). In other words, the promise here is that the overcomer shall enjoy life that was heretofore unknown to God's people. On the other hand, "a white stone" has reference to what in ancient Greek and Roman times was awarded to the victor in competitive athletic games: he was given a white stone with a new name inscribed upon it. Thus, the overcomer in the present age shall receive a reward in the age of the kingdom of the heavens to come.

Another promise of life the risen Lord shall fulfill to the overcomer includes all of the following: "he that overcomes, and he that keeps unto the end my works, to him will I give authority over the nations, and he shall shepherd them with an iron rod; as vessels of pottery are they broken in pieces, as I also have received from my Father; and I will give to him the morning star" (2:26-28).

The Lord also promised the following: "He that overcomes, he shall be clothed in white garments, and I will not blot his name out of the book of life, and will confess his name before my Father and before his angels" (3:5). "White garments" speak of the righteousnesses of the saints. It is to be the wedding garment of the bride of the Lamb (Revelation 19:7-8). But what is signified—both for the overcomer and the non-overcomer—by the phrase, "blot his name out of the book of life"? This requires a little explanation.

For the believer in Christ who nonetheless fails to overcome, his name shall be blotted out in the book of life. This statement of the Lord's, like the earlier one regarding the second death, has also troubled many Christians. Yet one's name being blotted out by the Lord does not mean a person's name is to be erased or removed from the book of life but is to be covered therein during the coming kingdom age. The name will still remain in the book of life, except that it shall be covered during that age. For the overcomer, however, his name will not be covered or blotted out but will be on display in the book of life for all to see. And furthermore, the fact that his name shall not be blotted out means that the risen Lord shall be most glad and willing to confess the overcomer's name before His Father and the angels during the Lord's second coming.

Yet another promise made by the Lord was as follows: "He that overcomes, him will I make a pillar in the temple of my God, and he shall go no more at all out; and I will write upon him the name of my God, and the name of the city of my God, the new Jerusalem, which comes down out of heaven, from my God, and my new name" (3:12). What an immense reward is to be bestowed upon every overcomer during the kingdom age! He will have a most intimate relationship with God and Christ and shall occupy a very responsible position in the kingdom of the heavens.

The risen Lord made one final promise: "He that overcomes, to him will I give to sit with me in my throne; as I also have overcome, and have sat down with my Father in his throne" (3:21). The Lord Jesus has overcome and is now seated with the Father in His throne, but one day He will be given the kingdom with His own throne, and the overcomers will sit with Him in His throne.

In the light of all that has been said, may each of us truly see why spiritual exercise can be so profitable and beneficial to all who overcome—not only for this age but also for the age that is yet to come. If we truly see and understand, how, then, for the sake of a little ease, pleasure and benefit, can we be so foolish as to willfully forfeit that which holds out the promise of so great, so glorious, and so marvelous a life. May the Lord therefore help us that we may make this our heart's true desire: to be an overcomer and a victor to the very last—and all for the glory of God.

Chapter 16

THE NEW JERUSALEM

I Timothy 4:8-10—Bodily exercise is profitable for a little, but piety [godliness] is profitable for everything, having promise of life, of the present one, and of that to come. The word is faithful and worthy of all acceptation; for, for this we labour and suffer reproach, because we hope in a living God, who is preserver of all men, specially of those that believe.

Revelation 21:1-7—And I saw a new heaven and a new earth; for the first heaven and the first earth had passed away, and the sea exists no more. And I saw the holy city, new Jerusalem, coming down out of the heaven from God, prepared as a bride adorned for her husband. And I heard a loud voice out of the heaven, saying, Behold, the tabernacle of God is with men, and he shall tabernacle with them, and they shall be his people, and God himself shall be with them, their God. And he shall wipe away every tear from their eyes; and death shall not exist any more, nor grief, nor cry, nor distress shall exist any more, for the former things have passed away. And he that sat on the throne said, Behold, I make all things new. And he says to me, Write, for these words are true and faithful. And he said to me, It is done. I am the Alpha and the Omega, the beginning and the end. I will give to him that thirsts of the fountain of the water of life freely. He that overcomes shall inherit these things, and I will be to him God, and he shall be to me son.

Revelation 22:1-5—And he shewed me a river of water of life, bright as crystal, going out of the throne of God and of the Lamb. In the midst of its street, and of the river, on this side and on that side, the tree of life, producing twelve fruits, in each month yielding its fruit; and the leaves of the tree for healing of the nations. And no curse shall be any more; and the throne of God and of the Lamb shall be in it; and his servants shall serve him, and they shall see his face; and his name is on their foreheads. And night shall not be any more, and no need of a lamp, and light of the sun; for the Lord God shall shine upon them, and they shall reign to the ages of ages.

During these past several months we have been considering together this vital matter of spiritual exercise—how spiritual exercise gives us the promise of life. Yet what is in view here is not physical life or soul- or self-life, but spiritual life: the life of Christ Jesus that God has given us. And by means of spiritual exercise we can possess that life not only in this present age but also in the ages to come. So today I would like for us to consider together how spiritual exercise can bring us into new Jerusalem.

GOD PUT ETERNITY IN MAN'S HEART

In Psalm 90 Moses declared: "from eternity to eternity Thou art God" (see v. 2b). Our God is the eternal One. Whereas in creating all other living things God made them beautiful for a time in their season, in creating man He placed eternity in his heart (Ecclesiastes 3:11 ASV). In other words, man was not created for a time or for a season but was created with eternity in view because God is himself eternal. So this is why man will never be satisfied in living only for today. Even if a person should live to the age of one hundred years, he will never be satisfied.

I remember during my college years always seeing at the entrance to the college a memorial pillar which had been placed there in honor of a particular individual. Yet that pillar had been cut off at its middle in order to represent the fact that this person, who had done so much, had nonetheless not fulfilled all which he had wanted to fulfill before he died. Is that not the sense we all have? The present heavens and earth will someday all pass away, including all the physical things—even the animals—which live for a season of time but not for eternity (II Peter 3:10; Revelation 21:1b). The cat or the dog which we love as a pet lives only for a season; and the flowers we so much appreciate blossom for merely a season as well and then their end is reached. However, that is not the way with man because God created him with eternity in his heart.

GOD'S ETERNAL PURPOSE FOR MAN

We cannot simply live for time—following the all-too-familiar philosophy of eating and drinking, for tomorrow we die. That is not God's will. He desires every one of us to enjoy life in eternity to come. We have already mentioned that in eternity past God had a purpose before He had created anything: He would never embark upon any project by chance. So that before the establishment of time God had conceived a purpose in His mind, and which we today call the eternal purpose of God. That purpose is ever and always concerned with His beloved Son, and with His Son and in His Son man is graciously included. We have also pointed out previously that time is continually being used by God to perform what He has purposed in eternity past. And with respect to this matter of time, we find in the Bible that there is this current age, which is the age of grace, that there is also the age to come, which is the millennial or kingdom age, and that there is eternity as well—what the book of Revelation in the Greek original has termed "the ages of the ages" (see 1:6b, 22:5b Darby; cf ASV mgn). Having already discussed the relationship between spiritual exercise and the first two of these three ages, I would today like for us to consider how spiritual exercise has its relationship with the ageless eternity to come.

Now when we look at ourselves, are we satisfied? When we look around us, can we say we are satisfied with what we see? I am afraid the answer is no. From the Bible we learn that the Lord Jesus is to have a glorious church without spot or wrinkle or any such flaw or imperfection (Ephesians 5:27). But as we observe the condition of the church today, do we see that glorious church? Most likely what we see is just the opposite. Moreover, the more we look at ourselves, the more we are dissatisfied; the more we look around us, the more we are unsatisfied; and the more we look at the church, the more we sense that it is anything *but* a glorious church. Instead, we find it is quite *in*glorious and even in some respects shameful. Let us praise God, however, that though man may fail, God never does. And as a way to encourage us, God has given us His final revelation.

THE LAST REVELATION GOD HAS GIVEN

Chapters 21 and 22 of the book of Revelation constitutes the last revelation God has given us. From these two glorious chapters we realize that in spite of our failures and weaknesses He shall be able to finish that which He had purposed in eternity past before time ever began. I believe the reason God has unveiled to us this final revelation, which is concerned with new Jerusalem in eternity to come, is to encourage us and to show us that in spite of all our weaknesses He is able to obtain fully what He had had in mind from the very beginning. He most surely will gain it for himself. God is using time to accomplish what He had purposed before creation.

In these two chapters there is described in great detail for us a new heaven and a new earth; all the old things have disappeared from sight. There is new Jerusalem descending out of heaven upon this new earth. Oftentimes believers have pictured this in their minds in the physical sense only. Hymns have been written and sung about God's people entering through pearly gates, walking on the golden street, and playing harps all day. Christians have been too physical and too material in their conception of what has been described in these two chapters. Here, God is unveiling for us a spiritual reality; and with spiritual reality there is far more to be seen and understood than just the physical and material aspect; it is heavenly and spiritual in nature. For instance, how can we ever imagine a city being a bride—the bride of the Lamb? That is physically impossible. Please understand that I am not trying to over-spiritualize things here; nevertheless, Christians must realize that when it comes to spiritual reality, there is more to be seen than only the physical and material side: the heavenly and spiritual side must also be discerned. What we can see physically is temporal, but what we cannot see and which can only be seen by the eyes of faith is eternal (II Corinthians 4:18).

NEW JERUSALEM: THE BRIDE OF THE LAMB

In this final revelation or vision God has given us we behold a holy city, new Jerusalem—prepared and adorned to be the bride for the Lamb of God, the Lord Jesus Christ. Now in visualizing this wonderful city with the eyes of faith, the spiritual impression we receive is that of a union: the uniting of new Jerusalem to the Lamb. And that has been the purpose of God from before the creation, that man may be united with Christ into one.

At the very beginning of the Bible, in the book of Genesis, a marriage is brought into view. After God had created man He said, "It is not good for man to be alone; I will make him a helpmate, his like" (see 2:18). So God put Adam to sleep and performed the first surgical operation: He took "something" out from Adam's side, some Bible versions stating it to have been a rib whereas in the Hebrew original the translated text reads as "something." And with that something taken from man God built a woman. He then led that woman to the man and they became one flesh—a union in marriage. That was the scene presented to us at the Bible's beginning (2:21-24). And at the very end of the Bible there is brought into view another marriage—the uniting of a city, new Jerusalem, to the Lamb of God, the Lord Jesus Christ.

UNION WITH GOD

"Union with God" is a term many of us have probably heard quite often. The theme and aim of the mystics has always been union with God. For example, the seventeenth-century Christian lady in France, Jeanne-Marie Bouvier de la Motte (Guyon) (1648-1717), known more familiarly as Madame Guyon, had described it as each of us believers being like a drop of water in a stream that gradually flows until it reaches the vast ocean, it then having become one with the ocean. Do we see anything wrong there? Union with God is the aspiration of most people in the world, but in the sense in which the mystics talk about it, there is a serious flaw. Such a notion as described by Madame Guyon could either become the error known as pantheism—which holds that everything is God and God is everything—or the error of the deification of man, signifying that in our being united with God we ourselves become God. Deification of man has sometimes been taught in Christianity.

Upon hearing the above discussion some Christians might react by claiming: "Is that not what Psalm 82 declares: 'Ye are gods'? And did not Jesus himself quote this verse as recorded in John 10:34?" Yes, He did quote that verse from the Psalms; but Jesus explained the matter by saying the following: "Is it not written in ... [the] law, I said, Ye are gods? ... he called them gods *to whom the word of God came* ..." (John 10:34-35a, emphasis added). The phrase, "the word of God" here, refers, of course, to the Old Testament Scriptures.

And we very much need to be aware of the use sometimes of the word gods in these Scriptures. For they at times have used this word to stand for judges who, as Jesus explained, had the word of God. Nowhere in the Old Testament is there the notion mentioned of men becoming gods or of their having been deified. Nevertheless, let us praise God that it is His will that we should be united with Christ into one for eternity, and through that union—and only by that union— are we united with God. The Scriptures never teach the idea of man—even Christian man—being united with God *directly*. The distinction between God on the one hand and man on the other is never blurred in the Bible: God always remains God and man always remains man, and so shall it be in eternity.

What the Bible therefore teaches is union with God *in Christ Jesus*, and that is what we see here in Revelation. We are told here that this new Jerusalem is to be brought into union with the Lamb of God because she is to be married to the Lamb. She is able to be brought into union with God only because the Lamb *is* God. We need to be very clear on this point; otherwise, we will be led into heresy. God's people are to be united to God in and through life and that is the life of the Lord Jesus. In other words, this union with God is through Christ Jesus: God's people are united with Christ and through *that* union they are to be united to God.

THE WIDTH, LENGTH, AND HEIGHT
OF GOD'S LOVE

According to her dimensions as described in Revelation, new Jerusalem is an incredibly huge city: "he that spoke with me had a golden reed as a measure, that he might measure the city, and its gates, and its wall. And the city lies four-square, and its length is as much as the breadth. And he measured the city with the reed—twelve thousand stadia: the length and the breadth and height of it are equal. And he measured its wall, a hundred and forty-four cubits, a man's measure, that is, the angel's" (21:15-17). Hence, this city is a cube—its width, length, and height are equal.

Let us recall that in the Old Testament period there was once a structure that contained within itself a room which was a perfect cube. The structure was the Jerusalem temple, which included three major parts: the outer court, the holy place, and the holiest place. And the holiest of all three was a cube: with its width, length, and height being perfectly equal (I kings 6:16, 19-20a). That, however, was just a *room* in an edifice of old Jerusalem, whereas in God's final revelation we have a *city*, new Jerusalem, in the shape of a cube! Can anyone imagine a city as a cube—with its length, breadth, and, more marvelously, its height all being equal? Consider for a moment new Jerusalem's cubist dimension: twelve thousand stadia. Now a mere sixty stadia measures out to about seven English miles; therefore, twelve *thousand* stadia measures out to some *fourteen hundred miles*. Has anyone of us ever seen a city that is fourteen hundred miles in length, width, *and* especially in height? None of us! This entity called new Jerusalem therefore cannot, in the first instance, be considered as something physical; rather, the description is meant to convey a spiritual impression: that impression most likely being the sheer immensity of the work of God which He has done in bringing His people into the new Jerusalem that will become the bride of the Lamb. Oh, the length, width, and height of the love of God is beyond human understanding! Hence what this passage in Revelation reveals and impresses upon us spiritually is the immensity of the love of God; and that it is through His tremendous love that His saints are being brought into this reality of being united with God through the Lord Jesus Christ.

TOTAL SEPARATION

"And he measured its wall, a hundred and forty-four cubits, a man's measure, that is, the angel's" (21:17). Wall in Scripture stands for or symbolizes separation. A cubit is the length of an arm and hand. The wall in new Jerusalem is therefore a great and high wall, signifying total separation. Christ is the wall of separation. God is about the business of performing the work by His Holy Spirit of building Christ in His people till they be totally separated from all that is not of God but preserves all that is of Him.

THE GLORY OF GOD FILLS THE CITY

What we spiritually discern in contemplating Revelation's description of this city which comes down out of heaven is nothing but glory. The glory of God fills that city. Her wall is made of jasper (21:18a); and we are told in Revelation 4 that the One who sits upon the throne is like jasper (v. 3a)—in other words, this betokens God's glory. The whole city is filled with the glory of God. This beautifully dovetails, does it not, with the Scripture in Ephesians 5 which declares: "It is a glorious church without spot or wrinkle or of any such sort" (see again v. 27). We realize from this that, prophetically speaking, God has done it. Man may fail, but God never fails in accomplishing His purpose and work: new Jerusalem is full of glory.

Now glory is nothing less than the manifestation of God. When fallen man is manifested, we do not see glory, we see only shame. But when God is manifested, we see glory. Every time God is revealed or manifested in the Scriptures we see glory. One day we will be delivered out of all the shame of our flesh and will truly be conformed to the image of God's Son Jesus Christ (Romans 8:29a). And when that day arrives, it will be all glory—nothing of self but everything of God.

THE MEASURING ROD GOD USES IN THE CHURCH

There is a measuring rod or standard of measurement in the Bible by which everyone and everything must be measured or evaluated. What, then, is the standard against which God would measure us individually, also His church, and everything else? God has but one standard—His beloved Son (Romans 8:29a). God will set forth His Son against whom He will measure every one of us to see whether or not we rise to His standard. Whatever in us does not will be cast away, and only that which meets God's standard according to Christ will last forevermore (I Corinthians 3:13-15a).

Are we building up the house of God with gold, silver, and precious stones or are we building ourselves up before God with wood, stubble, and hay (I Corinthians 3:11-12)? Today, what we too often see in God's house are wood, stubble, and hay because they are cheap and are therefore readily available. We can build a very large edifice with such cheap materials; but gold, silver, and precious stones are costly and cannot be easily seen because they are small due to the fact that this is "the day of small things" (Zechariah 4:10a). Yet let us not despise the day of humble accomplishments and costly undertakings for the Lord's church nor be attracted by that which is big. We by nature desire after and are drawn to big things—for instance, a mega-church. Yet what God is seeking after is what is of Him—gold, silver, and precious stones. Thank God, the day shall come when the church shall have no spot or wrinkle or any such imperfection. She will only be full of His glory.

THE CITY'S GATES AND FOUNDATIONS

We also learn from God's final revelation that this city has twelve gates, and every gate is a pearl (21:21a, b). Have you ever seen a pearl the size of a gate through which you can walk? The names inscribed on these twelve gates are those of the twelve tribes of Israel (21:12b). Then there are twelve foundations to the wall, whose names are those of the twelve apostles of the Lamb of God, and these foundations consist of twelve precious stones (21:14, 19). The spiritual impression to be gained from all this is that the day will come when God will gather together all the redeemed and all His works accomplished during both the Old Testament and New Testament eras and sum them all up in Christ Jesus. It is the summing up of all the works of God performed throughout time past and present (Ephesians 1:19-23; Colossians 1:15-20). Nothing will be lost. This can be likened to what took place after the Lord Jesus had performed the miracle of feeding the five thousand people with that boy's five loaves and two fishes. For after all the people were satisfied, the disciples gathered up all the bits and pieces, which amounted to twelve filled baskets. Nothing which God will have done is ever to be lost; all will still be there (John 6:1-13). Contrarily, whatever is not of, through, or for God (cf. Romans 11:36) will be cast out (I Corinthians 3:10-15a).

GOD ALMIGHTY AND THE LAMB ARE THE TEMPLE OF THE CITY

Now as we survey new Jerusalem more thoroughly, we discover an odd fact—there is no temple in this city of God (21:22a). During the Old Testament dispensation the tabernacle or temple had been the most important element present among God's people. We will recall that after God had delivered the children of Israel out of Egypt and brought them to Mount Sinai, He covenanted with them to make them His people (Exodus 19:3-6); and He also desired to dwell among them; nevertheless, despite having been delivered out of Egypt, they were not yet a holy people. Which meant that God, who is most holy, could not dwell directly in their midst. He therefore asked them to build Him a tabernacle, and He would live therein among His people (Exodus 25:8-9). Later, of course, the temple in Jerusalem came into existence.

But then, after many centuries had come and gone, God sent His Son to the earth. Twice during His several years of ministry Jesus was agitated in heart to cleanse the Jerusalem temple. When He first cleansed it at the beginning of His ministry, He declared this: "You cannot make my Father's house into a house of merchandise" (see John 2:13-16). But when He again cleansed the temple at the end of His ministry, Jesus discovered that its condition had gotten worse; for He now cried out: "This was to have been a house of prayer for all nations, but you have made it a den of robbers" (see Mark 11:15-17). Significantly, on the occasion of His first temple cleansing Jesus had declared to some Jews who had questioned His right to do this: "If you destroy this temple, I will raise it back up in three days." In saying this, however, Jesus had been referring to the temple of His body (John 2:18-20).

While the Lord Jesus was on earth He himself was the temple of God because God dwelt in Him and He dwelt in God. But then, once the Lord ascended back to the Father, the church—the body of Christ—ought now to be the temple of God on earth all during the present age. And we learn from Revelation that in eternity to come the whole city of new Jerusalem is to be a temple. No longer do we find the holiest place, the holy place, and the outer court; instead, we see that the entire city is the temple because God Almighty and the Lamb are its temple (21:22). So far as we are concerned, He is the temple, and so far as He is concerned, we too are the temple. Is that not marvelous that there shall be such a dwelling together in unity? Let us not overlook the fact that though there is no temple, the throne of God and of the Lamb is there in the very center of this spiritual reality known as new Jerusalem (22:1-3a). And let us not misunderstand that though in the ages of ages to come believers shall be united with God in Christ Jesus, the authority of God will still be upon them. We often hear it said today that familiarity breeds contempt. We may therefore think that because His people shall be so close to God in eternity, they can disregard His authority. Not so, for in the ages of ages to come there shall be no resistance in new Jerusalem to His supreme authority there.

THE GOLDEN STREET

In contemplating this immense city further we are faced with another and quite strange phenomenon: it has only one street (21:21c, 22:2a). People have tried to figure out how physically there can be but one street—one which touches every gate and runs throughout the city everywhere. Some have concluded, for example, that it must be spiral in shape, and that this single street spirals upward higher and higher until it touches the summit where the throne of God is. But let us not think here in terms of the physical but the spiritual. So what are we to assume is the meaning when the text indicates there is only one street? (see Revelation 21:21b)

Quite often, a street is a place where people walk along together engaged in fellowship. Therefore, we may say that in the Scriptures the word street can speak of fellowship, and we know that for the Christian there is only one fellowship. Today, unfortunately, we hear of this fellowship, that fellowship, and other assorted fellowships. How we Christians are divided! According to the Bible, however, there is only one fellowship—that of the Son of God (I Corinthians 1:9). It is the fellowship of the Lord Jesus with His Father in the Spirit, and this fellowship has been extended to all those who are His (I John 1:3b).

The wonderful thing is that new Jerusalem's street is golden. Have you ever seen gold that is transparent? There is no such gold on this earth. This street is of transparent gold like crystal so that everything upon the street is reflected.

God's people will not be able to hide anything because this fellowship is so open and thus will reveal everything. People today talk excitedly about walking on this golden street in the ages to come. Yet if it is able to reflect all which might be in anyone's mind, would anyone dare walk today on that street? People dare not. But one day that will become a fact, and God's people will be able to walk on that transparent golden street without hesitation or shame. Their fellowship will be without any shadow or shade—even like the fellowship between the Father and the Son. Will that not be most wonderful?

THE RIVER OF LIFE AND THE TREE OF LIFE

Then we find there is one river—the river of life flowing through the whole city. There is one Tree of Life, and it spreads itself not only in the midst of the river but along the two sides of the river as well, and all through the city (22:1-2a). New Jerusalem is a garden city because the Tree of Life is there bearing a different fruit every month of the year (22:2b). Such can be said to symbolize the fruit of life or the fruit of the Spirit of God (cf. Galatians 5:22-23a). And the leaves of this same tree are for the healing of the nations (22:2c). All this betokens the fullness of life and the enjoyment of life itself.

OUR RESPONSE

Would you like to be in new Jerusalem? It is God's will that all who are saved will be there. But let us be mindful of this, that before that time comes, God is intent on *preparing* us today to *be* there. During every moment of every day we live God is preparing us for that coming day. He not only has sufficient grace, He also has made every provision for us to enable us to be there. It is a full salvation Christ has won for us. He is to sanctify by the work of the Holy Spirit not only our spirit but also our soul and even our body. For all this to happen, however, God requires us to respond to Him. That is God's ongoing principle which He continually maintains— even in this matter of our getting saved. What the Lord Jesus has accomplished on Calvary's cross is more than sufficient to effect the salvation of everyone who is born into this world. Sadly, not all are saved because many do not respond in faith—they do not believe. Instead, their response is to reject Christ, and in rejecting Him, they must suffer the consequences of their unremitted sins. It is only by our receiving Christ Jesus on the basis of the blood He has shed for us at Calvary that we have remission of sin and are delivered from eternal death. If anyone rejects the Lord Jesus, that person's sin remains with him or her, which means that that individual must pay the wages of sin which is eternal death (John 3:14-18). Sadly, that person will be outside of new Jerusalem.

A similar situation will be true for us who have believed but who fail to overcome during our earthly life. Thank God, all who have believed are saved according to His unchanging will: once we are saved we are forever saved and will be saved to the uttermost, that is, saved completely and forever—even as it has been declared in God's word: "Whom He has foreknown, He has foreordained to be conformed to the image of His beloved Son" (see Romans 8:29a). This same Scripture goes on to indicate that a vital process is involved in our being saved to the uttermost: "Whom He has called, He has justified. Whom He has justified, He has glorified" (see Romans 8:30b-c). For us to be glorified—that is, for us to be brought into glory—a responsibility is ours to engage in spiritual exercise. Thank God that in His word He has shown us how to exercise our spirit. God has given us His life through Christ; He has given us the Holy Spirit who is in us to bring us ultimately into glory. But we have a responsibility to respond by agreeing and receiving in our spirit whatever the Holy Spirit speaks to us. If we exercise our spirit in such a manner, then by the grace of God we will be brought into the place of glory.

DISCIPLINE NOW OR IN THE MILLENNIAL AGE?

The foregoing discussion regarding our needful response to God's working to prepare us for the place of glory can perhaps help to explain further what was mentioned in the previous message concerning the kingdom and about those Christians who may need to be disciplined during that period. Today, many believers are comforting themselves by saying, "Once saved, forever saved"—in other words, they are overlooking the kingdom age to come and their relationship to it. As was pointed out last time, there *is* the kingdom age to come that shall precede the eternal age. Entrance into the kingdom, however, is for those who have overcome in the present age of grace. If, on the other hand, a saved believer in Christ does not overcome today, what will be the consequence for that person during the kingdom age? Now the Lord does not want us to engage in negative thinking, which we often do. It is my belief, based upon my understanding of God's word, that even though we do not respond to the working of the Holy Spirit today in exercising our spirit—even though we may continue to live in, by, and for our flesh during this present age—we will nonetheless be in heaven, in new Jerusalem, after all. Such non-overcoming believers will indeed be in new Jerusalem; nevertheless, they will need to endure the disciplinary experience of the kingdom age first. For if those Christians do not allow themselves to be disciplined today, they will have to be disciplined by God in the kingdom age to come.

God uses the kingdom age to discipline those believers who have not submitted to the chastening of the Lord in this present age of grace (cf. Hebrews 12:1-11). A son cannot grow into maturity without a father's discipline. It is absolutely necessary. None of God's saved people is able to avoid discipline. We may think we can avoid it for the duration of at most a hundred years or so of life on earth, but during the kingdom age of a thousand years we will be weeping and gnashing our teeth in deep regret for having avoided it. God is most positive. He wants everyone who is saved to be saved to the uttermost so that in eternity to come all His saved ones will be counted among all God's redeemed ones inhabiting new Jerusalem.

One further truth ought to be noted here. We who believe are saved to serve Him. If we are not faithful in our service today, our conduct can be likened to the one-talent servant in Jesus' parable who had one talent given him by his master but who buried it—he did not serve his lord and master as he should have. In those thousand years of the coming kingdom age we servants of God will regret it and will have to be disciplined. Now it is quite true that we believers are all sons of God, but it is equally true that we also are all His servants, and who are, or should be, engaged in faithful service to Him. Yet in a sense, our service to God today is only probationary in nature. Our real service begins in eternity—in new Jerusalem. In the ages of ages to come we will serve God according to His will. What a service that will be!

THE LAST REVELATION
IS TO ENCOURAGE AND WARN

I believe the Lord has given us this last revelation in order that we may be encouraged and also that we may be warned.

The apostle John knew the Lord so well, but twice in the book of Revelation we read of him doing something quite bizarre: he bowed down and worshiped the angel who had shown to him the vision of new Jerusalem. It was so spectacular and awesome that it took him by surprise. As a result, John was beside himself and worshiped the angel. He was lost in total wonder and amazement.

Are we, too, lost in wonder? Or do we think too little of what God has purposed and prepared for us? Oh, if we really see His immense plan for us, I wonder if we would do the same thing as John did. It is too marvelous! It should take our breath away and totally capture our hearts.

The Lord has graciously given us this final unveiling—that of new Jerusalem. May that vision, that revelation, captivate every one of our hearts. We do indeed look and long for that city, whose builder and maker is God (cf. Hebrews 11:10); but today we are pilgrims on the journey to there. Let us be willing to deny ourselves, take up the cross, and follow Him because we ought not live for time but for eternity. May the Lord help us all to exercise our spirits to that glorious end!

PART FIVE:
FOUR LIFE-CHANGING LESSONS OF SPIRITUAL EXERCISE

Chapter 17

CONSECRATION

I Timothy 4:7b-10—Exercise thyself unto piety [godliness]; for bodily exercise is profitable for a little, but piety [godliness] is profitable for everything, having promise of life, of the present one, and of that to come. The word is faithful and worthy of all acceptation; for, for this we labour and suffer reproach, because we hope in a living God, who is preserver of all men, specially of those that believe.

Romans 12:1-2—I beseech you therefore, brethren, by the compassions [mercies] of God, to present your bodies a living sacrifice, holy, acceptable to God, which is your intelligent service. And be not conformed to this world, but be transformed by the renewing of your mind, that ye may prove what is the good and acceptable and perfect will of God.

THE SPIRITUAL EXERCISE OF CONSECRATION

We are still considering this vital topic of spiritual exercise, and I do hope we really understand how important this is. Not only is it very basic to our spiritual life, it is also very essential. The Greek verb form for our English word exercise is *gumnazō,* and it means "to exercise naked." In other words, when we exercise, we must remove all heavy clothes and shoes in order to really exercise. The noun form of this Greek word is the basis for our English word gymnasium.

Are you still in the gymnasium of Christ or have you quit already? I do hope none of us will be a quitter but will daily and hourly be in the gymnasium of Christ and actively engaged in spiritual exercise because that is the way to experience the promise of eternal life. We not only have held out to us the promise of life in eternity but we may also experience that eternal life today. Thus, we can see that it is profitable for all things, and hence we cannot afford to neglect it.

Today I wish for us to consider—beyond what has already been said—the spiritual exercise of consecration which is the first truly Christian experience. If you have already believed in the Lord Jesus, you should have consecrated yourself to Him. If you have believed in the Lord Jesus as your personal Savior and are saved and thus have received His life but you have not consecrated yourself to the Lord, then something is radically, fundamentally wrong. For it is the will of God to save us so that we may be His and live our lives not only for Him but also by Him and to His glory. And consecration is the needful, essential spiritual exercise that can make this happen.

THE TRUE MEANING OF CONSECRATION

I am sure this word consecration is familiar to many of us, and probably you have already consecrated yourselves. But the more I meditate on this subject the more I have come to realize that many believers have missed the real meaning of consecration.

The entire letter of Romans tells us about the salvation of the Lord. From its chapters 1-11 we learn of all the mercies of God which have been bestowed upon us. We were once sinners in bondage to the law of sin and of death, having no hope, no God, and no eternal life. Yet God in His marvelous love sent His only begotten Son into this world to seek and to save us. What a great price His Son has paid for our salvation! Not only did He bear our sins in His body on the cross and shed His blood for the remission of our sins; He also took the old Adam in us with Him and crucified him on Calvary's cross. Salvation not only solves the problem of sins we have committed, it also solves the problem of the power of sin so that it may not any longer have dominion over us. And we will therefore be able to overcome the power of sin through the Lord Jesus Christ.

Moreover, by the mercy of God we are called by Him: "Whom He has called, He has justified; whom He has justified, He has glorified" (see Romans 8:30b, c). To sum up, by God's mercies His salvation towards us is full and complete. He not only saves us out from the place and position of a sinner but He also has made every provision to save us to the uttermost so that we may be conformed to the image of His beloved Son and be called and declared the heirs of Christ (Hebrews 7:25, Romans 8:29b, 17b).

CONSECRATION—THE DOOR TO SPIRITUAL LIFE

So when we contemplate the immensity of the salvation which the Lord Jesus has accomplished for us, we cannot but be touched in heart by the many mercies of God. And as we are touched by His mercies then the opening verse of Romans chapter 12 comes into view with greater force and meaning: "Brethren, I beseech you therefore by the mercies of God, to present your bodies a living sacrifice, holy, acceptable to God, and this is your spiritual worship or reasonable, intelligent service" (see v. 1). Now this is where spiritual life really begins. In fact, strictly speaking, we do not begin our spiritual life when we first believe. We do have a new life because we have believed, but we do not truly begin our spiritual life until we have consecrated ourselves to the Lord. To put it most succinctly, consecration is the door to spiritual life.

According to the word of God we are not our own; we have been bought with a price (I Corinthians 6:19-20). Once we were slaves to sin and to the enemy of God—Satan. We were in bondage, but thank God, the Lord Jesus came and set us free. In setting us free He paid the highest price for our souls. As the Bible declares: "We have been bought with a price." Out of slavery, as it were, God purchased us for himself with His Son's blood. That is the reason His word declares: "You are not your own; you have been bought with a price." Now we belong to God.

Formerly, we belonged to Satan. He was in control of our life and directed it. What a hardship it was! There was no hope. Now, though, we are set free by the Lord Jesus, but that does not mean we are set free to do whatever we wish. If that were the case, sooner or later, we would return to our old master, Satan, and again be under the bondage of sin and death. That is why when our Lord Jesus delivered us out of the bondage of sin, He saved us to God so that we may be under another and totally opposite kind of bondage—a benevolent, merciful, and glorious kind. In reality, by His life He binds us to the Father.

CONSTRAINED BY THE LOVE OF GOD

Now in our being moved by the mercies of God, what should be our response? Should we accept the salvation He has provided but then proceed to live our own life again? If that should be the case, we will return to our old master—Satan—and again be under the bondage of sin and death. But let us praise God for His wonderful provision in having purchased us for himself. Legally, though, in His having bought us for himself at such a cost, then by right we are His; however, He does not wish to deal with us on the basis of legal rights but has set us free to go our own way, if we so wish. Nevertheless, God has said in His word, as it were: "You whom I have redeemed at such cost to myself you may indeed go and do whatever you would like, but if you have truly been constrained by My love, you will want to come back, give yourself to Me, and tell Me that you wish to be My love-slave for life."

In the olden days among the children of Israel, if a Hebrew—usually a poor person or one in debt—sold himself to another Hebrew, he would serve him for six years. In the seventh year, that servant was set free to go his own way. If, however, he had grown to love his master and his master's family, he would tell the latter: "I do not wish to go out free; I want to serve you forever." The servant would then be taken to the door of the master's house and have his ear pierced with an awl—an action which signified that he was henceforth a bondservant forever to his master (Deuteronomy 15:12, 16-17). Accordingly, his service would thereafter be performed out of love—no longer on the basis of legal rights. And, incidentally, the piercing of the ears demonstrates how important the ears are to a real servant of

God. If we wish to be a true servant of His, we must be able to hear Him well.

PRESENTING THE SACRIFICE

So the very first thing to be noted here concerning consecration is that if we have truly been constrained by God's love in Christ, our initial response to God's mercies is to present our bodies as a living sacrifice. Why is it that the body is cited as that which is to be offered? Because we live and express ourselves through our bodies; therefore, man's body serves to symbolize his entire being.

The next thing to be noted regarding consecration is that it is to be a *living* sacrifice. Under the Old Testament dispensation before Christ came the sacrifices offered up were all dead. If an Israelite wished to give a sacrifice to God—whether a lamb, goat or bullock which he already possessed or had just then purchased for this purpose—it would be released from his hands willingly and would be presented to God. It would then be killed by the priest and burned on the altar. Hence the sacrifice taken from among the Israelite's flock or herd or just then purchased would be received by the priest out of the giver's hands and offered up to God, with all this being done out of the giver's gratitude. During the present New Testament era, however, the sacrifice and its presentation to God as described in Romans 12 is different in a number of ways. Unlike in the days of Israel when what was offered up to God was simply a possession which belonged to the givers, today's consecration involves the offering up not just what we have but also what we are. In other words, because our whole being has been bought and redeemed by God through Christ, we want to give our entire selves to Him. Hence, the sacrifice in view in Romans 12 is one that is out of our very selves to God and not merely out of our hands. Therefore, the right meaning of consecration is a giving of one's total self to God, allowing Him to have all of the giver for himself.

Moreover, a further facet to the real meaning of consecration is the giving up of our right to ourselves. In offering ourselves to God as a sacrifice we are to live daily for Him according to His will, not ours; that is to say, we yield up the control and management of our lives to God and let Him be the Controller and Manager. Too often our thought of consecration is that of our service to God, and, of course, that is included in the meaning of consecration: we wish to offer ourselves to God in order that we may serve Him. Formerly, we served God's enemy, Satan, and accordingly, we served sin; but now we want to serve God; therefore, we give ourselves to Him to serve Him. However, that is not the true and foundational meaning of consecration; rather, the basic meaning is a giving up of our right to ourselves by our willingly allowing God to control our lives. Such will make our life on earth wonderful and glorious and enable Him by His Spirit to transform us and conform us to the image of His beloved Son. That is what consecration in reality is.

Furthermore, let us realize that consecration is not a one-action event: that when a person is constrained by the mercies of God and presents his body to Him as a sacrifice, that one act does not constitute the meaning and fulfillment of consecration. Not so; for as we look into this issue of consecration more carefully, we notice that Romans 12 calls the body presented a *living* sacrifice—thus indicating that true consecration is to be a lifelong experience. To put it another way, the presenting of our bodies to God can be likened to a doorway through which we enter to begin our experience of consecration; but, then, because our consecration is defined in God's word as a *living* sacrifice, we are daily, even hourly, to present ourselves to God continually as an ongoing lifelong experience of consecration.

This understanding of consecration has been portrayed physically for us in the Old Testament sacrificial system ordained by God for His chosen people of old. Back then, there were many sacrifices presented. There was the daily sacrifice which consisted of one lamb in the morning and one lamb in the evening. In addition, at the beginning of each month there were more sacrifices added to the daily sacrifice. Moreover, if there was a festival, the sacrifices were increased further (see Exodus 29:38-42, Leviticus 23). From this we come to realize that consecration is meant to be an ever-increasing, ever-ongoing experience in the life of God's people.

Also, Romans 12 tells us that the sacrifice or consecration of ourselves is holy, and this simply means we are to be separated or set apart to God. In presenting our bodies as a living sacrifice we are separated—yet not only from the world but also even from ourselves. Each believer's totally consecrated self is to be holy for God. We have offered it up out of our own hands and placed it into the hands of God.

Then, too, we want to be acceptable to God, and the first and foremost way by which this can occur is for us to present our bodies a living sacrifice. If we have truly done this, we shall know we are acceptable to God. But if we fail to do this, and even though we may try to serve Him in some way, neither we nor our service will be acceptable.

Finally, consecration is additionally our spiritual worship; it is here that genuine worship begins. Not only that, it is our intelligent service. Out of consecration we are able to serve God intelligently and according to His will.

Consecration, therefore, is a major element in the believer's spiritual life, for it is to be an ongoing everyday experience. In fact, we cannot say we will ever graduate from consecration or that we can arrive at the point of claiming that it is behind us because we are more advanced spiritually. Never! If we remain faithful, we shall actually experience consecration to a deeper and deeper and deeper degree.

I would like for us next to consider together this matter of consecration further based upon the actual experience of several Christians and, of course, based also upon the word of God. If Christians have truly consecrated themselves to God, what kind of life should they be living and what type of service should they be engaged in until the coming of the Lord? In giving answer to this I would like for us to divide consecration into roughly three stages and to consider each one in turn by illustrating it through the experience of various believers both past and present.

THE INITIAL STAGE OF CONSECRATION: TRYING TO SERVE GOD

First, there is the initial stage of consecration. Assuming that upon our being saved we are moved by the Spirit of God and have been constrained by the Father's love, we realize that because we are now redeemed we cannot live for ourselves any longer and wish to live for God and serve Him. And because of that, we gladly present our bodies to Him as a living sacrifice, which constitutes the opening experience of consecration. It is especially marked by our trying to do things for God and serve Him in the best way we can.

In this connection, I recall that when I was first saved I was greatly touched by the love of God and so grateful to Him. Prior to this I had been under the burden of sin for a year, and then it all rolled away upon my being saved. I was now set free, and I was so grateful to God.

And then, on the last day of a conference I attended in 1930, the pastor who preached to us that day began to speak on consecration. He said to us that if we really love the Lord, we should serve Him as a preacher, evangelist, or Bible teacher. He added that we needed to express our love to the Lord in this way. So a huge map of China was placed on the wall and we were asked to choose wherever we wanted to serve. This pastor then instructed each of us to come up to the map and put our finger on the place where we wanted to serve. I was just fifteen years old at the time and in my youthful emotion I was filled with the love of God. So I walked up to the wall map and placed my finger on the area of Mongolia. That became my plan for serving God; and because I truly meant business, I began preparing myself for it. It being my last year in high school, I gathered all the information on Mongolia I could find. After graduation I chose a Bible school, thinking that this was the best way to prepare myself for serving God in the place I had chosen.

It should also be noted here that even while still in high school, I had already begun to serve God. I was leading meetings, including prayer meetings, and I even spoke at

Christian gatherings. I also went out to the countryside to evangelize. I had indeed been serving God already—but in *my* way. I was serving Him according to the best that I knew and with all the talents which I had. Yet that was all I had understood about consecration up to that point. Could this, however, be said to have really been consecration?

Let me also relate here the story of Mrs. Jessie Penn-Lewis, who upon becoming a Christian was greatly used by God. One day when about twenty years old she became very troubled about the return coming of the Lord Jesus. She took down a small Bible from her bookshelf and carelessly opened it up. It fell open on the page where Isaiah 53:6 appeared which stated that the Lord put all our iniquities upon His suffering Servant. Then she turned over many pages further till her eyes alighted upon John 6:47: "He that believes has eternal life." Now that is how Mrs. Penn-Lewis got saved.

After that she became very zealous for the Lord. At that time the work of the Young Women's Christian Association (YWCA) had just begun, which would be greatly used by God. She began to help in the YWCA by leading Bible classes, and the Lord used her to bring some girls and young women to salvation. Then she longed for the Spirit's power from on high, and she prayed that the Lord would endue her with that power, just as Peter had experienced on the day of Pentecost when he stood up and preached his first message and three thousand were saved (Acts 2:14-41).

One morning Mrs. Penn-Lewis had either a dream or a vision, in which she saw a hand holding a bundle of filthy rags. A voice came to her, which said: "This is all your works from the past years." Now suppose you had seen and heard that, what would have been your reaction? Mrs. Penn-Lewis herself responded by saying: "Lord, I have consecrated myself to You. This is all consecrated work." Then she heard a voice which declared: "Yes, but though it is all consecrated work, it is consecrated self. It is you yourself: you planned for it; you worked for it; and you used your own talent for it. It is all of you." Finally, she heard a voice saying: "Crucified." That transformed her life. As many of us know, her special message to the Christian world was ever and always the cross.

Now as I read this account of hers, it dawned on me that the assessment of Mrs. Penn-Lewis's Christian service made by her dream/vision's voice was an accurate description of what my consecration was at this time in my Christian experience. Yes, I had consecrated my life to God and had truly wanted to serve Him, but I was making my own plan and using my own talent. Everything came out from me—not out from God. The Lord did in fact bless somewhat; but just as He had spoken to Mrs. Penn-Lewis, He said to me: "It is consecrated *you*. It is you—not I."

Sad to say, we do not really understand what consecration is. As was the case with Mrs. Penn-Lewis and with myself, we think consecration is to work for God, but that is a wrong concept; to the contrary, consecration is letting God work in and through us. A second wrong concept we have about consecration is that we think we can serve God with our old self—*our* mind, thought, strength, and talent. Do we use our talent and strength for Him? Let us suppose that I am a person talented in administration; I would therefore probably think that I could serve as a local church elder. We Christians are too often urged to use our talent and strength in serving God and to put all we have into it. But let us pause and consider: Do we actually think God will accept our old man—that is, our fleshly self—to serve Him? Yes, we do in fact mean well, but we have missed the basic understanding of what consecration is. And I would therefore describe the initial stage of consecration as marked by good intentions but also by a gross misunderstanding of the meaning of consecration.

THE SECOND STAGE: CRUCIFIED CONSECRATION

Let us realize that unless we are crucified, God cannot and will not accept our service. The most important understanding we must have about consecration is that the self needs to be crucified. If self is not crucified, there can be no consecration. Hence, the second stage of consecration I would like to call *crucified consecration*. In other words, during this stage God will lead us on in our walk before Him until we come to a crisis, and that crisis will lead us to experience the cross in a deeper way. And there will most likely be additional crises along the way that if responded to positively will lead us to experience the cross further and more deeply as we continue to walk on the pathway of crucified consecration.

I remember when I was in college that the Lord began to reveal His way to me. I was trying very earnestly to obey whatever the Lord was showing me. In the city where I was going to school, the Lord at that time began doing something with seven of us Christian brothers and sisters who had started gathering together regularly. We had felt led to follow the Lord according to His will, and so He began to bless us. However, at one point a big struggle developed within me because, even though I wanted to follow the Lord all the way, I could see how difficult it would be. I commenced wavering. It was as though my two feet were planted on two boats, and they were gradually sailing apart. This well describes my internal situation.

At one point during that period a brother came and spoke to us on Luke 14:25-33. He reminded us that the Lord had said the following: "If you want to follow Me, and you do not hate your father, mother, children, wife, husband, and your very self, you cannot be My disciple. If you are not willing to lay down everything, you cannot be My disciple. If you are building a tower, you should first sit down and count the cost as to whether you can complete it. If you are fighting an enemy and he is coming to the battle with twenty thousand troops but you only have ten thousand, are you willing to meet him in battle?" The essence of that message was for the believer in Christ to count the cost to himself.

Upon hearing this message, I began praying: "Lord, perhaps my problem is that I have never really counted the cost to myself. Yes, I did respond to You and gave myself to You out of love and emotional feelings, but I never sat down and counted the personal cost. I am now going to do that." Yet the more I counted what the cost would be to me, the more costly it became. Moreover, Satan was busy putting all kinds of thoughts into my mind—such as, that I would be dismissed from the university, cast out of my family, etc., etc. So I told the Lord I could not do it. It was then that I beheld a vision of the Lord coming towards me, extending His bleeding hands, and saying, "I did all this for you, what have you done for Me?" This so broke me down that I told the Lord: "I give You everything." Nevertheless, I must acknowledge here that it was not that easy to fulfill. For after making this promise to the Lord, I could not sleep for three days and nights. I went to my classes, but I did not hear what the professors were saying. Finally, the Lord overcame all obstacles within me; and that marked a radical change in my life. In short, I had experienced crucified consecration.

We may perhaps remember my relating earlier an incident in the life of F.B. Meyer who had lived during the nineteenth and early twentieth centuries. At the time of the incident to be told he was a brilliant young pastor who loved the Lord very much. One day, two of the now famous "Cambridge Seven" visited him. This was in the late nineteenth century, and one of these seven, all of whom were at this moment poised to embark for China as missionaries with the China Inland Mission, was C.T. Studd, who just prior to this had been proclaimed the best cricketer in all of England. The salvation of these seven university students and their having been moved by God to go forth as missionaries had deeply stirred the Christian world in both Britain and America at that time.

Now it was C.T. Studd and Stanley Smith who were F.B. Meyer's visitors that day during the period when he was pastor at Melbourne Hall in Leicester. It was in November and very chilly. One morning during their stay with him, and while it was still dark, brother Meyer noticed that in his home's room where these two were bedded down, the candle was still burning. He was a little worried that something untoward had occurred, so he waited and waited for the light to be extinguished; but when it was not, he finally knocked on the door. Upon entering the room he saw C.T. Studd wrapped in a rug and studying the Bible. The young pastor said to him,

"You are rising early." To which brother Studd replied: "I love the Lord, and I am searching the Scriptures for His commands."

Is it not true that we search the Scriptures for God's promises—not His commands? Yet this brother was searching the Scriptures for His commands. F.B. Meyer was very touched and sensed that his visitor had something he did not have—the peace, rest, and also the overcoming experience in his life. So he asked C.T. Studd what his secret was, and his answer was: "Consecrate yourself to the Lord." "Well, of course, I have already done that," pastor Meyer responded. Brother Studd said, "No, you must go to the Lord, count everything in your life, and then turn it all over to Him."

The pastor said to him that he would do that. He went to the Lord in prayer and gave up everything in his life one by one to the Lord except that there was one thing he could not yield up but held it back from the Lord. This was when the Lord had come to brother Meyer in a vision and the latter had handed over to Him a bundle of keys to all the rooms in his life, but had held back the key to one small room. The Lord shook His head and said, "No." Pastor Meyer now tried to bargain with the Lord by promising to give up everything else in exchange for being allowed to hold on to that one small room. The Lord, however, kept on saying, "No." And then came forth from Him that now famous word: "If I am not Lord of all, I am not Lord at all." And with that the Lord turned and began walking away. In this moment of desperation F.B. Meyer cried out in prayer with what has become an equally famous line: "Lord, make me willing to be willing." The Lord graciously returned and took from His young servant all the keys in the bundle, including the key to that one small area of his life. And immediately thereafter, brother Meyer began spending the necessary time in clearing out every room in his life he had now offered up to the Lord.

These are but two stories of crucified consecration. How true it is that when we first consecrate ourselves to God, we are full of joy, but when we experience true consecration, it is not joyful. Rather, we pass through the valley of tears. Yet that is where the actual consecrated life begins.

THE THIRD STAGE: CONSECRATED LIFE ITSELF

The third stage is consecrated life itself. This does not mean that after we consecrate ourselves to God there will be no further crisis; to the contrary, there will be further breaking; nevertheless, we no longer retain any assurance in, or reliance upon, ourselves. It is now all in and of Christ; only He can preserve us. Essentially, we are today "over the hump," and now we are able to live a life that is truly consecrated to God.

PAUL'S CONSECRATED LIFE

In the light of all which has been said regarding consecration, I would finally like for us to consider the life experience of the apostle Paul. At the outset of his adult life this was an eminently wonderful young man. The other young men of his time were all seeking fame and fortune in this world, but Saul (who would later become Paul) was different. As a young man he sought after spiritual things. As an orthodox Jew Saul of Tarsus had accordingly been trained in that way in his family until he went off to Jerusalem and became a student under Gamaliel, the most famous rabbi at that time. After completing his studies under Gamaliel, Saul became a Pharisee.

When we hear of Pharisees today, we instantly conjure up the thought of hypocrites. Saul, however, was a true Pharisee. He tried his very best to keep all the letters of the Law because he had come under the great influence of the traditions of the fathers. He was so zealous for his religion that he persecuted the believers in Christ because he considered Jesus to have been an impostor of Judaism. As a result of his firmly believing this Saul went about seizing people of the Christ-way and having them condemned to death. When, for example, Stephen was stoned, he was present as a chief witness to the event. Nevertheless, God knew that Saul's heart was sincere; therefore, He allowed him to go as far as he could until he became bent on going to Damascus with a letter from the Jewish high priest authorizing him to seize the believers there, bring them to Jerusalem, and have them condemned. On the way, however, a light brighter than the midday sun shone down upon Saul and struck him blind to the ground. Then he heard a voice: "Saul, Saul, why do you persecute Me? It is hard for you to kick against the goads." It was a gentle voice full of sympathy and love. The voice continued: "It is for your sake; do not continue doing this. Turn around!" Thank God, Saul of Tarsus turned around, and from then on he became the apostle Paul (Galatians 1:13-14; Philippians 3:4-6; and from the book of Acts: 22:3; 26:4-5, 9; 6:9-15; 7:1, 54-60; 8:1; 9:1-2; 22:4-5; 26:9-11; 9:3-30; 22: 6-21; 26:12-23).

Now there is one writing of Paul's which reveals to us the secret of his Christian life. That is the letter he wrote to the

Philippians. In that letter he shows us how he lived a surrendered, consecrated life. In chapter 1 he declared: "For to me to live is Christ" (v. 21a); by which declaration he meant: "It is no longer I who live; it is not I Paul who can live such a life but it is Christ who lives in me." In chapter 2 he evinces having the meek and lowly mind of Christ; for elsewhere in his writings Paul called himself the chief of sinners and the least of all the apostles (vv. 5ff.; I Timothy 1:15; I Corinthians 15:9). Then in chapter 3 Paul described how in his life's pursuit as a Christian he considered all things as loss for the surpassing value of gaining the knowledge of Jesus Christ (vv. 7-8). Finally, in chapter 4 he tells us of his having found in Christ his all-sufficiency: "I can do all things through Him who empowers me" (see v. 13).

A consecrated life is the will of God—not only for Paul but for every one of us. We may not be chosen to be the great apostle that Paul was; even so, we all are chosen to live for Christ, by Christ, and as Christ. This is the sum and substance of what the Christian life is, and it can only be lived out through consecration. Perhaps you had consecrated yourself to the Lord five, ten, or more years ago; but are you still living that consecrated life today? This is a question we need to ask ourselves. It is only through exercising our spirit that we are able to live such a consecrated life. May the Lord have mercy upon each one of us!

Chapter 18

DIVIDING OF SOUL AND SPIRIT

I Thessalonians 5:23-24—Now the God of peace himself sanctify you wholly: and your whole spirit, and soul, and body be preserved blameless at the coming of our Lord Jesus Christ. He is faithful who calls you, who will also perform it.

Hebrews 4:12-13—For the word of God is living and operative, and sharper than any two-edged sword, and penetrating to the division of soul and spirit, both of joints and marrow, and a discerner of the thoughts and intents of the heart. And there is not a creature unapparent before him; but all things are naked and laid bare to his eyes, with whom we have to do.

We are considering together four key life-changing lessons to be learned in spiritual exercise. We know that unless we exercise our spirit, all that God has done for us through the Lord Jesus Christ will not become a living experience in us. That is how essential spiritual exercise is.

CONSECRATION

Last time we considered together the first of these four lessons—that of consecration. Let me briefly review what was shared. Upon our receiving all the mercies of God and having been constrained by the love of Christ, our only reasonable response is to present our bodies as a living sacrifice to God.

That is to say, we give ourselves to Him and allow Him to have absolute freedom to work in our lives according to His will. More often than not, though, when we first consecrate ourselves, we do not really understand what that means. We deem consecration to mean that we are now going to live for God and serve Him. However, He knows our hearts. And though we try to live for Him and serve Him, we still live, as it were, by our old, fallen, natural self-life. And even in our service it is the same story. We need to realize that consecration is not serving God or living for Him by our old natural life; rather, consecration means we give ourselves to Him and let Him deal with our natural life until we live by His life and serve by His Spirit.

We will recall what Mrs. Penn-Lewis learned. After she had served God faithfully for several years, she began seeking for more power from above so that she could serve Him better and more fully. One day the Lord revealed something to her in a dream or vision. She beheld a hand with a bundle of filthy rags, and a word was spoken to her: "This is what you have done all these years." Mrs. Penn-Lewis told the Lord: "No, I have served You with a dedicated and consecrated life." But a further word came to her that said: "Nothing but consecrated self!" Finally, she heard the word: "Crucified!"

In our consecration we need to grow into the real meaning of it. We need to learn subjectively the lesson of our self-life having been crucified with Christ so that whatever comes out of us in our daily living or service to God is Christ and not *I* (Galatians 2:20). If we learn this lesson, we will be able to live a consecrated life just as we saw in the life experience of the apostle Paul.

WHAT ARE WE?

Now I would like for us to continue with the second life-changing lesson to be learned in spiritual exercise. That lesson for today's message is knowing and experiencing the dividing of soul and spirit. We shall approach this subject not primarily from the doctrinal or teaching side but mainly from the personal, experiential side. Nevertheless, any spiritual experience that is not based on the word of God is false. Only those experiences which are according to God's word will have the right foundation and shall therefore be genuine spiritual exercise.

So, on the one hand, the chief emphasis in our consideration together concerning the dividing of soul and spirit shall be on how to experience this in our lives rather than on presenting a theological treatment of the subject. On the other hand, we cannot experience this dividing in a personal spiritual way without our having a sound understanding of the truth to be found in the word of God on this subject. Therefore, for the sake of clarity and of safety in avoiding error, I feel we need to have at least a basic understanding of our constitutional makeup as human beings. That is to say: How was man created? What are we? Even on this point there are differences in theological understanding, but I shall try to keep the presentation of it as simple as possible without going into any of several controversies surrounding this matter. We simply want to consider what God's word says to us.

The first part of Paul's writing in I Thessalonians 5:23-24 reads as follows: "Now the God of peace himself sanctify you wholly: and [may] your whole spirit, and soul, and body be preserved blameless ..." Let us take special notice of three words here. We read first that our God is the God of peace, and this word peace signifies harmony: He wants us to be at one with Him. We next read that God wishes to sanctify us. Because God himself is holy, therefore, He wants us to be sanctified, set apart and made holy for himself—in other words, we are to be holy as He is holy. And the final word to be noted is the word wholly which, because it means entirely or totally, is meant to convey the fact that God wishes every part of our being to be sanctified. And as though to make certain his readers understand what he has in mind, the apostle—inspired by God's Holy Spirit—goes on to write: "and [may] your whole spirit, *and* soul, *and* body be preserved blameless …" Therefore, we understand from these verses that we human beings are constituted as having these three parts or elements in our makeup.

MAN IS CREATED A TRIPARTITE PERSON

We each of us have been created a tripartite person possessing a spirit, a soul, and a body. The body element is most evident to us humans because we each live in a physical body which we can see, touch and feel. According to Genesis 2:7 God formed our body with the soil of the earth. That is how our marvelous body, as the psalmist of old declared, was "fearfully and wonderfully made" (Psalm 139:14a). Because it is made of the soil of the earth our body is composed of the same elements which are found in the earth; therefore, our body makes us world-conscious: we are aware of the physical world because we ourselves live in a physical body. We are in touch with the world around us by means of our five physical senses.

This Bible verse also tells us that God breathed into the nostrils of that form made of the earth, and by that process man became a living soul. Let me pause here before proceeding further concerning the soul of man and focus our attention for a moment on how man's spirit was formed. We know, of course, that God is Spirit and His breath is Spirit; and hence, through His Spirit the breath God breathed into man's nostrils could form, and did form, the spirit of man. By this human spirit of ours we are therefore able to communicate with God; otherwise, we have no way to have contact with Him. So it is by means of our spirit that we are able to have God-consciousness.

With the formation, then, of both man's spirit and body, there immediately occurred a mutual reaction by these two to each other, and the result was that man became a living soul. That was how man's soul came into being, and thus our soul provides us with self-consciousness. Moreover, we should take note of the fact that the Bible often employs the term soul or souls to refer to a human being or beings because that is what we human beings essentially are: souls. And our soul, being the seat of our personality, possesses the functions of emotion or feeling, mind or thinking, and volition or will and decision-making.

GOD PROVIDED FOR EACH PART OF MAN

So the Bible tells us that God created the first man, Adam, with a body, a spirit, and a soul. Now after God created Adam, He placed him in the Garden of Eden. In it He had already planted many trees which were good for food. These thus provided fruit for the body of man. Also, in the midst of that garden God had planted the Tree of Life and, by its side, the tree of the knowledge of good and evil.

In considering all these trees we need to have a basic understanding as to why God had planted them in the Garden of Eden. All the unnamed fruit trees were planted there to provide for the physical needs of the body since God would not have created a body without making provision for it. The tree of the knowledge of good and evil God had planted in the garden as that which could supply fruit for the soul because the soul is that element in man where human knowledge is gained. And, finally, in the midst of the garden God had planted the Tree of Life which could yield up fruit for the spirit. We can clearly discern, then, that God had made every provision necessary here for the entire makeup of man.

GOD GAVE MAN FREE WILL

Now we know from Genesis that God created man in His own image (1:26); and since one of the features of the divine image is that of free will, man was himself created with the ability to make choices and decisions freely on his own. God therefore had no intention of making a robot when creating man; on the contrary, He made him with the capacity to exercise free will. And God was about to confront man with a choice to be made. For if there is free will in man but no choice to be made, what is the point in giving man this free-will capacity? It would make no sense. Hence, that is why God placed or set apart these two specifically-designated trees— the Tree of Life and the tree of the knowledge of good and evil—in the Edenic garden together in order to provide man the opportunity to make a choice between two options—an historic choice, as it most surely turned out to be.

What was this choice that was presented to man to make? It was as though God in confronting Adam with this opportunity to choose, had said: "Since I have created you, you are now going to choose how you are going to live. You are going to choose your future. Will you choose to depend on Me by eating of the Tree of Life and thus live by Me? Or will you choose to live by relying upon yourself? If you choose to eat of the tree of the knowledge of good and evil, you will make yourself knowledgeable and can thus live by your knowledge of what is good or what is bad. You yourself are to decide how you are going to live."

MAN MADE THE WRONG CHOICE

Regrettably, our forefather Adam made the wrong choice—not only for himself but also for all those who come out of him. This means that in Adam we have all, as it were, made that wrong choice: we do not want God nor wish to depend upon Him or live for Him: we instead want to live in reliance upon ourselves and for ourselves (Romans 6:12, 3:10-12).

As a consequence of this wrong choice by Adam, when we his descendants are born into this world, our condition is such that the spirit God had originally created in us is dead. This does not mean that our spirit does not any longer exist; it is still there but it does not work or function properly. It can only function improperly (in contacting evil spirits, as the Bible has made abundantly clear). In short, we have no way of reaching God, for our communication with Him has been completely cut off. When we are born into this world, we are born with a live soul and a live body but our spirit is dead. That is why Genesis 6 declares that "man has become flesh" (see v. 3). For this term flesh signifies the combination of soul and body without the spirit. There is an echo of this to be found in the book of Jude in the New Testament: "[the] natural man without the Spirit" (v. 19b). That has been the condition of all people born into the world since Adam. Indeed, before we who are believers today were saved, that is what we were. Therefore, people may know everything about the world and be very knowledgeable, but when it comes to knowing God they are completely puzzled—they know nothing of Him and have no contact with Him.

THE SPIRIT OF MAN COMES ALIVE

Thank God, He has saved us. God loves us, and in His mercy He sent His only begotten Son into this world to become a man and to be our Kinsman-Redeemer. He died on the cross bearing our sin and taking all the judgment upon himself that we may be saved (Isaiah 53:4-6).

When we believed in the Lord Jesus and were saved, what was the result for us? Probably, the first thing we realized was that the burden or load of sin upon us had been rolled away. Our sins were forgiven and our conscience now had peace. Praise God for that! What emancipation! What joy! But having our sins forgiven is only the negative side of our salvation. God has done something positive as well. He has quickened our dead spirit back to life. He that is born anew of the Spirit is spirit (John 3:6). Moreover, Ezekiel tells us that God gives us a new spirit (36:26-27). In other words, our dead spirit has been restored to life. It is a new life, that life in our spirit being Christ himself who has come to dwell in us (Galatians 2:20). All who are saved not only have their sins forgiven but their dead spirit has been quickened into life. The resurrection life of Christ has come in and dwells in our spirit. Furthermore, the Holy Spirit of God also comes and dwells in our spirit. All that is what we gain positively when we are saved. Therefore, our condition now is that we are restored with a living spirit, a living soul, and a living body. We are alive!

A NEW CREATION

Before we were saved we lived by our old natural life— that is, by our self-life. We knew how to live, how to do things, how to decide on things—all on our own. But upon our being saved, how are we going to live our spiritual life? Are we going to continue to do so by our old self? No; we now have a new life in us, which is Christ himself dwelling in us. Therefore, we are supposed to live by *His* life. As a matter of fact, when we are first saved, we are experiencing our first love with God, and it does seem as though we are living wholly by the new life in us.

II Corinthians 5 says that "if anyone be in Christ, there is a new creation" (v. 17a). If we are now in Christ we are a new creation: indeed, "old things have passed away, everything has become new, and all things are of God" (see vv. 17b, 18a). During the initial stage of our salvation we do experience a new creation because in the flush of that first love of ours, we love God so much we are willing to give up anything for Him. There is nothing too hard or too great for us to yield up or to do for Him. We want to love Him, serve Him, and please Him. Thus, it seems as though we are actually living in the third heaven.

A DUAL PERSONALITY

Regrettably, such a situation does not last long. For some people, perhaps it will last a few months; for others, it may be longer or shorter. Sooner or later, however, we shall make a startling and troubling discovery—that we are not totally a new creation. It is true that we are of Christ, but in our daily life are we really living in Him? On the contrary, we find ourselves often coming out of Christ and wandering aimlessly about more than we are dwelling in Him. When this happens, it becomes more and more difficult to obey Christ. Or when we have problems or find ourselves in a quandary, it is more difficult to know what the will of God really is. We discover that there are two lives in us, thus creating in us what appears to be a dual personality.

Now a non-believer does not have that problem because he is all on the side of the enemy of our souls. But for us believers, it seems as though we have become two persons. There is one life being lived in our spirit—which is Christ—and there is another life being lived in our soul—which is self. Though our sins have been forgiven, the sinner we once were seems to still be there. The outcome of all this is that a civil war begins to rage within us.

Sooner or later you will experience this unless you have never consecrated yourself to God. If the latter be the case, you are totally living by your soul-life and will not have any problem of an internal civil war. If, however, you truly mean business with the Lord and you want to love and follow Him, then sooner or later you will discover that a dual personality is waging a civil war within you.

ON KNOWING THE WILL OF GOD

Young Christians oftentimes will ask this question: "What is the will of God?"—as though His will is the most difficult thing to know. There is one person within them who desires to do the will of God because these young believers have a new life. On the other hand, there is another person within them who hates the will of God. This creates an inner conflict within, and their reasoning often overcomes or overrules what the Spirit is speaking to their spirit. That is the reason young believers are always asking the question: "What is the will of God?"

Now if God in fact wants you to do His will, would He make His will known to you or would He keep it a secret and cause you to experience such a problem? Of course He would not keep His will a secret! Why, then, do young believers find it difficult to know the will of God? It is because of those two irreconcilable lives within. The life in their soul is the Adamic life—by age an old life, both strong and full of experiences. By contrast, the new life, which is Christ in them, is quite young. Furthermore, in terms of man's constitutional makeup, the soul is located in the body whereas the spirit is embedded in the soul. Therefore, the spirit is imprisoned within the soul.

Moreover, because of its longer age and experience the soul is much stronger in us than is our renewed spirit. It is hard, brittle, and insistent on having its way, and that is why we—both younger and older believers—are often puzzled and weakened and cannot follow the Lord all the way. A Christian who is truly seeking after God and finds himself in the kind of situation just described will become very nervous. I have often said that nervous Christians are good Christians. Well, if you are not nervous at all, you will simply do whatever you want. If, however, you truly desire to do the will of God, you will be confronted with one of two problems—either you do not know what the will of God is in a given circumstance, or you do not have the power to do His will even if you did know what it is. And either one of these two problems makes you very nervous.

How are you going to solve these problems? When you do not know what the will of God is—whether you should do this or that, whether you can go there or go here, what is the right decision you have to make—how are you going to deal with the situation?

There are two ways which especially a young believer will try to follow, neither of which, in the long run, will prove helpful. The easier of these two ways is to ask people who have been Christians longer than you. You will perhaps say to one of them something along the line of: "I am just a new Christian, but you have been so for years; certainly you must know what is God's will for me in this present situation of mine." And sure enough, you will find teachers available everywhere. Now we are all born with the inclination to be teachers: we want to teach others. Therefore, if and when the opportunity comes our way, we would say, "This question of yours is easy to answer and solve. Here, this is the will of God for you; do this in the present circumstance of your life and you will be all right." And such advice will seem to you to have solved your problem, but basically it has not solved it because your way in the Christian life is being directed by man and not by God.

Then there is another equally unhelpful way. In your frustration you end up analyzing your situation in your mind by attempting to reason the whole matter out. You engage in thorough introspection, looking deep within yourself to try to figure out the situation by weighing the pros and the cons. And in this way you come to a conclusion as to what is God's will. Yet Isaiah instructs us as follows: "Who is among you that feareth Jehovah, that hearkeneth to the voice of his servant? he that walketh in darkness, and hath no light,—let him confide in the name of Jehovah, and stay himself upon his God. Behold, all ye that kindle a fire, that compass yourselves about with sparks: (all right, if you insist, go ahead and) walk in the light of your fire, and among the sparks that ye have kindled. Yet this is what ye shall have of my hand: ye shall lie down in sorrow" (see 50:10-11).

WALKING IN OUR LIGHT

When we have no light on a given matter in our walk before God and are therefore in darkness, what are we do? Well, if we decide to kindle a light of our own and proceed to walk in that light, what—according to God's word—will be the result? We will lie down in sorrow. It can be concluded, then, that introspection or self-analysis never helps. Sadly, there is a teaching among Christians today that instructs us to search ourselves, delve back into our childhood, conjure up in our mind everything negative in our life, and repent before God accordingly; and then we will be all right. Such self-analysis will not help us; instead, it will bring us down into deeper and deeper darkness.

Now I recall the case of a man back in China who was a Christian leader, a well-respected writer, and well known within Christian circles throughout the country. Though he was older than I, I came to know him somewhat. At the time that I knew him it was during the early period of the founding and spread of the Oxford Group around the world from the 1930s onwards (known also later as the Moral Rearmament movement). People within this movement would try to make themselves perfect by examining themselves introspectively. After a person examined himself and repented of everything, that individual was considered perfect. This Christian leader was one of those who had involved himself in the Oxford Group; and whenever he became weak physically, this Group's teachings, it turned out, would adversely affect his mind. In self-examining himself, all this Christian man's past came back to him, and so he had to confess all over again in order to gain the inner peace he sought. Nevertheless, he had no peace.

I met with him and we talked together. He shared with me what had previously happened to him. During this particular time of interaction with me he once more became physically weak and was currently engaging in the same introspective examination of himself again and again. I tried to tell him: "Brother, no. It is the blood of the Lord Jesus that cleanses us once and for all. God forgives and forgets. Do not try to analyze yourself." Sad to say, he had remained entrapped within that kind of Oxford Group teaching. Self-introspection never helps.

In this connection, some of us may have heard the tale of the bewildered centipede. As we know from its name this particular insect-like creature has a hundred legs; therefore, it can walk very fast. One day, the centipede said to itself: "I want to know which one of my one hundred legs moves first when I wish to walk." So it set itself to patiently observing his legs, trying to figure out which would move first; but in so doing, the centipede became immobilized. Tired of watching and waiting, it finally said, "Oh, I give up!" and off it went. How often we are like this centipede. We analyze ourselves to exhaustion in trying to know what is of God and what is of self, what is God's will and what is our will. If we do that, we—like the immobilized centipede—will become paralyzed, and thus we are unable to follow the Lord. And this is what has happened to many good Christians—they become immobilized. Such is the human way, and it does not work.

GOD'S WAY: HEBREWS 4:12

What is God's way? It is very simple, and it is found in Hebrews 4:12: "the word of God is living and operative, and sharper than any two-edged sword, and penetrating to the division of soul and spirit, both of joints and marrow, and a discerner of the thoughts and intents of the heart." We know that what lay behind this Scripture was a graphic scene quite familiar to all Jews from the olden days when they each would bring their individual sacrifice to the altar and tie it there. The priest would come and kill the sacrificed animal and put it on the altar. He would then dissect it, cutting it into pieces. He was such an expert with his sharp knife that he could even cut through the joints. When the joints were penetrated by the knife and cut, the marrow within the bones was exposed (Leviticus 1:6-8).

A LIVING SACRIFICE

Now we know that the sacrificial animal obviously did not try to kill itself. It was bound on the altar, lying motionless. If it was a willing sacrifice, there would be no resistance from it, just as with the boy Isaac when his father Abraham offered him up to God: Isaac was a willing sacrifice, for after he was bound to the altar by Abraham, he lay there motionless: he was going to let Abraham use his knife to kill him. But we know that God mercifully intervened at the last moment to save him (Genesis 22:9-12).

Like those Jewish sacrifices of old, we today are to be pleasing sacrifices offered up to God, but we are *living* sacrifices. As a living sacrifice we willingly lie upon the altar doing nothing to ourselves but allowing God to do the work. We do not try to cut ourselves—that is, deal with ourselves spiritually—because we are not trained to do that, for if we ourselves do the cutting, the outcome will be a mess; yet oftentimes that is what we do. Like the priest's knife God's word is a knife, too, and if His word is living as it comes to us, it is sharp—sharper, even, than any two-edged sword. Now the written word which we find in the Bible is in and of itself not living and operative because it was written in letters which lie there on the pages of the Scriptures. Yes, God's word is true, but if it comes to us as mere letters, it is not sharp; that is to say, it is not living, penetrating, and operative. That is why, when we read the word of God, oftentimes it comes to us only as letter and not spirit, and because of that, the written word kills instead of quickens (II Corinthians 3:6).

Hebrews 4:12 declares that the word of God is living and operative. This means that God's word is not only written, it is also spoken directly and afresh to us by the Holy Spirit who dwells in us. In other words, *logos*—the written word— becomes *rhema*—the living word—to us. The Holy Spirit dwells in us, and by His revelation or enlightenment He will shine upon the written word of God and make it living until it seems as though it jumps off the page at us. And as *rhema* it is also operative: it works. That is why it is so important that we have the spirit of wisdom and revelation (Ephesians 1:17). Now, of course, we cannot have totally new and separate revelation outside of the Bible because all of God's revelations are complete in His written word. Nevertheless, the written word has to be quickened afresh by the Holy Spirit and spoken again to us directly and personally. From this we see that God speaks twice. On the first occasion He speaks through His prophets and apostles, and that speaking through these servants of God has become all the words which are recorded in the Bible (Hebrews 1:1-2, II Peter 3:15-16). On the second occasion, however, He speaks the same word but it is now breathed upon afresh by the Holy Spirit to you and me. When *that* word comes, it is living, penetrating, and operative; and thus it works effectually.

THE HOLY SPIRIT WIELDS THE SWORD

Like the priest of old with his knife, the Holy Spirit is the One today who is wielding His own sword-like knife. The Bible says that God's word is the sword of the Spirit (Ephesians

6:17b). Yet it is not to be treated as your sword nor mine. How often we wield the word of God as a sword to beat and to cut to pieces other brothers and sisters! How awful! Or sometimes we wield it even to cut up ourselves. Let us not do that because we are not trained nor are we experts. Let us allow the Holy Spirit to do this work, for He is like the priests of old: He is an expert. And He knows exactly what, for each one of us, the will of God is and knows how, accordingly, to deal with each of us.

Now as the Holy Spirit begins to reveal the word of God to us as *rhema*, it penetrates, cuts, and divides the soul and spirit. All our intents and thoughts are exposed just as the marrow in the bone is exposed (Hebrews 4:12b, c). We know that the bone is the covering surrounding the marrow, and marrow is the real-life substance in our body because it is what makes our life-blood. Life comes out of the marrow.

What, then, is God's way to deliver you from this darkness of not knowing what the will of God is or not knowing whether the decision you are proposing to make comes from the spirit or the soul? Obviously, if it comes from the spirit, it is Christ; if it comes from the soul, it is self. But you may be confused, not knowing which one it is. When you are in such a quandary, what should you do? You must not try to analyze yourself, but you must go to the Lord, rest and be at peace before Him, and look to His Spirit. Let the Holy Spirit reveal God's will to you and allow Him to do so according to His timing. Then, when God's will is revealed to you, it is so clear that you shall know what is of God and what is of man, what is of the spirit and what is of the soul. Not only that, God's *rhema* word shall be both operative and powerful in you: it shall give you the power to overcome.

So we see that the dividing of soul and spirit is another life-changing experience, and it comes through the revelation of the Holy Spirit. That is God's side. On our side, we need to exercise our spirit because if God sheds His light upon our spirit and we do not follow the divine light given, we will continue to walk in darkness. That is why spiritual exercise is so necessary.

Therefore, whenever you do not know what the will of God is and have a question about it—which question is actually raised by the Holy Spirit and not by yourself—you need to go back to the Lord, lie at peace on the altar as a willing sacrifice giving no resistance, and look for the Holy Spirit to wield God's word to divide your soul and spirit. The more you learn this life-changing lesson in spiritual exercise, the easier you will discern what the will of God is in every situation.

Chapter 19

THE BREAKING OF THE OUTWARD MAN AND THE RELEASE OF THE SPIRIT

II Corinthians 4:7-18—But we have this treasure in earthen vessels, that the surpassingness of the power may be of God, and not from us: every way afflicted, but not straitened; seeing no apparent issue, but our way not entirely shut up; persecuted, but not abandoned; cast down, but not destroyed; always bearing about in the body the dying of Jesus, that the life also of Jesus may be manifested in our body; for we who live are always delivered unto death on account of Jesus, that the life also of Jesus may be manifested in our mortal flesh; so that death works in us, but life in you. And having the same spirit of faith, according to what is written, I have believed, therefore have I spoken; we also believe, therefore also we speak; knowing that he who has raised the Lord Jesus shall raise us also with Jesus, and shall present us with you. For all things are for your sakes, that the grace abounding through the many may cause thanksgiving to abound to the glory of God. Wherefore we faint not; but if indeed our outward man is consumed, yet the inward is renewed day by day. For our momentary and light affliction works for us in surpassing measure an eternal weight of glory; while we look not at the things that are seen, but at the things that are not seen; for the things that are seen are for a time, but those that are not seen eternal.

John 12:20-28—And there were certain Greeks among those who came up that they might worship in the feast; these therefore came to Philip, who was of Bethsaida of Galilee, and they asked him saying, Sir, we desire to see Jesus. Philip comes and tells Andrew, and again Andrew comes and Philip, and they tell Jesus. But Jesus answered them saying, The hour is come that the Son of man should be glorified. Verily, verily, I say unto you, Except the grain of wheat falling into the ground die, it abides alone; but if it die, it bears much fruit. He that loves his life [soul-life] shall lose it, and he that hates his life [soul-life] in this world shall keep it to life eternal. If any one serve me, let him follow me; and where I am, there also shall be my servant. And if any one serve me, him shall the Father honour. Now is my soul troubled, and what shall I say? Father, save me from this hour. But on account of this have I come to this hour. Father, glorify thy name. There came therefore a voice out of heaven, I both have glorified and will glorify it again.

SPIRITUAL EXERCISE REQUIRED

We have been considering together some life-changing lessons to be learned from engaging in spiritual exercise. God has made every provision for us so that we may be transformed and conformed to the image of His beloved Son. This is the will of God for each of us whom He has saved. How are we going to enter into all which the Lord Jesus has accomplished on Calvary's cross in order that we may receive all which God has promised to do in our lives? This requires spiritual exercise. If we do not exercise our spirit, we will not be able to appreciate or appropriate all which God has promised and has done for us. And this is why spiritual exercise is so necessary for us as believers.

Now these life-changing lessons which we are considering together these days can actually be viewed as consecutive in their relationship to one another. That is to say, in the sequential order in which they are being presented they follow one upon another in our walk before God. Moreover, they are to be continually experienced throughout our entire Christian lives. Never is it to be the case that, having learned one of these lessons, we can thereafter forget it and move on to the next one; rather, to whatever we will have initially learned in each lesson there will be added, again and again, new and deeper experiences of it until all of God's purpose concerning us shall be realized. Now before proceeding to the third lesson in this series, I would like for us to briefly review together what has been shared regarding the two previous lessons—Consecration and The Dividing of Soul and Spirit—with some further thoughts added to what has already been presented.

A LIVING SACRIFICE

As was noted earlier, consecration is actually the beginning of our Christian life as we truly commence living as Christians. It is quite true that when we receive the Lord Jesus as our Savior we do receive His life into our newly quickened spirit, and the Holy Spirit also comes and dwells therein to see to it that this Christ who lives in us will grow until His full stature is built up in us. And upon our receiving all the mercies of God, the first reaction from us should be to present our bodies as living sacrifices. Have we been constrained by the Lord Jesus' tremendous love for us? And under that constraining love have we realized we cannot live for ourselves anymore? If this be true and real in us, it will bring us to the point that we have to present our bodies as living sacrifices to Him. That is to say, our prayerful attitude ought to be: "Lord, here am I, redeemed by Your precious blood and constrained by Your love. I do not want to live for myself anymore. I want to live for You."   And such is the consecration God is looking for from each one of us.

Now if we have truly given ourselves to the Lord, the Holy Spirit within us will begin to work in our spirit and lead us more and more into expressing Christ in our lives. Yet, though consecration is in fact our first Christian experience, it is not a spiritual exercise which we only engage in once for all; on the contrary, we must continually do so day after day—morning, noontime, evening: in short, throughout the entire day. Indeed, just as in olden times the burnt offering had to be offered in both morning and evening, we likewise in our day need daily to present our bodies as living sacrifices. In other words, as the Spirit continuously works in our lives, showing us daily what is of Christ and what is not of Christ, we are to respond continually with spiritual exercise and obey whatever the Spirit of God teaches us in our spirit. And if we remain faithful to God, such spiritual exercise will increase as the days go on until, by the grace of God, we are living an uninterrupted committed life that is wholly set apart for God.

THE INWARD STRUGGLE OF SELF VS. CHRIST

As noted in the previous message, however, after we have consecrated ourselves and the Holy Spirit begins to work in our spirit, we will come to realize that there are two lives in us. In an unbeliever there is but one life, and that is old fallen Adam. We believers, on the other hand, sooner or later discover there are two lives in us: the life of Christ residing in our spirit and, unfortunately, the old Adamic life—even our fallen self—still residing in our soul. Our fallen self still tends to think in the old way, yet not only thinks but even turns back to the old way of living and doing. Therefore, in consecrated Christians these two lives commence striving against each other: Christ in our spirit strives against self in our soul and self in our soul struggles against Christ in our spirit. And the consequence of this continual striving is that we believers—especially the younger Christians in the church—oftentimes become confused: that is to say, all of us want to do the will of God in every circumstance of life but because of the civil war raging within us, we wonder what God's will actually is: is the decision we wish to make coming out of self or is it coming from God?

When we find ourselves in that situation, the dividing of the spirit and soul is most necessary. How can these two lives be clearly divided so that we can know what is actually from God and what is not from Him? Very often, when we are in that kind of situation, we become quite nervous, and we begin to analyze ourselves. We begin to engage in self-introspection to discover the answer to this problem. However, this will never help because the very fact of introspection means that we have sunk back into the old fallen self residing in our soul.

405

THE WORD OF GOD OPERATING

The only solution to this problem is the application of the word of God found in Hebrews 4:12 which essentially tells us this: "the word of God is living and operative; it penetrates and divides the soul and the spirit, the bone, the joints, and the marrow; and it exposes all the thoughts and intents of our heart because everything is naked before God."

When we are in that kind of situation, we need to recall that each of us is a living sacrifice. All we need to do is to lie once more on the altar quietly, looking to the Lord Jesus who is the expert Priest. The Holy Spirit will wield the sword of God's word to penetrate and divide the soul and the spirit. As the marrow is in the joints, so the spirit is in the soul. The soul is as a shell or cover of the spirit. Only when the living and operative *rhema* word of God begins to work in our lives and cuts through the joints can the marrow be exposed. The word of God is not just letters appearing across the pages of the Scriptures; in and of themselves those letters kill, but the Spirit quickens (II Corinthians 3:6). Therefore, the Holy Spirit must be allowed to breathe afresh upon the written word of God and make it living and operative in us. And when that living *rhema* word comes to us, immediately we shall know what is of God and what is not of God.

However, upon experiencing the dividing of the soul and spirit and thus now knowing what is God's will and what is not, we discover another problem confronting us—to will God's will is in me, but the power to obey and do it is not in me. In our spirit we know the will of God and we want to do it but the old man in our soul objects and raises up many arguments and questions to weaken us so that we are not able to do what we want to do.

LIKE PAUL, UNABLE TO OBEY

This is exactly what the apostle Paul experienced, as he himself acknowledged in Romans 7. Here was a man who was saved and consecrated and was seeking after God; nevertheless, he lacked the ability to carry through in obedience. In so many words Paul wrote the following to describe what faced him: "I know what the mind of God is but when I start to do it, I find I cannot. I also know what is not the will of God, yet I cannot help myself in not doing it. It is as though the sin within me is doing it in spite of myself. O wretched man that I am! Who can deliver me from this body of death?" Have we not also found ourselves faced with the same difficult situation? We know the will of God, and we truly desire to do it, but at the same time we discover that we are bound. We are under bondage of some kind, and we cannot break through: we cannot live as Christ lived. As a result, we find ourselves sinking back into our old self-life ways. It is a most wretched situation, impelling us, like Paul, to cry out in frustration and even desperation: Who can deliver me from this body of death?

BREAKING THROUGH THE SOUL-LIFE

Which brings us to what I would like for us to consider together today: the breaking of the outward man and the release of the spirit—which is the third important life-changing lesson to be learned from our engaging in spiritual exercise. So far as man's construction or composition at his creation is concerned, we know that on the one hand our soul is in the body, and that makes us alive. If our soul leaves our body, then we are physically dead. On the other hand, our spirit is embedded in our soul; therefore, unless we can break through our soul-life, the Christ-life in our spirit cannot be released.

In II Corinthians 4:16 the following two terms are found—the outward man and the inward man. The outward man spoken of here in this particular context does not refer to the body; it refers to the soul. Accordingly, in the context of II Corinthians 4 the soul is the outward man and is therefore the one in whom my *self* resides. By contrast, the inward man refers to the spirit where *Christ* resides. Given this set of contrasting realities, it becomes necessary for our outward man to be broken if the inward man is ever to come forth.

THE TREASURE IN EARTHEN VESSELS

To make his point in what he is presenting in II Corinthians chapter 4, Paul employs a parabolic illustration, that of a treasure in earthen vessels (see v. 7). We know that the treasure he has in mind here is none other than the Lord Jesus. We also know that we are the earthen vessels being pictured here because we are made of earth: from the book of Genesis we know that that is our composition. The word treasure is cast by Paul in singular number here because no matter what treasure you or I prefer on earth or what may be deemed as treasure to you and me, in spiritual terms, God has only one treasure—His beloved Son. On the other hand, the words earthen vessels spoken of here by Paul are cast in plural number. Hence, metaphorically speaking, Paul is saying that each one of us is an earthen vessel, there in fact being many earthen vessels. Thank God, there can be only one treasure in all of us many earthen vessels, and that is Christ.

Now in contemplating such a priceless treasure, it ought to fill us with amazement in realizing exactly where Paul says God has placed this treasure! If you have a thousand dollars in your pocket and you are walking down the street, where will your hand most likely be? Will it not be carefully placed over that pocket where your treasure is? Moreover, if we had a choice, most of us would place our treasure in a golden box and not in an earthen vessel. Amazingly, only God selects this latter choice, and that is the incredible wonder of the gospel! God alone is willing to put the treasure of His heart—His beloved Son—into us who are but earthen clay pots. The treasure of God—even Christ—is full of light and full of radiancy (see v. 6 Darby footnote; cf. v. 4), but the earthen vessel into which He has placed His treasure is opaque. This means that though God's treasure is full of radiancy, yet, because it is hidden in us earthen vessels, the radiant light of God's Son cannot shine forth. Now this is precisely our spiritual situation.

BREAKING THE EARTHEN VESSEL

How can the surpassingness of the radiancy of God's treasure—even Christ—shine forth through an opaque, non-transparent earthen vessel? The only way is to *break* the earthen vessel. We see this beautifully illustrated in Mary, the sister of Martha and Lazarus (see John 12:1-8, Mark 14:1-9, Luke 10:41-42, Matthew 26:6-13). After the Lord Jesus called Lazarus out of death back to life, there was a supper held for Jesus. Mary's heart was so touched by the love of Christ that she wanted to give the best she had to the Lord. She had a treasure—an expensive, beautiful alabaster flask with a pound of costly nard inside. More than likely, she had kept it for her wedding; but we do not know for certain.

She was so touched by the love of God that when Jesus was reclining at the table, she took the alabaster flask, went into the dining area, and broke the flask so that the costly ointment would completely fall upon Him. Immediately the fragrance began to spread throughout the whole house. But, oh, how the disciples began to murmur: "What a waste! This could have been sold for three hundred denarii (at that time, the total wages for three hundred days' labor). Why, then, this great waste?"

THE LOVE OF CHRIST OVERCOMES

What do we consider ourselves to be? Do we look upon ourselves as earthen vessels? Never! We always consider ourselves as beautiful alabaster flasks. Such a flask is a precious, worthwhile object. It is worth a great deal to us. Are we willing to break it wide open? Perhaps our thought is, we will gently open it and let a few drops of the costly perfume fall upon the Lord and that will be enough; and we can keep back the rest for ourselves. But the love of Christ had so overwhelmed Mary that she could not wait to see Him fully anointed at the time of His burial after Calvary (see Mark 14:8). She literally broke the alabaster flask and poured its entire contents upon the Lord. Now that is a deep expression of love.

As we go on with the Lord and as the Holy Spirit continues to reveal to us what the mind of Christ is, causing us to want to obey and do the will of God, what will be our reaction? Will we deny our self-life? I'm afraid most of us love ourselves too much and want to preserve ourselves. That is fallen man's natural inclination. But when the love of God truly constrains us, we—like Mary—shall be willing for our earthen vessel, which we heretofore deemed to be a precious alabaster flask, to be broken. In the process we may feel hurt, we may sense a great loss, we may even weep over the experience; nevertheless, the love of Christ overcomes all. His love gives us the motivation and the strength for allowing our outward man to be broken. And though it may hurt and wound us, the radiancy of Christ is released. That is the way we experience the release of the spirit. We are supposed to live by the spirit and no longer by our soulish self-life.

Let us look again at Paul's short parable in II Corinthians 4:7: "we have this treasure in earthen vessels, that the surpassingness of the power may be of God, and not from us." How true it is that we have neither radiancy nor power. The power to overcome and the incomparable radiancy of the light can only come from God.

AFFLICTED BUT NOT FRUSTRATED

Yet how in practical terms, does this all come about? Out of his own experience Paul provides the answer in his succeeding verses of II Corinthians 4, beginning with verse 8a: "every way afflicted, but not straitened [or, crushed]." Sometimes we are afflicted, yet not because of our sin but because we want to obey God. Our flesh does not like it and will even resist it. Our fallen self-life will give us all kinds of reasons to preserve ourselves. If we are willing to be afflicted—that is to say, be willing to deny ourselves, as the Lord Jesus himself taught—then we will tell ourselves: "I do not know you; I do not care about you." Are we willing to do that? Another translation of this passage reads: "every way afflicted but not frustrated." If we are willing to deny ourselves in this way, we may be afflicted but we shall not be frustrated; for deep down within us we know we are doing the will of God, and that becomes our comfort.

AT ONE'S WITS' END

Paul continues by saying: "seeing no apparent issue, but our way not entirely shut up" (v. 8b). A clearer expression of this sentiment says: "You are at your wits' end but not at your life's end." Oftentimes we try to find some way out of our difficult situation, perhaps searching for some easier bypass; ultimately, however, we must finally acknowledge that we have reached the end of our wits. What, then, do we do? Let us realize that though we have come to our wits' end, that is not the end of life. As a matter of fact, it is the beginning of life.

PERSECUTED BUT NOT ABANDONED

Paul adds: "persecuted, but not abandoned" (v. 9a). We may be persecuted, yet not only by our enemy, but even by our friends—*and* by our very selves. For in denying ourselves, as the Lord has instructed us to do, we are in that sense persecuting ourselves. However, we are not forsaken, deserted or abandoned because there is One who holds us in His hands.

KNOCKED DOWN BUT NOT KNOCKED OUT

Paul is not finished: "cast down, but not destroyed" (v. 9b). I like the Phillips translation: "Knocked down, but not knocked out." So often in life's situations as a consecrated Christian we feel that we have been knocked down. Naturally speaking, we want always to have the upper hand just as Jacob had wished. Even when the angel of God came to wrestle him to the ground, he could not overcome Jacob because he was such a strong and determined wrestler. It was not until the angel touched his thigh with an impediment was he at all weakened (Genesis 32:24b-25). Now the thigh is the most important body part when it comes to wrestling—its condition will determine whether one can stand or not. For if the thigh is weakened, the person becomes crippled and his strength is gone. Oftentimes we find we are knocked down so far as our feeling is concerned; but let us thank God that we have not been knocked out, and thus we can rise up again. As the Scriptures declare, a righteous man may fall seven times but he will bounce back on each occasion (Proverbs 24:16). Such is the way of the cross. Our outward man can only be broken through the working of the cross in our lives so that the inward man—our spirit—may be released.

BEARING THE DYING OF JESUS

Paul adds still further out of his personal experience by declaring the following: "always bearing about in the body the dying of Jesus, that the life also of Jesus may be manifested in our body; for we who live are always delivered unto death on account of Jesus, that the life also of Jesus may be manifested in our mortal flesh; so that death works in us, but life in you."

The Calvary death of Jesus is a fact. He died on the cross two thousand years ago. That is what He accomplished on Calvary's cross, and hence the truth of Christ's death will never change but is eternal. However, the dying process of Jesus is another matter. In this phrase of Paul's used here, "the dying of Jesus," the word dying is what is called in English grammar a verbal noun: though the word is a noun, it also possesses the characteristic of a verb in that the act of death (the noun aspect) continues on in its effect (the verb aspect). And hence, the dying of Jesus, writes Paul, is to be an ongoing operating work in us of putting to death whatever in us does not correspond to God's will and purpose. The dying of Jesus, or the power of putting to death, is therefore not in the past but is always in the present. In other words, the dying of Jesus is the cross being continually applied to us by the Holy Spirit. Day by day He will apply the cross upon our flesh—that soulish self-life in us—to put it to death so that the Christ-life within us may be released in order that others may receive life: so that, in the words of Paul, "death works in us, but life in [others]." Indeed, that is what true Christian ministry actually is.

Are we experiencing the dying of Jesus daily so that the life of Jesus may be released? If, as the Holy Spirit is working in our spirit, we do not respond by exercising our spirit by permitting ourselves to be afflicted—to be put to death— then the life of Christ within us cannot be released. Only when we are actively engaged in spiritual exercise can the spirit be released through the breaking of the outward man. This dying daily of the outward man will not only result in our being transformed and gradually conformed to the image of Christ but also result in our being able to extend true ministry towards other people.

In conclusion, wrote the apostle Paul: "If our outward man dies daily, our inward man is [being] renewed day by day. The things that are seen are temporal but we are to seek the things that are unseen because they are eternal" (see vv. 15-18).

THE GRAIN OF WHEAT

There is another parable in the New Testament Scriptures, this one to be found in John's Gospel chapter 12, which further exemplifies the breaking of the outward man that the Christ-life within may be released for the sake of others. And this parable was uttered by Jesus. The background to this additional parable is as follows: Towards the end of His earthly ministry the Lord Jesus had made His way into Jerusalem for the last time in a triumphant entry. Many people had sung "Hosanna" to welcome Him as a prophet of God (v. 13). Moreover, while He was there some gentile Greeks, who had come to keep the Passover feast because they admired Judaism, wanted to see Jesus. Philip and Andrew went to the Lord and told Him that those visiting Greeks wished to see Him. Humanly speaking, therefore, it could be said that this was the most glorious time for Jesus during His entire life on earth. Indeed, the whole world, lamented the criticizing Pharisees, was going off after Him (v. 19); and in response to all this Jesus remarked: "This is the time of My glory" (see v. 23; cf. v. 16b). Yet His terming this moment as His time of glory meant something quite different to Him from what we would think. If the whole world were following after us, we would consider that as an incredible display of glory. However, the Lord Jesus was speaking about another and far different glory; for He went on to utter the following parable that appeared to belie the whole notion of glory: "Truly, truly, I say to you, unless a grain of wheat falling into the ground dies, it abides alone. But if it dies, it bears much fruit" (see v. 24).

In our interpreting this parable it is obvious that Jesus is himself that grain of wheat that falls into the ground, and this speaks of His Incarnation. Jesus came into this world and lived on earth for some thirty-three years. And when, near the end of His earthly ministry, He was on the Mount of Transfiguration, He did not ascend and return to heaven, which would have been His legitimate right to do; for He had lived on earth a perfect life which proved His absolute sinlessness. He therefore had every right to return to God. However, had Jesus done so, there would have been no salvation for the world. He came into the world not to live but to die. And because Jesus as that grain of wheat did die, He has been the bearer of much fruit ever since: in fact, we ourselves are a part of that much fruit.

SAVING OUR SOUL FOR ETERNITY

Now immediately after teaching this parable the Lord Jesus began enunciating a most important principle. On the one hand, Jesus said that if anyone loves his soul-life he shall lose it. On the other hand, He said that whoever in this world hates his soul-life (because it is against God) shall save it for eternity (v. 25). Jesus applied this principle not only to himself, He set an example and applied it to all of us as well: "If anyone would serve Me, let Him follow Me; that where I am, there also shall My servant be" (see v. 26a, b). The Lord Jesus went to the cross in order to grant us salvation. He opened a new and living way for us to the Father. He wants us to follow Him because if we do, the Father will honor us (v. 26c).

JESUS IS TROUBLED

Jesus followed up these words by next saying to His disciples: "My soul is now troubled" (v.27a). Let us not think that when Jesus was on the earth His soul was so pure it could never be troubled. Obviously, His soul would not be troubled by sin since He had committed none; but His soul could and would be troubled by the very thought of His laying down His life for all *our* sins.

Let us pause for a moment and consider: If you are a very clean person and someone visits your home who is also clean and keeps everything in order, that would make you feel good. But suppose there comes a visitor who is disorderly and unclean: he tosses one shoe here and one shoe there; he is untidy and messes up whatever he touches. Would your soul not suffer from such conduct when contrasted with your cleanliness and orderliness? Doubtless, you would find this person unbearable and would want to drive him out of your sight!

In that light, then, let us consider the life of the Lord Jesus. How could He, the spotless One, live those thirty-three years amidst such a dirty, sinful world? How much He must have endured and suffered for us! Far beyond that, though,

He had to bear all these things in His body and die. The Bible describes it this way: "He who knew not sin was made sin for us" (see II Corinthians 5:21). It was not that He who knew no sin merely took up some of our sins. To the contrary, Jesus was made sin for us—that is to say, He became sin itself. One could say, or almost say, that Jesus became sin incarnate! All the sins in the world were centered and laid upon Him (Isaiah 53:6b). It can be likened to the notion of an immaculately clean person becoming a totally dirty person physically: all our uncleanness and dirt was placed upon the spotless Lamb of God. Consider, then, how you would feel if you were the Lord Jesus at this moment. Would not your pure soul rebel against it and be deeply troubled?

We know that Jesus was deeply troubled, yet not only at this moment (v. 27a); for later, while agonizing in the Garden of Gethsemane, He was heard to say: "My soul is exceedingly sorrowful unto death" (see Mark 14:34a). It was as though the Lord was saying: "I am so troubled. What shall I do? I can easily and rightly save myself since the sin is not mine; going to the cross is therefore not necessary for me. I am not obligated in the least to do that. Nevertheless, Father, I came into this world for this very purpose. Therefore, glorify Thy name in this hour" (see vv. 27-28a). Then came a voice out of heaven declaring: "I have both glorified it and will glorify it again" (v. 28b). The Lord Jesus has thus set the example, and He is calling each one of us to follow Him.

These two parables shared out of their personal experience by the Son of man and His disciple Paul provide the how and the way for experiencing the breaking of the outward man and the release of the inward man—our spirit. Whenever our spirit is released, that is, when Christ is released through our spirit, not only will we sense life but others will do so as well: they shall be the recipients of the life of Christ. And as was noted earlier, that is what true Christian ministry really is.

Finally, let us be reminded again that such spiritual exercise is not done once for all. It must be our hour-by-hour and day-by-day experience. As long as we live, we as consecrated believers in Christ ought to be continuously bearing about in our body the dying of Jesus so that the life of Jesus may be released and manifested through our body. Are we willing to do that? If we love the Lord, such is the path He has called us into. He has walked before us in opening the way, and has committed it to each of us. Said Jesus, "Come and follow Me." If we truly love Him, we can do no other.

LIFE WITHIN THE VEIL

Hebrews 6:18-20—By two unchangeable things, in which it was impossible that God should lie, we might have a strong encouragement, who have fled for refuge to lay hold on the hope set before us, which we have as anchor of the soul, both secure and firm, and entering into that within the veil, where Jesus is entered as forerunner for us, become for ever a high priest according to the order of Melchisedec.

Hebrews 10:19-25—Having therefore, brethren, boldness for entering into the holy of holies by the blood of Jesus, the new and living way which he has dedicated [consecrated, inaugurated, opened] for us through the veil, that is, his flesh, and having a great priest over the house of God, let us approach with a true heart, in full assurance of faith, sprinkled as to our hearts from a wicked conscience, and washed as to our body with pure water. Let us hold fast the confession of the hope unwavering, (for he is faithful who has promised;) and let us consider one another for provoking to love and good works; not forsaking the assembling of ourselves together, as the custom is with some; but encouraging one another, and by so much the more as ye see the day drawing near.

In recent weeks we have been considering together several life-changing lessons to be learned in spiritual exercise. And today I would like for us to consider a fourth and final one in this series. This does not mean, of course, that there are only four such lessons. As a matter of fact, spiritual exercise touches every aspect of our Christian life; but I have limited ourselves to considering just a few of the most fundamental ones in spiritual life. Without these foundational lessons learned we will not have a firm or steady spiritual life.

DWELLING IN THE PRESENCE OF GOD

We come now, therefore, to the final life-changing lesson in spiritual exercise I wish for us to consider together: the life within the veil, or, dwelling continually in the presence of God. As a matter of fact, this is—or should be—the objective of our spiritual pursuit. We want to live in the presence of God every day. Moment by moment, day after day, we want to live a life that is within the veil—nothing hiding us from the face of God. And we know from the history of man that this is what people have been searching for throughout the past ages of mankind.

All over the world, people are searching for this one special experience—their union with God. And hence, the question arises, How can man be united with God and know His constant presence? One seventeenth-century Christian, today known the world over as simply Brother Lawrence, wrote a little book entitled, *The Practice of the Presence of God*. It later became a very popular book among Christians, but I am afraid most people in our day have never read it. It is still considered a beloved Christian classic.

Born Nicolas Herman, Brother Lawrence lived in France from c.1614-1691. He was a quite ordinary person and very poor. Because of his poverty Nicolas enlisted in the French army, since this would at least provide him with clothes, food, and a small income. While in the military he fought in the terrible religious conflict known as the Thirty Years War. But it was while in his first year in the army that he, at the age of 18, experienced what he would later deem to have been "a supernatural clarity into a common sight" rather than "a supernatural vision." One winter day he spotted a totally barren tree stripped of all leaves and fruit. And in contemplating this not uncommon sight, young Nicolas came to realize that—like this tree that by nature was assured of a spring revival and summer abundance—he, too, now had the assurance from God of experiencing a similar revival in his heart and life. As it turned out, this "common-sight" experience served as the beginning of his personal subjective conversion to Christ, and within six years thereafter he would enter as a lay brother in a Catholic Carmelite monastery in Paris, where Nicolas took upon himself, appropriately, the religious name of "Lawrence of the Resurrection."

Now his occupation, whether in the military or the monastery, was that of a cook. And we know how busy a cook can be in the army or even in a monastery. And as a cook, of course, he labored amidst all the noise of a large kitchen with its clatter of dishes, pots and pans, and other types of vessels. Nevertheless, Brother Lawrence learned through spiritual practice the secret of how to live always in the presence of God in spite of all life's varied circumstances. He wrote in his little book that he could sense the presence of God in the midst of his busy work as well as when he was alone praying and meditating before Him.

Now it so happened that our brother Watchman Nee in China, after being saved for a few years, obtained a copy of that book and read it. He was convinced that this was what he himself must experience. So he began to try to practice the presence of God in the manner of Brother Lawrence. He tried remembering God all the time; but when he was busily engaged in various tasks, he forgot. Brother Nee discovered that it was very difficult to remember to practice the presence of God all the time.

Have you had this same experience? Obviously, if you have never practiced the presence of God, you will not have had that experience. If you do start to practice it, you will find that when you remember, it seems to work; but when you forget, the presence of God disappears. It is very difficult to do. Perhaps only a few monks can do that; I do not know.

How can we really live a life that is always in God's presence? How can we live from morning till night, as it were, within the veil? This has been the quest of God's people throughout the centuries.

THE TABERNACLE

In Old Testament times, after God had delivered the children of Israel out of Egypt He brought them to Mount Sinai, and there He first gave them the Law—the Ten Commandments (Exodus 19:1-3a; 20:1-17; 24:1-4, 12-18; 31:18; 34:1-4, 10a, 27-28). Why did God do that? It was through the Law that He made them His possession as His people (Exodus 19:3b-8). After giving them the Ten Commandments God instructed them to build for Him a tabernacle because, He said, "I want to dwell in your midst" (Exodus 25:8, 29:42-46). But, God went on to say, "since I am the Holy One, you are not holy enough to be My dwelling place, for I cannot directly dwell among you who are unclean sinners" (Leviticus 19:1-2, 11:44-45); therefore, make Me a tabernacle, and within its precincts I will be able indirectly, as it were, to dwell with you and be present with you."

So Moses had the Israelites build the tabernacle according to God's exact specifications (Exodus 39:32, 42-43). It was composed of three parts—an outer open court (Exodus 26:36a, 27:9, 16), the holy place where the priests would serve (Exodus 39:1), and the holiest of all where God was to dwell (Exodus 26:33b).

The Outer Court

First was the outer court open to all. Here was the brazen altar to which the people would bring their sacrifices to be offered to God and placed upon the altar

(Exodus 40:28-29). In type the altar represented the cross of the Lord Jesus upon which He was sacrificed as the sin offering to take away our sins before God and as the burnt offering that He offered to God for our acceptance (Leviticus 1:3). Here, too, was the bronze basin or laver filled with water with which the priests were to wash their hands and feet before entering the holy place to serve God (Exodus 30:18, 40:7, 30-32).

The Holy Place

Next was the holy place where the priests would serve. Here were three objects—the golden candlestick, the golden table of bread, and the golden table of incense (Exodus 40:22-27). Again, in type, we who have been made priests unto God through Jesus' sacrifice on the cross are able to serve God in the holy place where we can light the candlestick, set the showbread on the table, and burn incense on the altar.

The Holiest of All

Finally, there was the holiest of all. There was one very special object in it—the ark of the covenant with the two stone tablets within it on which the Ten Commandments were written (Exodus 25:10a, 16; Leviticus 16:2; Hebrews 9:3-4). Upon the ark, there was the mercy seat, and the presence or glory of God rested upon the mercy seat (Exodus 25:10-22, Hebrews 9:5). Between the holy place and the holiest of all, there hung a heavy veil or curtain—not unlike a doorway—that separated those two places (Exodus 26:31-33). Only the high priest could go behind the veil into the holiest place and only once a year to offer a sin offering for himself, his family, and for all the people of Israel, and then he had to quickly withdraw from God's presence (Leviticus 16:2-34, esp. v. 34; Hebrews 9:7).

THE VEIL THAT SEPARATES WAS RENT

The Bible tells us in Hebrews 9 that as long as the holy place existed, the way to the holiest of all would not be opened (v. 8). Nobody could enter into the presence of God because God is so holy. The priests could serve before God in the holy place, but they could not go into the presence of God; that is to say, they could not live in the presence of God because the way inside was not opened. Thank God, however, that we are told in the New Testament book of Hebrews that the separating veil has at last been broken through.

We will recall that during the final hour of Jesus' crucifixion He uttered the words, "It is finished!" And then He expired on the cross, His work of salvation having been finished (John 19:30). At that very moment the veil in the Jerusalem temple was rent in two from top to bottom (Mark 15:37-38). We know that the temple veil was very heavy, but at Jesus' moment of death it was rent from top to bottom. This signifies the fact that it was not rent by human hands, for had it been so, the veil would have been rent in the opposite direction: from the bottom to the top. It had to have been God himself, therefore, who tore that veil in two.

Hebrews 10 reveals that the veil represented the flesh of the Lord Jesus (v. 20). And John chapter 1 declares in further revelation: "the Word became flesh, and tabernacled among man, full of grace and truth. We have contemplated His glory, even the glory of the Son with the Father" (see v. 14). The Word is the Lord Jesus, for at the very beginning of John's Gospel we read this: "In the beginning was the Word, the Word was with God, and the Word was God" (v. 1). That is what our Lord Jesus was in eternity past, but the Word became flesh; thus speaking of Jesus' incarnation and how He came into this world to be a man who physically tabernacled among mankind. And while He was on the earth He lived a most perfect, beautiful, righteous, holy life: He knew no sin, never yielded to temptation, and was always obedient to His Father. In brief, Jesus lived as man *should* live according to the mind of God.

THE TWO SIDES OF THE VEIL

Now let us bear in mind that this temple veil that separated the holy of holies from the holy place naturally had two sides. One side faced outward towards the holy place and the other faced inward towards the holiest of all. As we continue to consider this temple-tabernacle veil in what is next said, let us bear in mind as well that it represents the flesh of the Lord Jesus.

So while Jesus was on the earth, He showed the world in His outward walk what in God's mind a human life should be. It was such a beautiful, obedient, and holy life. At the same time that Jesus was demonstrating to the world that kind of life outwardly, inwardly—on the inner side of the veil, as it were—He was always in the presence of God. Throughout his entire time on earth for some thirty-three years He was always in the presence of His Father. He said, "My Father is [always] with Me" (see John 16:32c). He never left the Father's presence except during those last three horrific hours on the cross when He with great anguish of heart cried out: "My God, my God, why hast thou forsaken Me?" (Matthew 27:46b) This cry arose from the fact that He had become the sin of the entire world (II Corinthians 5:21a), and thus the Father with equal anguish had to turn His face away from Him. Except for those three hours the Son of man always saw the Father while He was on earth.

Now if Jesus, having lived those thirty-three years on earth, had then ascended to heaven from the Mount of Transfiguration, thus avoiding the cross, where would that have left us? Moses and Elijah, appearing in glory at this moment, were there on the mount talking with Jesus about His departure that was about to be accomplished at Jerusalem (Luke 9:31). He had every right to depart back to the Father from there, but if He did, nobody else could ever see the face of God. Let us thank God that Jesus did not exit back to heaven from the Mount of Transfiguration! Instead, He came down from the mountain and set His face towards Jerusalem and the cross which awaited Him there (Luke 9:28-37, 43-45, 51). That is overwhelming love.

Now in His speaking to His disciples about the coming of the Holy Spirit the Lord Jesus mentioned several things the Spirit would convict the world about (see John 16:8-11). One of them was that the Spirit would convict men of guilt concerning righteousness because, said Jesus, "I am going to the Father" (v. 10). This seems an odd thing to say—that the world would be convicted concerning righteousness because Jesus would be going to the Father. However, the underlying meaning is that He alone of all human beings was righteously perfect and therefore qualified to go to the Father—no one else— and that that reality convicts men of their guilt before God as sinners needing redemption by the blood of the Holy One of God.

Therefore, the Lord Jesus must die. If in coming to the earth He had never died, He would have remained alone, not having produced any lasting fruit (see again John 12:23-24). But He came to the earth for this very purpose: to die—yet not for himself, since He was sinless perfect on earth, but for all of us sinners. And as He died, the veil was rent from top to bottom. In other words, as a result of His sacrificial death on the cross a new and living way was opened up for us (Hebrews 10:20); therefore, we are living at a time when the veil has already been torn into two, thus giving us who believe the privilege to enter the holy of holies and behold the face of God day by day. And not only can we enter in, we also can *dwell* there—not having to withdraw quickly upon having entered once a year, as the high priests of old were required to do. What an unparalleled privilege we have today!

MAN'S QUEST TO DWELL IN GOD'S PRESENCE

We have mentioned before that the world is seeking after this very thing—to be in God's presence, to live within the veil, to be united with Him. I believe this is the deep heart-searching of the world. In this connection, let us consider once again the mystics, whom earlier I very briefly touched upon in the message on new Jerusalem. Generally speaking, we are all mystics because we are a people who seek the presence of God, to be united with Him. In that sense, that makes all of us Christians mystics. But there is a certain group of individuals who are actually called by the term mystics. Reading about these mystics and looking into their writings is a very fascinating exercise. Many Christians whose lives we are familiar with and who truly knew the Lord benefited greatly from reading the writings of these mystics. Unfortunately, when delving more deeply into mysticism, we find that there are certain serious flaws or errors in their theological understandings and/or teachings.

First Error: Deification of Man

Many of us have heard or read about Madame Guyon who was previously mentioned earlier in the message on new Jerusalem. Born in France in 1648 she became an intensely devout Christian lady who as a Catholic had mostly spent her life living in the country of her birth. When I was young living in China, there were many people who read the life of Madame Guyon in a published biography which was not her own. Someone (a non-Chinese) had produced a biography on her life that was an abridgment, the author having deleted from its text all of the superstitious aspects of her life and thought—aspects which, of course, became known later among evangelical Christians. This volume was translated into Chinese and spread widely throughout China. Many Christian brothers and sisters wanted to be like Madame Guyon because she had lived such a wonderful and beautiful life; and her influence at that time was great. She lived during the time of French King Louis XIV and was imprisoned in the infamous state prison in Paris, the Bastille, from 1695-1703 because of some of her beliefs that were considered by both State and Church as heretical. She died in 1717.

Now we may recall from the earlier discussion of the mystics that Madame Guyon had described her understanding of the Christian's union with God in the following terms (paraphrased): "We each are like a drop of water in a stream flowing gradually towards the ocean, and upon reaching the ocean the water drop merges with the vast ocean, it having become one with it." Do we discern any serious flaw or error here? In maintaining such a theology, a person is bordering on advocating the notion of pantheism—everything is God and God is everything—or else actually embracing the deification of man. However, a Christian's union with God does not mean that, because he has God's life, therefore, he becomes God or a part of God. Such teaching is nothing less than the deification of man.

Sad to say, when Christians seek to know about and/or experience mysticism, they often fall into this very trap. I know of a famous Christian whose name, were I to identify it, would be quite familiar to some of us because we have read his books. He eventually fell into the snare of embracing the teaching of the deification of man. If we study the so-called Church Fathers, we shall discover that some of them, too, fell into this trap. In their teaching and writing they actually taught man's deification.

Let us clearly understand that we are in union with God *in Christ*. The Bible never teaches the notion of our being brought into union with God *directly*. Rather, it is union with God in Christ Jesus because we receive the life of Christ in us. In such union God is always God and man always remains as man. So this is the first error of the mystics, of which we need to be most careful.

Second Error: Man's Effort to Reach God

The second error with the mystics is their understanding on the way of reaching or obtaining God in one's life, which can readily be pictured in our mind's eye as man reaching up to God instead of it actually being the case of God reaching down to man. To put this another way, mystics attempt to gain God by their own efforts rather than having a true understanding that it is God who comes down, touches us, and rescues us. The whole theory with the mystics is of man reaching up to heaven and not heaven reaching down to man. In brief, it is man's work, not God's. However, both Scripture and personal Christian experience belie this theory, which is nothing less than a gross religious error; for we are saved by God's work of grace through our faith in Christ: it is not of ourselves but the gift of God (Ephesians 2:8-9).

Third Error: Ill-treating the Body

The third error of the mystics is that because they did not know the dividing of the soul and the spirit, we find there was mixture in their efforts. One has to admire them for their zeal and determination to gain God, but one must deplore the way they went about it: how they abused themselves unnecessarily! Many, for example, beat themselves unmercifully and lay on beds of nails. They ill-treated their bodies because they came to believe that sin and evil reside in matter and, since the body is matter, it therefore must be evil. So they tried to become holy by ill-treating their bodies. Even the great Reformer, Martin Luther, a professor of rhetoric, when convicted of sin and the fear of death, left his professorship and knocked at the door of an Augustinian monastery and became for awhile an ascetic monk there. How he continually ill-treated his body! He nearly died in attempting to become holy by that method.

We have to admire their determination, but what they practiced was not God's way. We do love our body too much, that is true, and hence we need to deal with it, but Biblically—that is, we are to buffet the body and bring it into subjection but not ill-treat it as though the body itself were evil. Because of their earnestness and zeal these mystics were willing to suffer as much as their bodies could physically tolerate. God, of course, knew their hearts, and in many cases He eventually told them to abandon those negative practices, and many of them did. For it was because of their earnest quest for God that He was able to reveal himself to them.

Obviously, we should all have that willingness to seek the Lord at any cost, but we should not be so foolish as to try accomplishing this spiritual objective by ourselves but recognize that union with God is all by His mercy and grace through Christ alone. This serious error of the mystics is likewise something about which we need to be most careful.

HOW TO LIVE WITHIN THE VEIL

What should we therefore do? How can we live within the veil? How can we live in the presence of God? Once again, we find that He has already made it possible through Christ. Christ has already accomplished it for us. Hebrews 10:19 tells us: "Having therefore, brethren, boldness for entering into the holy of holies by the blood of Jesus." We now have the boldness to enter the holy of holies and live in God's presence.

The Blood of Jesus

But from whence does that boldness come? First of all, it comes "by the blood of Jesus." Jesus shed His blood; therefore, our sins have been forgiven. He has given us the right and position to come before God as our Father. Since this is where our boldness comes from throughout our Christian life, we can never leave the blood of Jesus behind as though we have advanced so far that we do not need it anymore. The closer we are to God, the more we shall realize how precious the blood of Jesus is. We need His blood more at that time than at any other time because we realize how sinful, unrighteous, unholy, and dark we still are. We need the blood of Jesus all the time. Whenever the Lord shows us where we have sinned and fallen short of the glory of God, we must repent and claim His blood for cleansing and God's forgiveness. It is our most precious provision throughout our Christian life; therefore, we can always be clean before God.

A New and Living Way

A second provision is explained in the next verse: "The new and living way which he has dedicated [opened] for us through the veil, that is, his flesh" (v. 20). We have the boldness to enter the holy of holies because we have a way made for us. The Lord Jesus has opened a new and living way. It is new, having never been known before; and it is living, not dead. What is that new and living way? It is a way that has been inaugurated for us through the veil, that is, through Jesus' flesh. In other words, because His flesh was broken on Calvary's cross, the veil within the temple was rent, and the doorway was opened for us to go in. We must never forget that He consecrated this way for us. This means that whereas formerly we had no way to go behind the veil, now the Lord Jesus has opened a new and living way for us. He went in first by means of the cross and now He entreats us: "Follow Me." The way is there, but if we do not follow, we will never arrive inside the veil. That is precisely our problem.

The Lord has willingly allowed His flesh to be afflicted and broken for us, but our problem is that we are not willing to have *our* flesh—that is, our self-life—broken. We love our self too much and that hinders us from walking in that new and living way which Jesus pioneered for us. In the New Testament Scriptures we read how the Lord instructed His would-be followers again and again with these words: "Deny yourself, take up your cross, and follow Me." To deny our selves simply means: "I do not know you nor care about you." We love ourselves and think and care about ourselves far too much. But one day, by the grace of God, we will have the holy courage to say to ourselves: "I do not know you; I do not care for you." When that happens, that will be the cross working in us to enable us to follow the Lord through the veil into God's presence. If our flesh is never dealt with, there can be no way for us to live in the presence of God. This shows us again how very necessary spiritual exercise is. We cannot merely receive the word of God objectively. Yes, on the one hand, we need to take God's objective *logos* word by faith; but on the other hand, we need to have God's subjective *rhema* word come to us by His Spirit and follow through in obedience. Yet for this to become our daily experience, thus enabling us to dwell within the veil, it will require us to exercise our spirit, and to do so continually.

A High Priest

Now as we exercise our spirit to walk in that way, we shall find that we have not the strength to follow through in obedience. Do any of us think we have the power to deny ourselves? Let me observe that it is like trying to lift ourselves up physically by ourselves: we may be able to do anything else but we cannot physically lift ourselves up; that is impossible! How, then, can we possibly have the ability to go against our natural inclination to favor our self-life and deny ourselves? Thank God, we have been given a third provision, and what a provision it is: a High Priest who ever lives and intercedes for us—even *the* high priest, the crucified-risen-ascended Lord Jesus! He is thus able to save to the uttermost—that is, completely and forever—those who come to God through Him (Hebrews 7:25). He is there to supply to us the willingness, the ability, the power, and the strength to deny our self- or soul-life and take up our cross and follow Him.

Draw Near in Faith

When we contemplate all these provisions before us, let us not consider the life within the veil to be an impossibility or as that which only a few zealous determined mystics could strive after and achieve. On the contrary, it is an opened way for everyone to enter into and experience. As the writer of Hebrews advised: "Let us approach [draw near] with a true heart, in full assurance of faith" (10:22a). In other words, let us believe that it *is* possible and that the way is now open for us. Let us therefore desire to enter within the veil, nothing doubting. Indeed, our entering within is very much a matter of faith, for we realize that the Christian life throughout is grounded in faith, but faith's source is never to be found in us; rather, faith is that which is outside of us. That is why the author of Hebrews has further advised us to look away from everything and look off to Jesus, the Author and Finisher (or Perfecter) of faith (see 12:2a ASV). That, and only that, is where the faith we have comes from.

Our Hearts Sprinkled

"Sprinkled as to our hearts from a wicked conscience" (v. 22b). That is to say, every time we have an evil conscience or we sense something wrong or sinful in our life, immediately a supply of the blood of Jesus is applied and sprinkled upon our hearts to cleanse us from such a conscience so that we may live all the time—hour by hour, day after day—with a clear conscience.

Our Bodies Washed with Pure Water

"And washed as to our body with pure water" (v. 22c). Here we are reminded of Ephesians 5:26—the Lord Jesus will apply the water of God's word to wash us day by day in order that we may be able to serve Him. This can be likened to the bronze laver within the outer court of the tabernacle-temple that was used by the priests for washing and purifying themselves (Exodus 30:18). The word of God is like the water, and the life of God is like the water. When God's word comes to us and the life of God's Spirit within us responds to it, we are cleansed by that word.

Hold Fast the Confession of Hope

"Let us hold fast the confession of the hope unwavering, (for he is faithful who has promised;)" (v. 23). It is not an easy undertaking to seek to be within the veil in the presence of God all the time; for there shall be many failures. Many times our conscience will not remain pure or we will be contaminated by the world. We will fail again and again, yet let us not waver nor give up but let us hold fast the confession of hope. We have a confession to make repeatedly, and it is this: "Jesus is Lord." He is our living hope and He is able, as well as faithful, even as the parenthetical statement in this verse reminds us. So we hold on to Him and press forward, never wavering nor giving up.

Provoking One Another to Love

In this way of living as much as we can in the presence of God, we need one another. We are not able to proceed alone. That is why the next verse declares: "let us consider one another for provoking to love and good works" (v. 24). We need to help one another and encourage one another.

Not Forsaking the Assembling of the Saints

To be able to do that, however, we must "not ... forsake the assembling of ourselves together, as the custom is with some" (v. 25a). A custom is the result of having done something so often that it becomes a regular habit. Regrettably, some believers have acquired this custom.

I would plead with you: Do not forsake the assembling of yourselves with the other saints. Yes, you may fear that to assemble with the saints where you are might sometimes hurt you. However, as odd or cruel as it may sound, you ought to thank God that assembling together may in fact hurt you. Yet this is what you need. If you do not gather with the saints, you will obviously be free from any hurt feelings or harm to your pride; in that case, for you there will be no discipline to undergo whatsoever. You may indeed be free, but in the process your Christian life will be on the decline: you will find yourself departing further and further away from the Lord. You do not realize what blessing there is in assembling together with other believers.

I have seen people who, loving the Lord, drew back from gathering with the saints and were thus all by themselves. Though they still loved the Lord, gradually that love faded away and eventually they even fell into false teaching. How pitiful! Let us never fall into the habit of forsaking to gather with other Christian brethren even though in assembling with them they may step upon us. Let us view such experience as the particular cross which the Holy Spirit has provided and arranged for us in order to teach us some valuable lessons. We need to learn from one another just as we need to learn from the Lord himself. Such is the necessary exhortation which the writer of Hebrews has given us.